Martyn Cornell is an award-winning writer on beer and brewing history. He still remembers, when he was fourteen, drinking a pint of Fremlin's bitter from the Faversham brewery in Kent, which made him first realise how good beer could be. In 2000 he won the British Guild of Beer Writers Budvar trophy. Today, he lives in west London with his wife and young daughter, close to several excellent pubs and bars.

To Emer and Mara without whom . . .

BEER:
THE STORY OF
THE PINT

The History of Britain's Most Popular Drink

Martyn Cornell

headline

First published in 2003
by HEADLINE BOOK PUBLISHING

First published in paperback in 2004
by HEADLINE BOOK PUBLISHING

Martyn Cornell would be happy to hear from readers with their
comments on the book at the following e-mail address:
goneforapint@cornerpub.com

10 9 8 7 6 5 4 3 2

ISBN 0 7553 1165 5

Typeset in Garamond by Palimpsest Book Production Limited,
Polmont, Stirlingshire

Every effort has been made to fulfil requirements with regard to
reproducing copyright material. The author and publisher will be
glad to rectify any omissions at the earliest opportunity.

Printed and bound in Great Britain by
Mackays of Chatham plc, Chatham, Kent

Papers and cover board used by Headline are natural, recyclable products
made from wood grown in sustainable forests. The manufacturing processes
conform to the environmental regulations of the country of origin.

HEADLINE BOOK PUBLISHING
A division of Hodder Headline
338 Euston Road
London NW1 3BH

www.headline.co.uk
www.hodderheadline.com

CONTENTS

TIMELINE

Date	
*c.*8000BC	First domestication of grain plants in Middle East
*c.*6000	Pottery appears in Middle East
*c.*4000	First real evidence of beer drinking in Middle East. First farmers arrive in Britain
*c.*2000	'Hymn to Ninkasi' composed in Sumer. Beaker Folk arrive in Britain
*c.*800	Celts in Europe brewing with bread
*c.*300	Islanders of Britain brewing 'honey ale' with emmer wheat
AD100	Ale brewing widespread in Roman Britain
301	Emperor Diocletian sets price of beer at 4 denarii a pint
*c.*450	Saxon ale-drinkers start to settle in Britain
*c.*600	Germans start referring to 'bior', ancestor of our modern word 'beer'
*c.*800	Hops begin to be used in beer alongside other herbs
*c.*1250	Hops begin to take over from gruit as flavouring for beer in Europe
*c.*1420	Beer brewing, with hops, starts in England
*c.*1520	Hops first grown in England
1643	First tax on ale and beer in Britain
*c.*1700	All ale and beer in Britain now brewed with hops
*c.*1720	Development of porter
*c.*1795	London-brewed pale ale becomes popular in India
*c.*1822	Burton brewers began producing India Pale Ale
1842	Pale lager invented in Plzen, Bohemia

c.1845	Bitter starts to appear on brewers' lists in Britain
c.1880	Mild becomes dominant beer style in Britain
c.1895	Britain loses position as biggest brewing nation to Germany
1917	First World War restrictions see beer strengths dive
c.1930	Own-brew pubs now a rarity
c.1940	Demise of porter in Britain
c.1944	Experiments with keg beer in Britain
c.1965	Lager begins to take off in Britain: sales of mild begin to fall
1970	Effective domination of 'Big Six' national brewers
1971	Campaign for Real Ale (Camra) founded in Britain
1976	Microbrewery revolution begins in Britain
1990	The 'Beer Orders' begin split between brewing and pub owning

BEER AND BRITANNIA

*If [beer] is . . . the people's beverage – and
nobody, I take it, will deny that it is just that –
its history must of necessity go hand in hand, so to
speak, with the history of that people, with the
history of its entire civilisation.*

John P. Arnold, 1911

Beer is Britain's favourite drink – and has been for a long time. Two thousand years ago the most important political power in Britain, the Celtic king Cunobelin, was already consciously advertising beer as the national beverage by minting his gold coins with an ear of barley on one side. It was a deliberate political statement against the legions of Rome, which threatened just across the Channel. The barley-coins were a visual proclamation that Cunobelin and his people were patriotic drinkers of good British beer, and had no time for the Romans or nasty Roman habits like wine supping.

When the grape-loving Romans came in force in AD43, and conquered the independent British kingdoms right up to the Solway Firth and beyond, they failed to eliminate beer drinking from these islands – no big surprise, since the evidence is that beer had even then been drunk here for 4,000 years. More than that: within a short while the Roman army itself was drinking British ale. The legions had become part of a river of liquid history that stretched back to the sacred beers of the first Neolithic farmers in Britain, and forward another two millennia, taking in the *ealu* of the Angles and Saxons, the nut-brown *cerevisia duplex* of medieval monks, the strong pale ales drunk by the seventeenth-century country gentry, the stout dark beers that sustained London's hard-working street porters, and the draught bitter and lager drunk today.

Beer has formed an important strand in the British national identity for millennia. When the Reverend Sydney Smith asked in the nineteenth century: 'What two ideas are more inseparable than beer and Britannia?' he was expressing the same sentiment that Cunobelin had declared through his ear-of-barley 'beer money' in the first century. Another beer-drinking monarch, Queen Elizabeth I, also backed brews made from East Anglian barley against foreign tipples when she rudely told the Spanish ambassador, who was threatening to cut off wine supplies from his country: 'A fig for Spain, so long as Royston shall supply such plenty of good malts.'

By 1763 the economist Joseph Massie could call beer 'a common necessity, which Britons deem part of their birthright'. The same idea was proclaimed more robustly in a drinking song from 1757:

> *Let us sing our own treasures, old England's good cheer*
> *The profits and pleasures of stout British beer;*
> *Your wine-tippling, dram-drinking fellows retreat*
> *But your beer-drinking Britons can never be beat.*

We may not be quite so jingoistic in the twenty-first century; but beer is still, in terms of quantities consumed and money spent on it, easily the most popular drink in Britain. 'Beer money' is now worth £14 billion a year, with 27 million pints of beer drunk every day in the UK – meaning that two millennia after Cunobelin, we still drink almost six times as much beer as we do wine. Two out of five adults, and three out of five men, drink beer at least once a week. Beer and Britannia look like being inseparable for a long time still.

CHAPTER ONE

IN THE BEGINNING

how the search for a pint brought us civilization (maybe)

There were three Kings into the east,
Three Kings both great and high
And they hae sworn a solemn oath
John Barleycorn should die.

'The Ballad of John Barleycorn',
as recorded by Robert Burns
(1759–96)

On a calm spring day around 6,000 years ago a leather-skinned boat some fourteen feet or so long sailed across from the coast of continental Europe to land in Britain. On board were a small group of men and women, perhaps a pregnant cow or sheep, and several bags of barley or emmer wheat. The first farmers had arrived in these islands. The first brewers had also arrived: the grain they would plant and reap here meant the earliest agriculturalists to cross the Channel would also be also our earliest beer makers.

The history of beer, like so much other history, began in the Middle East, in this case some three to four thousand years before the first brewers reached Britain. Stands of wild wheat and wild barley still grow and seed today on the hills that flank the so-called 'Fertile Crescent'. This is the wide sweep of land that curves north from the

Persian or Arabian Gulf, through modern Iraq and Syria, and down the Mediterranean coast to the Nile Delta, and it is where European and West Asian agriculture began. Seeds from these tall wild grasses were probably part of the human diet from the time modern men and women first walked out of Africa into Asia. But 10,000 or so years ago, groups of Stone Age humans moved on from simply collecting ripened wild grain to begin a new relationship with these plants. Rather than go up to the hills every season to gather grain, they saved their best seed and planted it down in the valleys, where it could be harvested more easily: thus began the cultivation of wheat and barley.

These first farmers erected permanent or semi-permanent valley settlements, close to where they planted the seed, so that they could guard and nurture the plants. For one school of archaeologists, the reason why the previously happy roaming hunter-gatherers settled down in one place and turned from a relatively easy lifestyle to the hard and sweaty grind of farming can be summed up in a word: beer.

Did civilization begin in order to provide our ancestors with a regular supply of ale? It is an attractive theory for beer drinkers. The speculation is that, by 10,000 years ago, the grain-gatherers had learned how to make beer from the wild wheat and barley they harvested up in the hills. These Mesolithic (Middle Stone Age) people were so thrilled with the invention of brewing that they planted their own grain fields in more accessible places, to ensure they did not have to travel miles into the hills to fetch the raw material for their beer. They then built homes near the fields, thus setting up the world's first villages, entering the Neolithic era and laying out the literal foundations of civilization. That, succinctly, is the claim.

It is hard for us to imagine what the people who invented beer must have felt when they first tasted it, and discovered its effects; for today we live in a society that has known alcohol intimately for millennia. The best we can do for an authentically ancient picture of man's reaction to his initiating encounter with ale appears in a long poem from the early Babylonian era, four millennia ago, called the *Epic of Gilgamesh*. The Gilgamesh tales were originally oral poetry current around 2200BC in Sumer, southern Mesopotamia, thus putting them around halfway between the first beer brewers and today. In the poem, Enkidu the wild man has been lured from the fields by Shamhat the harlot, who has instructions to bring him to King Gilgamesh in the Mesopotamian city of Uruk. On the way they meet some shepherds, who offer Enkidu refreshment.

> *Bread they set before him, ale they set before him.*
> *Enkidu ate not the bread but looked askance.*
> *How to eat bread Enkidu knew not,*
> *How to drink ale he had never been shown*
> *The harlot opened her mouth, saying to Enkidu:*
> *'Eat the bread, Enkidu, essential to life, drink the*
>   *ale, the lot of the land!'*
> *Enkidu ate the bread until he was sated, he drank*
>   *the ale a full seven goblets.*
> *His mood became free, he started to sing, his heart*
>   *grew merry, his face lit up.*

There was probably a religious side to the early farmers' beer brewing, as well as a 'let's get merry' one. Around the world today, tribal peoples in places such as the south-western United States, Mexico, Bolivia, Kenya, India, the Philippines and Japan still make beer from maize, millet, rice or palm sap with social ceremonies that involve a recognition that something sacred is involved in the brewing and consumption of these drinks. Often some of the beer is sacrificed – poured on the ground – as tribute to the gods or goddesses who ensured a good grain harvest. Two Americans, Solomon Katz and Mary Voigt of the University of Pennsylvania, advocates of the theory that brewing was the impetus behind civilization, suggested in 1986 that similar ceremonies and significances could have emerged with the earliest discovery of beer in the Middle East. If beer was incorporated into the social/religious systems of the hunter-gatherers of ten millennia ago, they say, this association would have provided a further motive for the first brewers to found the first organized farming communities to secure supplies of grain for beer making.

How exactly beer was invented we do not know and we may never establish. Some modern writers have surmised that the first beer was brewed by complete accident. According to this theory, a Mesolithic grain-gatherer left a bowl of wheat out in the rain, and came back a few days later to find that it had sprouted and been infected by wild yeast. He or she was happily surprised on tasting the accidental alcoholic outcome, they suggest, and quickly learned to reproduce the accident on demand.

Unfortunately for the supporters of the 'lucky accident' theory, when this idea was tested by the Canadian palaeontologist and home brewer Ed Hitchcock in 1993, the result was so disgusting it gave a deadly blow to the idea of accidentally rain-deluged grain as a route to beer.

In an attempt to reproduce what might have happened 10,000 years ago, Hitchcock soaked whole raw barley grain in water to get it to sprout, just as might have happened according to the 'grain in the rain' theory. The plan was to pound the newly sprouted barley into gruel, place that in the sun to mash, leave it outside overnight to attract wild yeasts and watch the result.

The experiment never got beyond stage one. Within a day and a half of being placed in water, Hitchcock's grain was churning and bubbling with bacteria and yeast activity, and dead weevils were floating on the surface. Another day and white mould had spread across the water, the smell was awful and the bubbling was still furious. Wisely, Hitchcock decided he did not wish to taste the product. It's a fair bet that no Neolithic farmer would have been likely to try drinking it either.

Hitchcock's other experiment involved sprouting grains in jars, baking bread from the sprouted grains, and making a mash from the bread. Ancient farmers must occasionally have found their grain had sprouted accidentally, and they would have used the now sweet, soft grains in making bread rather than waste it or let it spoil by leaving it in water. Such 'green' (that is, undried) malt was a valued food in the early Middle East, and one Mesopotamian calendar had a month called 'the eating of green malt'. Hitchcock soaked his grain for only twenty-four hours, which avoided infection problems, and then left it to sprout. Wheat grains were ready in two to three days, but barley took seven days to sprout sufficiently, which may be a clue to the popularity of wheat over barley with early brewers.

When the grains were sprouted, Hitchcock ground them and baked the ground grains into biscuits. The biscuits were then broken up and mashed in hot water along with more ground sprouted barleycorn, thus adding extra flavour and colour. As Hitchcock heated this 'bread soup' it reached the temperatures which would have encouraged the enzymes in the malted grain to convert more starches into sugar, the

The Middle East, showing some of the places in the 'Fertile Crescent', such as Sumer, associated with the early history of brewing.

substance yeast turns into alcohol. Once the wort (unfermented beer) from the biscuits and grain had been brought to boiling, to sterilize it, and then cooled, it could be fermented.

For his experiment Hitchcock used a yeast cultivated from unpasteurized cider, imitating what we know of ancient brewing practice, which involved adding fruit to the grain wort in order to bring in wild yeasts, which live on the skins of fruits. The original gravity or OG (a measure of the fermentable sugars available) of Hitchcock's bread beer wort was 1071, and the final gravity a high 1033, suggesting an alcohol content of around 5 per cent by volume. The wort contained a lot of starch, which settled out with the yeast by the end of fermentation to leave a pale, cloudy, dry beer, with little carbonation. The aroma, Hitchcock said, was bready, yeasty and cidery, with a soft, slightly spicy flavour – 'good enough to warrant a second glass'.

These two experiments suggest that the invention of beer was not the result of an accident with wet grain, but a more complex process. Neolithic farmers would have found that sprouted grain tasted sweeter than raw grain, as the enzymes in each sprouting seed turned starch to sugar. They must have experimented with making sprouted grains into gruel or bread or, as the Danes still make today, bread soup; and, if you flavour the malted gruel or bread soup with fruit, which introduces wild yeast into the recipe, you are on the way to an early beer.

The Mesolithic first farmers, by deliberately planting grain (whether for beer or not) rather than just gathering it in the wild, set off the selection processes that changed a wild plant, which 'shattered', releasing its seeds from the stalk once they were ripe, into a domesticated, non-shattering variety, whose seeds, though ripe, stay on the stalk for later harvesting by humans. Early farmers would, semi-deliberately, favour the non-shattering plants, which were more easily gathered, and gradually these types began to dominate their fields.

The earliest evidence of domesticated barley (shown by a toughened or 'shatterproof' rachis, the part that attaches the seed to the stalk) comes from seeds found at a site called Netiv Hagud, north of Jericho, which dates from around 7750BC, or 9,750 years ago. It was mixed in with the wild kind of barley, but its existence implies that organized, regular farming was already taking place and had been for some time. Was the barley at Netiv Hagud grown for use in brewing? The technology of that period, even before the invention of pottery, was almost certainly capable of the processes needed to turn grain into beer. Baking and boiling, with hot stones, could provide the temperatures needed for some saccharinification of the starches in the grain, thus providing the sugars that wild yeasts would turn into alcohol.

Merryn Dineley of Manchester University believes the remains of early Neolithic villages show all the requirements for brewing. Smooth, level surfaces inside a building on which to spread the steeped grain as it germinated are a feature of almost every known Neolithic site from the ninth millennium BC onwards; hearths and ovens, which could have been used to dry the malt for storage, have been found; and quernstones, which could have been used to crush the malt before mashing, are common. Outside, they needed only a stream for steeping harvested grain in, just the way Norwegian farmer-brewers did up to the nineteenth or twentieth centuries. Dineley also suggests that a by-product of beer brewing helped with the domestication of animals: even today cattle and pigs are fed on spent brewers' grains, and left-over brewing grains around Neolithic villages may have attracted wild ruminants, making it easier to catch and domesticate them.

Many have doubted the possibility of brewing before the invention of pottery, around 7000BC, some time after the beginnings of agriculture. The only containers available for brewing in before pottery were organic: gourds or baskets (which could be lined with pitch or resin), or animal skins. But gourds are still used today in West Africa to brew palm wine in (the yeast that remains on the walls of the gourd starts the fermentation of the next brew). Baskets can be made to hold liquid: Zulu women in South Africa make 'beer baskets', tightly woven, rigid and with a small lid. When the basket, made of lala palm leaves, is filled with home-made beer, the coils swell and the basket 'sweats', cooling the liquid inside.

No traces of ancient pre-pottery brewing equipment, or ancient

Neolithic malt, have been found to tell us definitively that Katz, Voigt and Dineley are right and that brewing is as old as, or older than, farming. But this is not surprising: organic materials such as gourds and baskets rot swiftly away and do not survive into the archaeological record. The same is true of malted grain: the earliest surviving identifiable brewers' grains found by archaeologists come from the dry climate of Egypt, 7,500 years after the start of farming.

The first real indicator of the existence of brewing comes three to four thousand years after farming began, and well after the invention of pottery. A 6,000-year-old seal used for stamping designs on wet clay, discovered at a site called Tepe Gawra, north-west of Nineveh in Mesopotamia (modern Iraq), shows two figures drinking through long straws or tubes out of a large, wide-mouthed pot. Doubtless the Tepe Gawra seal, with its pictogram of beer drinkers, was used to mark pots or jars used for holding beer, to show what was in them. The tubes were probably used so that the drinkers could avoid bits of debris left in the brew. Even today in Africa home-brewed beer is drunk through reeds or straws out of large jars: groups of two or more men will gather around a big pot of sorghum beer with three-foot-long reed straws, in scenes that look identical, except for the clothes,

The Sumerian symbol for beer, based on the internally grooved, pointy-bottomed jar the drink was brewed in, from a clay tablet recording the allocation of beer dated to around 3100–3000BC, probably from southern Iraq.

to those depicted on Sumerian seals. Beer drinking through straws is also known elsewhere: in Russia, where the Cossacks are said to have drunk their *kvass*, or bread-mash beer, from the barrel through straws; and in Nepal, where traditional chang or millet beer is drunk through a bamboo tube with a strainer at one end.

The first 'solid' (literally) evidence for brewing is three or four centuries later than the Tepe Gawra seal. Pottery fragments from the late fourth millennium BC, about 5,500 years ago, found at a site called Godin Tepe in the Zagros mountains of Iran, show traces of calcium oxalate on what was the inside of the jar. This is 'beer stone', a naturally occurring deposit in beer brewing. While it might have come from spinach or rhubarb, two more sources of calcium oxalate, both found locally, there is another clue to suggest these pots were used for brewing. For the jars contained criss-cross grooves inside, below the shoulder, which were very likely designed to trap sediment. This yeasty remainder would have helped start the next brew when fresh ingredients were added. The grooves are similar, moreover, to those that occur on the shouldered-jar symbol that is the early Sumerian written sign for 'beer', in use around 5,300 years ago.

The Tepe Gawra seal was made at around the same time that the first farmers to set up in these islands were coming across the sea with grain and domesticated animals. The main wheat the earliest British farmers brought with them was a bearded type called emmer, the prime brewing grain of the Sumerians, of dynastic Egypt, and also of the later Celts (emmer is a hulled grain, which makes it easier to malt). It took more than a thousand years for the skills of agriculture to travel from south-eastern Europe, where farmers were active 7,000 years ago, to Britain. Evidence from the earliest British Neolithic sites, however, suggests that the knowledge of how to brew arrived from continental Europe in the same boats as the knowledge of farming.

We can at least be reasonably sure what sort of beer the first brewers made – porridge beer or bread-mash beer, the most primitive types known. Brewing beer made from bread or malt cakes soaked in water seems to have been the earliest method used by the Sumerians, and also the dynastic Egyptians, as shown in models and paintings in tombs of the Fifth Dynasty, from around 2510–2460BC until at least 1500BC. The earliest Egyptian brewing method we know of, illustrated by tomb models and wall paintings from 3,500 years ago, involved baking grain into loaves, soaking the bread and then pressing out the water from the soaked bread through basket-like sieves into pottery jars, where it fermented. It is doubtful the method used by the first British brewers was any more advanced.

Eventually brewers moved on, technologically, from brewing with bread to brewing with malt. We have already noted that the ancient Sumerians made green (undried) malt for use as food; they were doing this before 2400BC, and were drying the sprouted grain, which preserved it and made it available to the brewer at almost any time, by around 2000BC (there are hints in Sumerian writing that the malt was dried by spreading it on rooftops). For a while after the invention of 'proper' malting, however, beer was made from a mixture of bread and malt. About 1800BC an anonymous Sumerian composed a hymn of praise to Ninkasi, the goddess of beer and daughter of Enki, the water-god; she was called the goddess who 'satisfies the heart' in Sumerian mythology. The description of brewing in the 'Hymn to Ninkasi' shows that Sumerians at the time made their beer, or *kash*, from a mixture of *bappir*, or hard-baked barley bread, and soaked malt. Working out from this poem, written about 4,000 years ago, precisely how Sumerian brewers made their beer is rather like trying to construct a recipe for eighteenth-century ale from a reading of Robert Burns's verses on the story of John Barleycorn – with the added difficulties of translation from the Sumerian cuneiform. However, it is clear that the Sumerian brewers also added an extra sweetener to their raw, unfermented beer, quite possibly dates or honey.

We also know from the surviving writings that the Sumerians were brewing several different types of beer; three kinds could be on the table at once, at least if you were dining in the temple. A 'praise poem' written for King Shulgi of Ur, who ruled between 2094BC and 2047BC, says that in honour of the goddess Ninlil the king 'despatched dark beer [*kash-gíg*], *kurun* beer, and brown beer [*kash-su*] to her great dining hall for the evening meals'.

Across in Egypt, archaeological research at the kitchen complex of El Amarna, which was in operation around 1350BC, and at Deir el-Medina (1550–1307BC) shows that by this time beer was being made solely from grain, malted and unmalted (specifically, mostly emmer wheat), with no bread involved. Dr Delwen Samuel of the University of Cambridge, using a scanning electron microscope on brewing residues from El Armana, found evidence in 1996 that suggested by 1350BC Egyptian brewers appeared to be using a 'decoction mashing' process involving mashing malt, some of which was then taken away, brought to boiling and added back to the cold mash. This way the whole mash reached a temperature suitable for maximum starch conversion to sugar. The mixture was then strained of husks, and yeast was added for fermentation to take place.

The contemporary tomb paintings and tomb models, which still seem to show beer being made from soaked bread pressed through sieves, probably depicted the earlier method of brewing for religious reasons: if you were recently dead you would not want to upset the older people in the afterlife by making your beer in some new-fangled way with which they were not familiar.

The methods used by the dynastic Egyptians 3,350 years ago look to be exactly the same, except for the grain used, as those used to produce *pombe* beer in East Africa, described by the explorer Richard Burton in 1860. In a chapter on 'Village Life in East Africa' in his book *The Lake Regions of Central Africa*, Burton wrote:

The principal inebriant is a beer without hops, called *pombe*. This [beer] . . . dates from the age of Osiris: it is the *buzah* of Egypt and the farther East, and the *merissa* of the Upper Nile . . . It is usually made as follows: half of the grain – holcus [sorghum], panicum [millet], or both mixed – intended for the brew is buried or soaked in water till it sprouts; it is then pounded and mixed with the other half, also reduced to flour, and sometimes with a little honey. The compound is boiled twice or thrice in huge pots, strained, when wanted clear, through a bag of matting, and allowed to ferment: after the third day it becomes as sour as vinegar.

Porridge-beer and bread-mash beer, meanwhile, are still being brewed in the eastern Baltic and parts of eastern Europe, where the brew is known as *kvass* in Russia, *gira* in Lithuania and *taari* in Finland. One modern recipe for Russian *kvass* reads in part exactly like the method used to make beer in Egypt in 1500BC, according to tomb inscriptions of that time. Bread (black or rye bread in the case of *kvass*) is dried in an oven, then placed in a tub where boiling water is poured over it. The water is allowed to cool, and the liquid strained through a cloth, before yeast is added. Today *kvass* makers add other fermentables such as treacle and (very frequently) raisins to the brew, just as the Sumerians added dates or honey to theirs. Modern *kvass* is low in alcohol, and often undergoes a second or acidic fermentation, which makes it sharp and refreshing.

The earliest British beers were most likely made in the same way as ancient Egyptian or modern Baltic bread-mash beer. But it looks as if the first beers made in Britain were drunk by Neolithic farmers in special religious ceremonies, rather than as an everyday intoxicant. Simple equipment that could be used for brewing bread-mash beer, that is, an oven or hearth and a large fireproof pot, are frequently found by archaeologists at British Neolithic ritual sites dating from around 6,000 years ago, just after farming (and brewing) arrived in Britain. Merryn Dineley believes the bucket-shaped Late Neolithic pottery known as 'grooved ware' was used for brewing beer to be drunk on ritual occasions. Grooved ware pots, baked in a 'kiln' made from dung and reeds, are often found deliberately broken and buried at Neolithic cult sites such as henges around Britain, hinting that they were used for a religious purpose and then ritually smashed. Their capacities varied from one to six gallons, ideal for use as home brewing vessels.

As for what kind of brew this was, our evidence comes from recent analysis of a green, slimy residue found in 5,000-year-old Neolithic grooved ware pottery by archaeologists at a site near Skara Brae in Orkney in 1929. Pollen in the residue came from meadowsweet, *Filipendula ulmara* (which was probably used for flavouring and preserving the brew), and also from henbane, hemlock and deadly nightshade, three highly poisonous plants which produce (if they do not kill you first) strong hallucinatory effects. Henbane, *Hyoscyamus niger*, is a narcotic herb containing scopolamine, which causes delirium, delusions and stupor. Deadly nightshade or belladonna, *Atropa belladonna*,

Two Egyptian brewers squeeze soaked bread through a basketwork sieve into a jar, where the bready water will ferment into beer. From a tomb wall painting of around 2500BC.

contains another narcotic alkaloid, atropine, which also causes delirium. Both were allegedly used in medieval Europe by witchcraft and devil-worship cults to produce hallucinations: the cultists spread an ointment containing extracts of belladonna and henbane on their skin, which induced vivid delusions of flying in the air. Hemlock, *Conium maculatum*, contains the alkaloid coniine, which brings a brief initial stimulation, but is highly likely to be followed by severe depression of the nervous system, paralysis and death.

The Orkney mind-altering beer was not an isolated taste. Burnt 'porridge' containing traces of henbane – again, very likely the remains of a cereal mash from a Neolithic ritual or religious brew – was found attached to a fragment of another Neolithic 'grooved ware' vessel at a ritual site apparently used for burials at Balfarg/Balbirnie in Fifeshire, Scotland. Henbane was a Mediterranean plant originally: it is tempting to think the first farmers in these islands brought it with them from the south, along with wheat and barley, to flavour their psychotropic sacred beers and give them a hallucinatory kick.

So these Neolithic brewers were using powerful herbal drugs; and it is difficult to avoid the conclusion that this hallucinogenic brew was used for special ceremonial, shamanistic occasions when visions and delirium were sought – used to alter consciousness for religious purposes. Indeed, religious ceremonies involving alcoholic drinks made from grain are found so often in indigenous societies around the world today that it would be astonishing if the first British farmers did *not* brew beers to drink at ritual events, such as ceremonies to mark the planting of the corn in spring, or the end of the harvest, or a farewell to the dead.

Very likely Neolithic British beers had other fermentables besides cereals added to the mixture, such as honey or fruit; the later Bronze Age people certainly drank mixed brews using whatever fermentable materials were around. A clay pot found in a burial of a woman aged about twenty-five at North Mains, Strathallan, Scotland, dating from 3,600 years ago, contained a residue that suggests it once held a drink made from wheat and honey, flavoured, again, with meadowsweet.

In other words, this Bronze Age lass was accustomed to knocking back a cross between beer and mead – a brew known to Britons of the millennium just ended as bragget.

Over the North Sea in Denmark, at Egtved on the Jutland peninsula, another woman was buried around 3,370 years ago with a bucket made of birch bark. When the dried-out contents of the bucket were analysed in the early 1920s, they indicated it had contained a drink made from honey, wheat and cranberries, flavoured with bog myrtle or 'sweet gale': bog myrtle, which grows, as its name implies, in peaty wetlands, was a regular flavouring in ale until well into the last half of the second millennium AD across northern Europe, and was used to make 'gale ale' in Yorkshire.

What had changed by the late Bronze Age, however, was the circumstances under which beer was drunk. Early in the Bronze Age, around 4,000 years ago, a culture known to archaeologists as the Beaker Folk or Beaker People arrived in the British Isles. They are named after the distinctive pottery drinking vessels found in their graves – vessels which, given their size and shape, really ought to have earned these people the name 'pint mug folk'. Some of the 'beakers' that have been found in their graves look astonishingly like nineteenth-century pottery beer mugs. The typical Beaker culture grave, normally a single burial under a tumulus, contains, as well as the drinking mug, archery equipment and a dagger. Clearly drinking was extremely important to these people, who spread from Spain over much of Atlantic Europe, if they needed to be buried with their mugs. But what was it they were drinking?

The archaeologist Peter Fowler wrote in 1983: 'It has for long been traditionally thought that the "beakers" of the Beaker People could well have been (communal?) beer-drinking containers, but although the possible contemporary rise in the production of barley could allow precisely this interpretation, the argument is insecure and circumstantial.' Insecure and circumstantial or not, nobody has put forward a more likely suggestion for what the Beaker People drank from their mugs than beer, or mead, or a beer-and-mead mix.

As it happens, the rise in barley production in Britain about the time the Beaker People arrived is irrelevant to the argument, since the archaeological evidence shows that brewers at the time used emmer wheat, not barley. But what the beakers do represent, the archaeologist Andrew Sherratt of Oxford University suggests, is a change from the sacred community beer drinking of the Neolithic farmers to a culture of male warrior elites who would gather to drink beer and feast. Sherratt wrote in 1987: 'Alcohol was a precious substance, hard-won (no doubt with much ritual and mystique) from a temperate environment, and often adulterated with other things. Its effects would have been a remarkable experience, perhaps not available to society at large, and monopolised by the powerful.'

What happened with the Beaker People, Sherratt suggests, is that the social significance of alcohol shifted: hitherto the prerogative of individuals acting on behalf of the community, in a shamanic role, its consumption became a hallmark of status in general, of chiefs and heads of families. Four thousand years ago, in short, beer drinking stopped being a ceremonial act and became a secular expression of hospitality and your standing in the community: a role 'getting the beers in' still fulfils today.

CHAPTER TWO

CELT AND ROMAN

how the legions learned to love British beer

Will you have a pint of ale?
We are the Romans.
Will you have a pint of ale?
For we are the Roman soldiers.

A pint of ale won't serve us at all,
We are the British,
A pint of ale won't serve us at all,
For we are the British soldiers.

Will you have a barrel of ale?
We are the Romans.
Will you have a barrel of ale?
For we are the Roman soldiers.

Yes, we'll have a barrel of ale,
We are the British,
Yes, we'll have a barrel of ale,
For we are the British soldiers.

Part of a traditional children's challenge game

Some time around the beginning of the last millennium BC, 3,000 years ago, the British Isles became part of the firmly beer-drinking, warrior-dominated Celtic culture that controlled Europe north of the Alps.

Today's Celtic and Germanic-speaking inhabitants of the British Isles have common linguistic ancestors in a people known to us as the 'proto-Indo-Europeans'. These people, whose daughter languages, as their name implies, are now spoken from western Europe to northern India, were living probably somewhere north of the Black Sea around 8,000 years ago. Originally their favourite intoxicating beverage was mead, the fermented drink made from honey and water. We know this because of the wide range of words from the same Indo-European root that cover the meanings 'mead', 'honey', 'drunk', 'intoxicated' and so on that are found today in Indo-European languages from Cork to Calcutta.

Millennia before they arrived in Britain, the ancestors of the Celts and Germans had been introduced to cereal agriculture and ale brewing. For those that could not afford mead but wanted some of the prestige associated with this upper-class intoxicant, a cheaper drink could now be brewed that was a mixture of honey and wheat. As we saw in chapter 1, archaeological finds from the Neolithic to the Bronze Age in Scotland suggest that a honey-and-grain alcoholic drink was being consumed in Britain three to six millennia ago, probably in ritual circumstances. The main flavouring seems to have been mead-owsweet, a marsh, fen and woodland plant whose name actually means 'mead sweet': modern experiments show that meadowsweet has a preservative as well as a flavouring effect on alcoholic drink, preventing brews going sour for two weeks longer than drinks made without it.

No one has been able to put a firm date on when the Celts arrived in the British Isles: between 1200BC and 800BC is the best guess. Although invasion might seem the obvious way, there are no archae-ological signs for anything but gradual change. There was certainly not much difference between the beers brewed in Iron Age Celtic Britain and their predecessors in Bronze Age Britain. But beer drinking had become more democratized, with none of the evidence for the elite nature of alcohol consumption shown by the Beaker People: beer mugs were beer mugs, with no hint that they carried the status implications late Bronze Age mugs evidently did.

The tradition of wheat-and-honey beers continued well into the Iron Age. Around 320BC the Greek explorer Pytheas of Massilia (modern Marseilles) came to Britain. His original writings have been lost, but a later Greek writer, Strabo, who died in AD21, quoted him saying about the natives of Britain that 'where there is grain and even honey, the people get their beverage from them'. Strabo's quote is mildly ambiguous, since it is just possible he is talking about Thule, further north than the 'Pretannic Islands'; but, given what else we know, it seems certain that Pytheas, the first literate traveller to reach Britain from the Mediterranean, found the British Celts making beer from grain and honey 2,300 years ago.

The grain used for this mixed drink was the one known to the Celts as *bracis*, generally identified as emmer or bearded wheat. From *bracis* came the name of the honey-and-grain drink: in Old Welsh, *bragaut*; in English, 'bragget'. However, since *bracis* is linked to early words for malt, it may be that the Celts called emmer simply 'the malting grain'. *Bracis* is the root of the French words for brewer (*brasseur*) and brewery (*brasserie*).

By the time the Romans arrived, the Celts had moved from bread-beer to malted-grain brews. There were certainly maltings in Roman Britain, and since the Romans never introduced malting, the Celts must have been doing it before Caesar and his legions arrived.

The Celtic word for beer was *curmi*: it appears in a Gaulish personal name, Curmisagios, which literally means 'beer seeker' or perhaps 'beer hunter', though 'beer steward' is probably a politer translation. Around the first century of the Christian era a pronunciation change took place in Britain and among the mainland Gauls in which *m* became *v*. Thus the word for ale changed from *curmi* to something closer to *corvi or *corev. In medieval Welsh the word was spelt *cwrwf* (single *f* is pronounced *v* in Welsh), today altered to *cwrw*, while in Cornish it became *coref* or *cor'f* (*coreff* in Breton, the continental version of Cornish). It is from this late Celtic word that the Latin for beer, *cervisia* or *cervesia* (several spellings exist) is derived; and it is from the Latin, of course, that Spanish gets the word *cerveza*, meaning beer, and the Portuguese get *cerveja*. In French *cervoise* means (unhopped) ale.

A Greek writer, Posidonius, who lived from around 135BC to 50BC, gave a description of the drinking methods of the Celts of southern Gaul that probably applied to their cousins in the British Isles as well: the 'masses' consumed a wheat-and-honey beer called *corma*, Posidonius wrote, and while 'they sip a little, not more than a small mouthful from the same cup [that is, a common cup] . . . they do it rather frequently'. The cups used in southern Britain, at least, for drinking beer around AD20 came in two styles: a tall thin pot known to modern archaeologists as a butt beaker, and small cone-shaped cups.

The first-century Roman writer Gaius Plinius, better known today as Pliny the Elder, wrote in his *Natural History* that the 'peoples of the west' had their own intoxicant made from grain that was '*madida*' with water. The ambiguity of *madida* – a word which, like 'sodden' in English, can mean 'soaked' or 'boiled' – means we cannot be certain if Pliny knew the Celts used hot water to mash the grain for their beer; but he knew enough to say that Celtic brewing practices were not exactly the same everywhere: 'There are a number of ways of making it in Gaul and Spain, under different names, although the principle is the same.' He also told posterity that Celtic ale was not the undrinkable-after-a-couple-of-days concoction it is sometimes made out to be, writing that the Spanish provinces 'have by this time even taught us that these types [of liquors] will bear being kept for a long time'. Whether this was because they were strong in alcohol,

Footnote: the asterisk indicates that this is a presumed form of an unrecorded ancestor-word.

or because they used preserving herbs such as meadowsweet, he did not say.

Like other Roman writers, Pliny appeared shocked that beer drinkers did not dilute their cups with water, as wine drinkers did – 'they actually quaff liquors of this kind neat'. He also mentioned that the *spuma* or froth of all these brews (presumably the yeasty foam on top of the fermenting beer) 'is used by women as a cosmetic for the face'. If this use of yeast to improve the complexion was a British practice, it was still taking place 1,900 years later. In the 1930s, sufferers from skin complaints would collect excess yeast from Adey and White's brewery in St Albans, Hertfordshire, making a small donation to St Albans City Hospital at the same time.

A description of Celtic brewing practice comes through the Spanish-born historian Paulus Orosius, who was writing in North Africa in the early fifth century AD. In his *History against the Pagans*, which told the story of the known world from the Creation to AD417, Orosius wrote about the siege by the Romans of the Celtiberian city of Numantia in 133BC. Numantia stood on the Douro river in Soria, north central Spain, and the siege was the culmination of sixty years of ultimately unsuccessful local resistance to Rome's armies. Orosius wrote that the land of the Numantians was not fertile enough to produce wine, and instead they drank 'the juice of wheat skilfully treated', which they called *celia* (one of the types of Spanish beer mentioned by Pliny).

To make this 'juice of wheat', *succo tritici*, Orosius said, 'the young shoots of the crop are soaked', a fair if slightly garbled description of steeping the grain, 'and their potency is kindled by being heated'. This sounds like the malting process, where the sprouting grains will heat up as the enzymes inside each one turn starches into sugars. The grain is 'then dried' – kilned – 'and afterwards pounded into flour, and mixed with *molli succo*'. This expression translates literally as 'soft juice'. However, *molli succo* is also an occasional Latin expression for fresh water, which is probably what is meant here.

The result, Orosius said, was a fermented drink 'to which an astringent taste and the heat of drunkenness is added'. It was powerful enough to encourage the Numantians, trapped in their city during Scipio's siege, to burst out of the gates after 'extensive drinking', and try unsuccessfully to take on the surrounding Roman legions before their final defeat and the city's complete destruction.

Between the two brief invasions of Britain by Julius Caesar in 55 and 54BC and the successful one by Claudius in AD43, the Celtic tribes of southern Britain were split between those who saw themselves as allied to the great power in continental Europe and those whose strongest desire was to remain out of Rome's hands. The anti-Roman 'Eurosceptics', to use a 1990s expression, were led by the Catuvellauni, who ruled in modern Hertfordshire and Essex, with their capital at Camulodon, modern Colchester. The 'Europhiles' were chiefly the Atrebates, whose land lay between the middle Thames and the south coast. The two sides used their coinage as propaganda: Verica, the Europhile king of the Atrebates, called himself *rex*, Latin for king, on his coins, which carried on one side a vine-leaf, symbol of the Romans' favourite drink, wine. On the other hand, Cunobelin, Eurosceptic king of the Catuvellauni, used the native word *rigonus*, Celtic for king, on his coins – which, as noted in the introduction, bore on one side an ear of bearded barley or emmer wheat, the symbol of beer, the British drink.

The Catuvellauni were not as purist about their alcoholic drink as their propaganda declared: archaeologists have found the remains of many amphorae, vessels for storing wine, at Catuvellaunian sites. But the Romans were not solely wine drinkers either. There are plenty of signs of the legions in Roman-occupied Germany drinking local beer, and in the 1980s archaeologists found the evidence that Rome's soldiers in Britain sustained themselves on Celtic ale. A series of domestic and military accounts dating from AD90–130, dug up at the Roman fort of Vindolanda in modern Northumbria, reveal the garrison at Vindolanda buying *ceruese*, or beer, as the legions doubtless did throughout the rest of Roman Britain, almost certainly from local brewers.

One list of accounts from Vindolanda mentions 'Atrectus the brewer' (*Atrectus ceruesar[ius]*), the first named brewer in British history, as well as the first known professional brewer in Britain. Around the end of AD110 one of the few clearly dated Vindolanda tablets shows a *metretam* (twelve gallons) of *cervese* being bought for eight asses, or four-fifths of a silver denarius. The accounts also show purchases of *bracis* or *braces*, emmer wheat (or malt), doubtless for brewing. Quite possibly the garrison bought the malt, and hired a local brewer to make beer from it for the troops.

At least two stand-alone Romano-British malting/brewing complexes have been excavated: one at Loudwater, Chorleywood, Hertfordshire and the other, from the third century, at Scole in Suffolk. Their similarity suggests they represent a common plan for Roman breweries in Britain. Each involved a leat or channel dug across a bend in the local river (the Chess at Loudwater, the Waveney at Scole) which supplied a large tank where raw grain must have been steeped for malting. Close to the steeping tank at each site was a large 'corn-drying oven' or maltings. At Loudwater the leat ran down to a water mill where the dried malt would have been ground before it was mashed. Another likely brewery was uncovered at a fourth-century Roman villa at Woodchester, Gloucestershire.

All of these breweries were rural, but brewing went on in towns and cities as well. The archaeological evidence shows that a small cookshop/brewery was in operation on a street corner opposite the public baths in Roman Verulamium (modern St Albans) for 300 years. In the third and fourth centuries British potters were making fine drinking vessels that very frequently held a quart or more. This suggests that customers of the Verulamium home-brew establishment sank their ale in pottery tankards similar to those used by eighteenth-century Britons, who also preferred quart pots.

Brewing in Roman Britain, domestic and retail, must have been widespread: remains indicating the existence of Roman-era malting or brewing operations have been found from Somerset to Northumberland, and South Wales to Colchester. In the third and fourth centuries AD Roman 'hypocaust' technology, for supplying central heating to homes, was adapted in Britain to build permanent corn dryers/maltings, and the remains of these double-floored buildings, with underground flues, are found in Roman towns as well as on Roman farms.

Most archaeologists have insisted on calling them 'corn dryers'. However, when a replica of a fourth-century example that had been excavated at a gravel quarry at Foxholes Farm, near Hertford, in the late 1970s was built and tested, it showed that the design made it a poor dryer of large quantities of grain but an efficient maltings. The temperature in the 'dryer' reached an average of 60–70°C, and would have been able to produce an amber malt perfectly capable of making good ale.

The stone-and-tile Romano-British maltings replaced the earlier method of drying grain and green malt, which involved placing the grain on a wheel made of brushwood which was supported on posts over a fire. The apparatus was called a *zabulum*, and it must have needed careful watching to stop the brushwood flaring up and burning the grain to charcoal.

Beer was included in the list of goods and services laid out by the Roman Emperor Diocletian in an edict of AD301 setting maximum prices in the empire, an (unsuccessful) attempt at curbing price inflation. Among dozens of different goods and services, three types of beer were named in the edict, which was written on stone pillars erected in important cities around the empire. The beers were *cervesia* and *camum*, to be sold at 4 denarii the 'Italian pint', and *zythum*, Egyptian beer, to be sold at 2 denarii a pint. For comparison, the very best Falernian wine, the finest the Romans knew, was priced by Diocletian at 30 denarii a pint, and ordinary wine, *vini rustici*, was 8 denarii a pint. Other prices included cheese at 12 denarii a pound, beef at only 8 denarii a pound, a pair of chickens for 60 denarii – and ten dormice for 40 denarii (meaning a pint of ale cost the same as one tasty but tiny dormouse). A haircut cost 2 denarii, while a mule driver was to be paid 25 denarii a day.

In AD410 the imperial powers finally pulled out Rome's troops from Britain and told the locals they would have to look after themselves. Native lords and kings took control of the country and Britain became once more a Celtic land under a man with the title Vortigern – a Celtic word meaning 'high lord'. Rents and tributes to these Celtic rulers would have been payable, or 'rendered', in food and drink. Welsh law books surviving from the twelfth century show what was expected in tribute from a township in the medieval period, and the same 'renders', or something very similar, must have been demanded by local British kings from the fifth century onwards. As far as payments in alcohol were concerned, the most valuable drink was mead (*medd* in Welsh), the least valuable was ale (*cwrwf* in Old Welsh), while in between was bragget, *bragaut*, the wheat-and-honey brew of the early Celts.

In Ireland, meanwhile, Celtic brewing traditions had continued uninterrupted, and when Christian monks bought literacy to the island the rules and traditions surrounding brewing were finally written down. The records show that ale was an important part of the tribal way of life, and a king's relationship to his people involved supplies of drink. A law tract called the *Crith-Gablach*, compiled about the middle or end of the seventh century AD, declared that the 'seven occupations in the law of a king' were: 'Sunday, at ale drinking, for he is not a lawful *flaith* [lord] who does not distribute ale every Sunday; Monday, at legislation, for the government of the tribe; Tuesday, at *fidchell* [a popular Celtic board game]; Wednesday, seeing greyhounds coursing; Thursday, at the pleasures of love; Friday, at horse-racing; Saturday, at judgment.' Clearly, being an Irish king was tough.

A glorious poem to Irish ale occurs in a telling of the life of a Scots Gaelic prince called Cano, who fled to Ireland and was killed in AD687. The poem, which was written about the eighth or ninth century, lists more than a dozen different ales from Kerry to Antrim.

*Though he were to drink of the beverages of flaths
  [lords]*
Though a flath may drink of strong liquors
He shall not be a king over Eriu
Unless he drink the ale of Cualand

The ale of Cumur na Tri nUisce
Is jovially drunk around Inber Ferna.
I have not drunk a juice to be preferred
To the ale of Cernia.

The ale of the land of Ele
It belongs to the merry Momonians;
The ale of Fórlochra Ardaa
The red ale of Dorind.

The ale of Caill Gortan Coille
Is served to the king of Ciarraige
This is the liquor of noble Eriu
Which the Gaedhil pour out in friendship.

In Cuil Tola of shining goblets —
Druim Lethan of good cheer
An ale-feast is given to the Lagenians
When the summer foliage withers.

Ale is drunk in Feara Cuile
The houses are not counted.
To Findia is served up sumptuously
The ale of Muirthemne.

Ale is drunk around Loch Cuain
It is drunk out of deep horns
In Magh Inis by the Ultonians
Where laughter rises to loud exultation.

By the gentle Dalraid it is drunk –
In half measures by [the light of] bright candles
[While] With easy-handled battle spears
Chosen good warriors practise good feats

The Saxon ale of bitterness
Is drank with pleasure about Inber in Rig
About the land of the Cruithni, about Gergin
Red ales, like wine are freely drank.

One brew not mentioned in Cano's poem was heather ale. The legend of heather ale, 'the most delicious drink the world has ever known', is a folk tale once told right around Ireland: sixty years ago most Irish country folk seemed to know about the fabled drink brewed from heather. It was also found throughout Scotland, from the Shetlands to Galloway. The legend's basic theme is almost always the same, whoever is telling it, and wherever: a father and son (or two sons), the last survivors of their race, the only people left alive who know how to brew the heather ale, are captured and ordered to reveal the secret of making the drink, or die. The father says he will disclose the recipe, but only if his son(s) are first killed, because he is afraid his offspring will murder him for divulging the ingredients and methodology of this rare and famous liquor. The son (or sons) despatched into the yonder, the father then laughs at his captors and tells them that they have done what he wanted: weak youth might have given away the secrets of heather ale in return for life, but old age cannot be compelled. The recipe, the old man says, will die with him: he will reveal nothing.

In Scotland the possessors of the secret of heather ale are usually given as the Picts, the race that inhabited the northern half of the country from pre-Roman times until their lands were conquered by the growing kingdom of the Scots under Kenneth mac Alpin around

AD843. However, in almost all the Irish tales the people who know how to brew heather ale and who refuse to tell anyone else are the Vikings. In most of the Irish-language versions the heather ale is actually called *bheoir Lochlannach*, or Viking beer, from the Old Norse *bjorr*. Before about AD1000, confusingly, *bjorr* seems to have signified a strong, sweet, honey-and-fruit drink rather than grain-based beer. Perhaps, therefore, *bheoir Lochlannach* was a heather-flavoured mead or something similar.

It is a mystery why, when the Irish told the tale, the people who held the secret of heather ale changed from the Picts to the Vikings. The Irish certainly knew who the Picts were: several Pictish tribes lived in Antrim and Armagh. The Irish called them, and their Scottish brothers and sisters, *Cruithin*: this is the Irish version, substituting *k* for *p*, of the British Celtic name for the Picts, *Priten*. Pict appears to be a Latin translation of *Priten*, since both mean 'picture', implying the Picts were covered in tattoos. (*Priten*, via the Greek Pretanoi, is the origin of the Latin Britannia and thus Britain, the 'land of the tattooed people'.)

The 'drinking Pict', an engraved slab from Bullion in Angus, Scotland. Is that heather ale in his drinking horn? (*National Museums of Scotland*)

The change in nationality of the heather ale brewers in Irish stories may have occurred because there was no tradition of the Irish Picts being wiped out, while there was a strong folk recollection in Ireland of a massive defeat for the Vikings. Just as many of the Scottish versions mention a last battle between the Picts and the Scots, many of the Irish tales about heather ale feature the last big clash involving the Irish and the Vikings, the battle of Clontarf, which took place just outside Dublin in AD1014. Just as in the Scottish stories, two sons and a father were captured after the battle, this time Danes rather than Picts. As in the Scots tales, the eldest Viking then allows all three to be killed rather than reveal the recipe for heather ale.

The story in all its versions excites folklorists because of its basic theme: captive cleverly achieves desired death of companion by falsely promising to reveal valuable secret to captors. This is identical to one of the plots found in the Norse Eddas and the Germanic *Niebelungenlied*, and turned into opera by the nineteenth-century composer Richard Wagner – except that the secret Attila, the king of the Huns, wanted to get from Gunnar the Niebelung was the whereabouts of the Rhine gold, rather than the recipe for a famous beer. Much debate has taken place in folkloric publications about which tale came first, the Rhine gold or the heather ale. Most scholars feel the Vikings told the Gaels the original story, and somewhere the real gold of the Nibelungs became the liquid gold of the heather ale.

Hints do exist that heather ale really was made by the Vikings in Ireland, and by later brewers as well. The Victorian journalist John Bickerdyke, writing in 1889, said that 'as late as the commencement of this century', that is, around 1801, 'an ale flavoured with heather . . . was brewed in many parts of Ireland. The practice, it is believed, is now almost if not quite extinct'. The method, Bickerdyke said, was to let the wort drain through heather blossoms placed at the bottom of tubs, so that during its passage the wort gains 'a peculiar and agreeable flavour'.

Heather may have been doing more than adding flavour. The nectar in the heather flowers would add extra sugar to a brew, and wild yeasts growing on the flowers would have helped with fermentation. But the plant is also 'reputed' to be narcotic, as are several of its relatives in the Ericacea family. In addition, a moss or 'fog' (*fog*, sometimes spelt *fogg*, is the dialect word for moss in Scotland and the north of England) that grows on the heather stems produces a white powder which itself has narcotic and at least mildly hallucinogenic effects.

The strongest evidence of an enduring tradition of brewing heather ale comes from Scotland, where the practice seems to have lasted long after the Picts were history. The writer and traveller Thomas Pennant wrote in 1772 that on the Hebridean island of Islay 'ale is frequently made of the young tops of heath, mixing two thirds of that plant with one of malt, sometimes adding hops'. Just over half a century later, in 1831, James Logan, in a book called *The Scottish Gael*, said that 'in the Highlands it was an almost invariable practice, when brewing, to put a quantity of the green tops of heath in the mash tub, and when the plant is in bloom it adds much to the strength and flavour of the beer. The roots, also, will improve its qualities, for they are of a liquorice sweetness, but their astringency requires them to be used with caution'.

The grain generally used for brewing in Ireland was barley, and the barley that grew on rich land was the most prized; but ale was also brewed from rye, from wheat and from oats. One of the best-known Irish brews was *cuirm Cualann*, the ale mentioned in the first verse of Cano's poem referred to above, 'once a famous kind of ale brewed in the Cuala district' (the rich farmland of east Leinster), drunk by the kings of Leinster out of vessels made from wild ox horns.

Among the flavourings that went into Irish ale were the leaves and twigs of bog myrtle (*Myrica gale* in Latin) – known to have been used throughout northern Europe – also known as sweet gale or, in old Irish, *ridiog* (*roid* in modern Gaelic). Also used was bogbean, buck-bean or marsh trefoil (*Menyanthes trifoliata*), whose leaves give a bitter taste: one nineteenth-century writer said 'large quantities' of 'pressed and exhausted' leaves and stems of buck-bean had been found near raths (old native Irish castles), the suggestion being that they were left over from ale brewing.

All farmers would have brewed their own ale: a description of an Irish farmer of the first few centuries AD says he had in his house 'strainers with their cries always at work, *ag sgagadh leanna*, "a-straining ale", in hospitable preparation for guests'. But there were also professional brewers, each working in a specialized brewhouse known as a *coirmthech*, or *cuirm-teac*, an alehouse.

Brews that would not ferment were occasionally a problem: an ancient account says one 'stuck' wort was kick-started into yeasty life by having a fragment of the cross of Saint Aéd dropped into it. (In the nineteenth century, illegal poteen distillers in the hills of the Irish west who could not make a ferment begin would sometimes drop a piece of turf into the mash to get the yeast going.) The brewer in Colmán Elo's monastery asked the saint to help with a wort that failed to ferment, and got a gushing non-stop fountain of beer as a result, one of the chroniclers wrote. Monastic brewing was universal: the British cleric Gildas, writing about AD545, mentions *cervisa* in connection with monks, and just as other landed estates had brewed their own beer, there would not have been a monastery in Britain or Ireland without its brewery to sustain the brothers.

Irish priests in the first millennium seem to have been connoisseurs of ale, since there are records of their complaints about the standard of drink they found while travelling on the European continent. One said the local beer was so bad he 'threw his boots at it'. Sedulius Scottus ('Sedulius the Irishman'), one of the most famous expatriate Irish scholars of the ninth century, once gave a list of grievances to his patron, the Bishop of Liège, which included the 'really horrible' local ale. 'No child of Ceres this,' Sedulius said, 'though it has the yellow of her hair . . . a beast of prey in a man's inwards.' Things have improved over the past 1,200 years: Jupille, just outside Liège, is now the home of Interbrew, Belgium's biggest brewing company, which also owns a fair slice of the British brewing industry.

CHAPTER THREE

A THOUSAND YEARS OF ALE

from the Saxons to Dick Whittington

Or hi parra
La corveyse vos chanteres
Alleluia
Qui que aukes en beyt
Si tel seyt comme estre droit
Res Miranda

Let it now be taught
If ale is made as it ought
Alleluia you will sing
What a wonderful thing

Part of a thirteenth-century Norman French chanson

The Germanic invaders who came over the North Sea to raid and settle in the early fifth century AD were – like the Celtic Britons before them – warriors from a beer-drinking culture. The Jutes, Saxons and Angles met and celebrated in the beer-hall, which was central to their lives, and to their myths. In the Old English epic *Beowulf*, a story brought across the North Sea, a vital role in the plot is played by the great beer-hall of Heorot, where Queen Wealhtheow brought round the 'flowing cup' and bade her king: 'be blithe at the beer drinking'.

If the pagan tribes of Jutland and the north German coast who invaded Britain in the fifth and sixth centuries AD were like the pagan south Germans the Irish monks were trying to Christianize in the seventh century, then the Angles and Saxons used ale in sacrificial ceremonies to the gods. The Christian Irish, who were beer drinkers themselves, were disgusted by this German habit. The saint Columbanus, who was born in Leinster about AD545, was in Bregenz, by Lake Constance, in or about AD611, preaching to the local German tribe, the Suevi (or Swabians). One day, his biographer Jonas relates, he found them 'preparing to make a profane offering', 'and they placed a great barrel, which in their language they called a *cupa* [a word for a beer cask from which we get cooper, cask maker], which holds twenty measures or more of ale, in the midst of them'.

Columbanus went up to the Suevi and asked them what they were going to do with the ale, Jonas says, 'and they said that they were going to sacrifice to their god Woden'. Not surprisingly this 'evil project' angered the saint, who blew on the cask, 'and it burst with a mighty crack and the ale poured out'. The Suevi, of course, 'were astonished, and said that they had a great man of God among them, who could thus dissolve a barrel fully bound with hoops as it was'. Columbanus 'preached the word of God to them, and urged them to refrain from these sacrifices', and many of his audience, impressed by the miracle of the bursting cask, 'turned to the Christian faith and accepted baptism'.

The story reveals more than the use of ale in sacrifices: it shows that the German tribes knew how to make large hooped casks, big enough to contain perhaps forty gallons of ale. For those seeking a non-miraculous explanation of why the barrel exploded, it also suggests that the ale made by Germanic tribes went through a secondary fermentation in the cask, which could build enough carbon dioxide pressure to shatter the hoops.

The Anglo-Saxon or Old English settlers in what was to become England recognized at least three different types or styles of ale. These are regularly mentioned in surviving charters and laws from the seventh century onwards, which set out the food rents required from an estate. The first was *hlutres aloth* in the Anglian dialect, *hluttor eala* in that of Wessex: 'clear ale'; what later centuries would call stale or old ale. This had been left standing long enough for whatever was in suspension – yeasty bits, proteins – to settle out. Its existence shows that either ale before the introduction of hops was expected to keep for at least the several days it takes an unfined brew to clear, or the Old English were using something to clear it. One possibility for the Saxon clearing or fining agent is the plant called alehoof or ground ivy, *Glechoma hederacea*, which Culpeper's *Herbal* in the 1600s said would clarify new ale 'in a night'.

Modern experiments with brewing unhopped medieval-style ales suggest that they start to go sour after four or five days, which is before they have cleared properly (though this is without using herbs such as ground ivy). The sourness, however, is no more than will be found in wild-fermentation Belgian beer styles such as *gueuze*. The idea that clear ale was normally an astringent, sour or bitter drink is strengthened by the warning in an eleventh-century leechdom, or medical text, to sufferers from lung disease to stay away from *geswet eala*, sweet ale, and drink *hluttor eala*, clear ale, instead.

The contrasting brew to *hlutres aloth* was *lithes aloth*, mild (or sweet) ale, which would have been newly brewed and still unacid, and probably still rather cloudy as well. The third and final drink regularly mentioned in charters as a currency in which rents could be paid was *Waelsces aloth*, Welsh ale. This was probably the same as bragget, or honey beer, and obviously a novelty to the early English, if they named it after their enemy the Welsh, who had been brewing honey beer for centuries.

By the early eleventh century, just before the Norman invasion, a leechdom written in Old English could mention nearly a dozen different types of ale for mixing with medicinal herbs. They included (in the Wessex dialect) *Wilisc ealath*, Welsh ale; *strang hluttor eala*, strong clear ale; *hluttor eala wel gesweted*, well-sweetened clear ale; *sur ealath*, sour ale; *niwe ealath*, new ale; *eald ealath*, old ale; *awylled ealath*, either 'boiling' or 'bubbling' ale (possibly still-fermenting ale); *twibrowen ealath*, 'twice-brewed' or strong ale; and *niwe ealo aer thon hit asiwen sie*, new ale before it has been strained or filtered.

This last description suggests that freshly brewed Anglo-Saxon ale was full of yeasty 'bits', an idea reinforced by the 'sieve spoons' with which high-born Anglo-Saxon women were buried. The spoon was a symbol of the lady's role as hostess for her lord, as fulfilled by Queen Wealhtheow, who came round with the ale in the *Beowulf* epic. If the guest wanted new, sweet, mild ale, it would have to be strained first by the hostess.

The many compound words in Old English that contain the word *ealu* give a good picture of Anglo-Saxon pub life: down at the *ealu-hus*, or alehouse, the *ealu-sceop*, brewer, is standing over the *ealo-faet*, ale-vat or fermenting vessel, engaged in the *ealo-geweorc*, 'ale-working' or brewing. When the brewing is completed, the finished drink will go into the *ealu-cleofa*, cell or chamber for storing ale.

Once it is ready it will be served to the *ealu-wósa*, 'ale-wetter' or ale drinker, who is sitting on the *ealu-benc*, or ale bench. He is drinking from his *ealo-wáege*, ale cup, getting happily *ealo-gál*, 'ale-drunk' and listening to the *ealu-scop*, 'ale-poet' or ale-minstrel, one who recites poetry where there is drinking. Priests, incidentally, were repeatedly forbidden in canonical edicts from ale-minstrelsy, which suggests that a degree of ribaldry was expected in the performance, and it was fun enough for the Anglo-Saxon clergy to risk angering their archbishops by taking part.

More lastingly, the word for ale also appears in the compound *brydealu*, 'bride ale', or wedding feast (the use of the word for ale as the word for feast also occurs in Old Irish; and in Sumerian, 2,000 years earlier, the word for banquet or feast was *kash-dé-a*, literally 'the beer pouring'). 'Bride ale' survives as the modern English adjective 'bridal'. There was also the *ealu-gafol*, the ale tax, or tribute paid in ale. This was one of three types of tribute a Saxon 'boor' or peasant could be made to pay his lord for the land he farmed, the others being 'honey tribute' and 'meat tribute'.

Rents were sometimes also payable in malt, so that the recipient could brew with it later. The usual Anglo-Saxon malting grain seems to have been barley, or, more likely, the hardier, more primitive variety of barley known as bere (pronounced 'bare', in older times 'barr'), which is still grown today in Scotland. Dozens of English placenames incorporate the word 'bere', including most of the Bartons, Barwicks and Barfords. (Barley, which actually means 'bere-like', is not found as a noun in English until the twelfth century, while a barn, etymologically, is 'a house for storing bere'. However, 'bere' has nothing to do with the origin of the word beer.) Most Old English references to the processed grain are simply to 'malt', *mealt*, but occasionally leech-doms talk specifically about *hwaetene mealt*, wheat malt. Oats do not seem to have been malted, though they are known to have been in the later medieval period.

Malt was made in the *mealt-hus*, and later ground and mashed, after which the wort – *maesc-wyrt*, mash-wort – was drained off and fermented. Fermentation did not always go well, and Anglo-Saxon brewers would resort to spells and the like to get things moving, to the despair of their religious leaders. Aelfric, the early eleventh-century abbot of Eynsham in Oxfordshire, wrote: 'It shames us to recount all the shameful sorceries which you foolish men practise . . . *on brywlace* [in brewing].' One leechdom suggested that if the ale was spoilt, the brewer should 'take lupins and lay them in the four corners of the building and over the door and beneath the threshold and under the ale vat', and also 'put holy water into the wort of that ale'.

Brewers knew about yeast, which they called *beorma* (root of the modern dialect word 'barm', and etymologically linked to the word 'fermentation') or *doerst*, from *dros*, the word for dregs, or *gest*, source of our modern word 'yeast'. But how they added yeast to their wort to get it to ferment is not clear. They may have waited for wild yeasts to begin fermentation; they may have added the dregs of the last brew to the new one; or they could have dipped twigs into the froth on top of a fermenting wort and let that dry until it was needed for the next brew, as nineteenth- and twentieth-century Norwegian home brewers did. Probably each brewer had their own technique, and different brewers would use different ways of getting yeast into the wort: it would be a mistake to assume a universal brewing method throughout Anglo-Saxon England. A drying bundle of yeast-covered twigs, incidentally, is sometimes said to be the origin of the 'ale-bush' that hung outside a house where ale was for sale, but there is no evidence for this.

In both Anglo-Saxon and medieval England, anyone who had ale for sale announced it by erecting an 'ale-stake' or 'ale-pole', decorated with a green bush or garland, outside their home. The implication of the ale-stake is that householders who brewed for sale did it seldom enough that their neighbours could not expect to find ale available without being visually informed of it by the sign of the bush. (Today in Lesotho, southern Africa, women who make sorghum beer let neighbours know a fresh batch is on sale by flying a white flag from a long pole.) Nor were the neighbours the only people who needed notifying: a tenant who brewed for sale was often liable to pay a 'tax', called a *tolcester*, to his lord of a gallon or so from every batch, and the ale-stake was a way of telling the lord's servants that the *tolcester* should be collected.

The universality of ale drinking is reflected in a sentence from the *Colloquium* written by Aelfric when he was schoolmaster of Cerne Abbas around AD987 to 1002. In a series of questions and answers designed to help pupils master Latin (which give us, moreover, an unmatched picture of life in pre-Norman England), a young man is asked what he drinks, and replies: '*Ealu gif ic haebbe, oththe waeter gif ic naebbe ealu*' – 'Ale if I have it, water if I have not ale.' Ale was such an essential part of life that the authorities were tough on brewers who failed to make a satisfactory brew. In eleventh-century Chester, in the time of Edward the Confessor, any brewer who made bad beer was either put in the dung-stool or fined 4s, a substantial punishment.

Domesday Book recorded four places where dues were payable in ale, all in areas with strong Celtic connections. In Helston in Cornwall, a county which had been under proper English rule for only around 130 years, there were forty *cervisarii*, which must mean men whose rent was paid by supplying ale. At St German's, also in Cornwall, a hide of land paid *una cupa cervisae* (a cask of ale) and 30d to the church. In Bistre, Flintshire, the Welsh King Gruffydd had a manor that gave him 200 loaves, *una cupa plena ceruisia* and a vessel of butter. In the village of Llanmartin, Gloucestershire, a rent was paid to the local church of two pigs and 100 loaves 'with ale' (*cum cervisia*).

William the Conqueror's great survey of England also gave an insight into the economy of a large early medieval abbey. Domesday Book's scribes wrote that, at the abbey at Bury St Edmunds, there were seventy-five 'bakers, brewers, tailors, washers, shoemakers, robe-makers, cooks, porters and bursars' to serve the abbot and brethren (that is: thirty priests, deacons and clerics, twenty-eight nuns, and unnumbered 'poor persons'). How many brewers this total included, sadly, the scribes did not say. However, a community that size would be consuming at least seven barrels of ale a week, very probably more: a substantial brewing operation for the time.

In Anglo-Saxon England, most brewing outside the monasteries was done by women, as it probably always had been. Domesday Book records that in Hereford before the Normans arrived the customary laws included one that said 'any man's wife who brewed ale', 'inside or outside the city', had to pay 10d to the city authorities. And, except in the monasteries, ale making continued to be women's work for the first three centuries after the Norman King William seized the English throne. A study of one small place, Brigstock in Northamptonshire, between 1287 and 1349 listed more than 300 villagers who brewed for retail at least once; of those, nineteen in every twenty were women 'brewsters', not male 'brewers'.

It was certainly medieval society's assumption that brewing was one of the specifically female occupations. When Edward I was at his castle in Conwy, North Wales, in March 1295 and running alarmingly low on supplies, he sent a message to his clerk, William Hamilton, at Chester. Hamilton was told to enlist the help of Chester's mayor and bailiffs, and assemble all the brewsters (*totes les braceresses*). The women – no mention of any male brewers – were to be ordered to brew good ale for the king and his army. As late as 1364, in the reign of Edward III, a law was passed banning men from having more than one trade, but 'women, that is to say brewers, bakers, corders and spinners . . . may freely use and work as they have done before this time, without any impeachment or being restrained by this ordinance'.

These women were not regular, professional brewers, however. The considerable numbers of different women found in manorial records in connection with offences against the regulations surrounding ale brewing suggest very strongly that the brewsters or ale-wives of the eleventh to fourteenth centuries were generally each only occasional producers of ale for sale. They would take turns to brew for the local community, using their domestic pots and buckets and fitting the boiling, mashing and fermenting in around their other domestic tasks. Dedicated brewing equipment was not normally needed: among the few specialist domestic brewing vessels used in medieval England were large curved pottery jars in which the ale was either brewed or, more likely, stored to settle out. A thirteenth-century example found at Churchill in Oxfordshire was around two feet high and had a capacity of approximately 16 gallons; the jar had a bunghole about one and a half inches above the base so that ale could be drawn off without disturbing the sediment.

English medieval brewers had their own saint: Thomas Becket, the Archbishop of Canterbury assassinated on the supposed instructions of King Henry II. Thomas was born in London in or near the year 1118, of wealthy Norman French parents, and it is said he was given his first post in the Church by the Abbot of St Albans. Around 1142, one tradition says, the abbot made him priest at Bramfield, a small village about five miles north of Hertford. While at Bramfield, its village historians claim, Thomas brewed ale using water from the old rectory pond, which is still known as 'Becket's pool'. If this sounds unhygienic (particularly as tradition also says Becket and his monks used to wash in the pond's water), it is worth recalling that using pond water to brew ale and beer was a very common practice. The farmer and diarist John Carrington, whose son ran the Rose and Crown at the nearby village of Tewin, was taking water from his farm pond at Bramfield to make his harvest ale with as late as 1800. The village clerics also drank home-brewed ale for hundreds of years – one history of Bramfield says the rector still brewed his own beer until the nineteenth century.

Thomas Becket's career soon took him away from Bramfield to work for the then Archbishop of Canterbury, Theobald; then, in 1154, King Henry appointed him chancellor, and for sixteen years the two worked closely together. At one point, in 1157, Thomas visited France on Henry's behalf to demand a French bride for the English king's son, taking with him a deliberately showy cavalcade designed to proclaim the glories of England. It included 250 footmen singing anthems in English, twenty-eight packhorses bearing gold and silver plate, English-bred mastiffs, greyhounds and hawks, grooms holding monkeys dressed in English livery and, according to a widely quoted passage supposedly from a contemporary chronicler, two chariots 'laden solely with iron-bound barrels of ale, decocted from choice, fat grain, as a gift for the French, who wondered at such an invention, a drink most wholesome, clear of all dregs, rivalling wine in colour and surpassing it in flavour'.

The passage is significant in showing that ale could travel before the use of hops, and could keep the fortnight or more it must have taken in the twelfth century to get from England to the French king's court. It also shows that, on special occasions at least, ale casks were hooped with metal.

Thomas was appointed Archbishop of Canterbury by Henry in 1162 and immediately found himself in opposition to the king's policies. Eventually this conflict led to four knights, supposedly acting on the king's orders, murdering Thomas in the cathedral at Canterbury on 29 December 1170. Within three years the former Bramfield brewer was canonized, and his shrine at Canterbury became one of the most popular destinations for pilgrims. Thomas's associations with ale seem to have led the Brewers' Company in London to claim him as its founder, tracing its origins to the late twelfth century and the 'Guild of Our Lady and St Thomas Becket'.

In Becket's time most people drank ale: only the wealthy few drank wine, only the young drank milk and only the poor drank water. In the thirteenth century, for example, as London's water supply began to worsen under the impact of a growing population, a scheme was given royal approval to pipe water from the River Tyburn, which flowed into present-day St James's Park, 'for the poor to drink, and the rich to dress [that is, prepare] their meat'. Many intelligent people thought drinking water was actively dangerous: the Abbess Hildegarde of Bingen, in Germany, in her writings on medicine made around 1150, said: 'Whether one is healthy or infirm, if one is thirsty after sleeping, one should drink wine or beer, but not water. For water might damage rather than help one's blood and humours . . . beer fattens the flesh and . . . lends a beautiful colour to the face. Water, however, weakens a person.'

With ale thus the only drink both widely available and considered safe, consumption was high: medieval household accounts regularly stipulated an allowance of eight pints a person a day. Society thought of ale, along with bread, as one of the two essentials of life. From the start of the twelfth century brewers began to be an increasing concern of the authorities in town and manor as worries were raised about supposed high prices and poor product. The lords and leading citizens thought that as law enforcers they ought to be ensuring regular supplies of wholesome, fairly priced bread and ale; they did not believe in leaving this to the free market and the honesty of the bakers and brewers.

From at least the time of Richard I, in the mid-1190s, the state took a legislative interest in the activities of the brewers, through a device called the Assize of Bread and Ale. This was meant to regulate the price of these two necessities throughout the kingdom, tying the retail prices of bread and ale firmly to the wholesale prices of wheat and barley.

The statute governing the assize was periodically restated, most formally in 1266–7 under Henry III. When wheat was 3s to 3s 4d a quarter, barley was 20d to 2s a quarter and oats 15d a quarter, for example, town *braciatores*, or brewers, were to sell 2 gallons of *cervisia*, ale, for a penny, and country brewers 3 gallons for a penny, with the price of ale rising a farthing a gallon for every shilling rise in the price of a quarter of grain. (The first implication is that yields were expected to be 48 gallons to the quarter, suggesting an original gravity of around 1065–1085. The second is that ale, being tied to the price of three different grains, was a mixed-grain brew; this is confirmed by other sources.) Two gallons for a penny was the bottom end of the price range, however: the normal prices for ale legally laid down in the thirteenth and fourteenth centuries were 1½d a gallon for the best ale and 1d a gallon for weaker ale. Under another statute made in 1267, offenders who broke the stipulations of the assize were to be fined, and regular offenders threatened with the *judicium tumbrelli*, or cucking-stool, where the guilty party was strapped into a chair at the end of a long pivoted beam, and ducked into a river, lake or pond.

Custom and practice settled into a set of standard regulations across the country. Local juries were appointed to review grain prices at least once a year, usually more often, and set a matching price for ale. Local courts appointed officers, generally known as ale-tasters or, rather less often, ale-conners, to sample ale before it was put on sale and judge whether it was fit to be sold at the regulated price. The ale-tasters also presented brewers at court for breaches of the regulations, such as brewing for sale without giving notice (which was required so that the ale could be tasted first); using unstamped ('unsealed') measures that had not been checked to see if they would hold a standard quantity; or selling at too high a price.

In London the ale-conners were required merely to swear that they would always be ready to taste ale when required, and would uphold the assize and ensure that all drink was of the required quality and price. However, in Scotland the rules were stricter: 'taisters of aile' were ordered not to 'fill their bellies or drink overmuckle in the time of the tasting' in case they 'tine and losse the discretion of gusting or tasting'. Nor could they go into the alehouse to test the beer. They had to 'stand without in the middes of the street' while someone else went in and chose 'the pot quereof he will taiste'.

The opportunity the statutes gave to the local powers (generally the lord of the manor) to raise revenue through fines meant that in many places the assize of ale quickly became an excuse for a de facto tax on anyone brewing commercially, rather than a means of punishing bad or unscrupulous brewers. In Norwich in 1288–9, for example, 290 brewers were fined for 'infringement' of the assize, an unbelievable number if they were all bad brewers, but realistic if they were occasional brewers-for-sale paying what was in effect a licence fee.

Although the use of corporal punishment against brewers or brewsters who broke the assize was rare, since it was more lucrative to fine them, the tumbril or cucking-stool was certainly used occasionally for serious offenders.

A similar punishment for the makers of bad ale existed in medieval Scotland. The Scottish jurist Sir John Skene, writing in the 1590s, noted that under borough law, 'if a brewster makes gude aill, that is sufficient. Bot gif she makes evill aill, she sall paye une unlaw [fine] of aucht shillinges, or sall suffer the justice of the burgh, that is, she sall be put upon the cock-stule, and the aill sall be distributed to the pure folk.' What the poor folk were expected to do with their free 'evil ale', and whether they were meant to be grateful for it, is not clear.

However, the Scots were more open about payments for permission to brew than the English, enacting around the time of King David I a 'burrow lawe' that 'ane Browster quha brewes ail, all the year sall pay to the Provost four pennies; and for ane half year twa pennies; And he may brewe thrie times, payand na dewtie, And for the fourt browst he sall give the dewtie of ane halfe year and nae mair (quhether he be man or woman).'

In a few places in England, in place of the fiction of 'fines', a specific ale toll was paid by anyone who brewed for sale. From at least 1260 to at least 1592 Leicester's brewers, for example, were charged something called *cannemol* when they brewed. In Alfriston, Sussex, tolcester or canale was imposed by the lord of the manor at a rate of two gallons of the best ale per brewing. In Crowle, Lincolnshire a *tolnetum cervisie*, or ale toll, is mentioned in court records around 1320, while in Cranborne, Dorset, around 1480 the lord of the manor was due a 'custom of ale' of between 1½d and 3d a brew.

Attempts to impose price and quality control were sometimes age-specific: in Coventry in 1421 the mayor commanded that 'no brewstere sell no derre a galon of good ale will hit is new under the here syve [that is, recently finished fermenting and just strained through a hair sieve] but for 1¼d and when hit is good and stale for 1½d'. The two points to note here are that ale obviously still needed sieving of 'bits' after it was brewed, and stale or matured ale, which would have cleared through standing (the original meaning of stale) – a process that would have taken three or four days – fetched a higher price than the same beer when new (or mild). Mature ale had similarly cost more than fresh ale in Saxon times, and it would do so through to the nineteenth century.

The ubiquity of women in brewing meant that attacks on the makers of ale for poor quality, high prices and other low practices were inevitably attacks on brewsters, women brewers. The condemnation of the wicked ale-wife to eternal punishment in hell is a common, and clearly popular, theme in medieval art and literature. The first example that survives is an illustration of the Last Judgment in an illuminated manuscript known as the Holkham Bible Picture Book, which was produced around 1325–30. It shows a cleric, a male baker and an ale-wife, all seen as oppressors of the poor, being borne off by devils to a boiling cauldron. The ale-wife is carrying the symbol of her trade, a large jug. In medieval churches at Ludlow, Shropshire, and Castle Hedingham, Essex, carvings on the bases of misericords (wall seats designed to give some support when standing during long services) show ale-wives being carted to hell by devils, as does a carving on a late fifteenth-century roof boss in Norwich Cathedral. In one of the plays of the Chester mystery cycle, a 'folk drama' composed around the early fifteenth century and performed yearly, after Christ has emptied hell of all the deserving souls (the 'Harrowing of Hell'), only a brewster is left behind, condemned for her sins of selling short measure and poor-quality, adulterated ale.

Feminist historians have interpreted these dark portraits of women brewsters as a sign of medieval misogyny: they are, however, no more

The view inside a 14th century brewhouse: the Bishop of Tournai, in Hainault in modern Belgium, receives his tithe of a cask of beer at a local brewery, in an engraving of a scene from one of the windows in Tournai cathedral. In the background, brewery workers are, from right to left, stirring the mash; emptying the copper; and filling a cask. In the top left corner a 'coolship', a shallow vessel for cooling the hot wort, can be seen: it empties into the fermenting vessel below. The Bishop's beer has been loaded onto a sled for transportation.

misogynistic than the 1930s song about the 'very fat man who waters the workers' beer' was a general attack on overweight people. Elizabethan writers condemned sixteenth-century brewers for growing rich from selling 'boiled water', and at the end of the eighteenth century denunciations were regularly made of the London porter-brewers for allegedly using poisonous substitutes in their beer instead of malt and hops. Drinkers have probably always had a tendency to suspect that the brewer/brewster was cheating them or poisoning them – or both.

The best-recorded medieval brewing operations are, unsurprisingly, those supplying great houses and religious establishments. The accounts of John de Braynford, keeper of the brewery of St Paul's Cathedral in London, for 1286 show the cathedral brewery making precisely 67,814 gallons of ale in 100 brewings over twelve months: that is, roughly twice a week. Only a wild stab can be made at the strength of the ale, but it was probably not less than 5 or 6 per cent alcohol by volume. With the normal allowance of one *bolla* or gallon of ale a person a day given in the accounts, the cathedral brewery was supplying around 185 people. The brewery had its own maltings, which used grain from the cathedral's farms in Hertfordshire and Middlesex; it brewed 22½ barrels at a time, using a total of 175 quarters of wheat, 175 quarters of barley and 708 quarters of oats (a ratio of 1:1:4 by volume, perhaps 4:3:8 by weight).

Oats, generally used in roughly this proportion, were a common ingredient in medieval ale in both Britain and continental Europe. Continental practice was to leave the oats unmalted, since having just a quarter or a third of the grain malted meant a big saving on space and, in particular, fuel. Ungerminated oats need the enzymes in germinated barley and wheat to turn their starches into sugar, but only a quarter of the total grain needed to be germinated to supply enough enzymes to convert all the starches. However, oats can be malted, though they take longer than barley: Norwegian farm brewers used malted oats in their ale up to the twentieth century, and a Norwegian who was a couple of gallons short of the full barrel was sometimes said to be 'like oats malt' – a little slow.

The brewing at St Paul's was under the control of the *braciator* or brewer, who was paid 10s a year; below him were two *servientes bracini*, brewery servants, paid 5s 4d a year each, and a *tractor cervisiae*, or 'beer puller', who presumably moved the 30-gallon casks of ale from the brewery to the refectory. He was called a puller, probably, because the full casks were pulled on a sled (see picture, page 48; sleds were still used 600 years later, see Barclay Perkins picture between pages 160–161). There was also a *circulator*, or cooper, who was paid 4s a year, and a water-drawer, or *aquaeductor*: it is not clear if the brewery was supplied with water by a well or from the nearby Thames.

The St Paul's brewery brewed every three to four days. However, surviving accounts for big private households from the fourteenth and fifteenth centuries show ale being brewed or bought in at intervals of anywhere between a week and thirteen days, which gives an indication of the 'shelf life' of medieval ale. John Russell, author of the *Boke of Nurture* in the mid-fifteenth century, said ale should be five days old before it was served, as did Andrew Boorde, the sixteenth-century physician and writer, which suggests that medieval ale, even though it was unhopped, was quite capable of staying drinkable for at least a week. (Another writer later in the sixteenth century, Reynold Scot, said that unhopped ale would 'endure a fortnight'.) An establishment such as that of Richard Mitford, Bishop of Salisbury, was storing around 300 gallons of ale at a time in 1406–7.

Breweries at great houses and religious establishments were usually sited away from the main residential buildings, because of the smells, and often next door to the bakehouse. The Plan of St Gall, an idealized depiction of the layout of a Benedictine monastery drawn up in southern Germany around the beginning of the ninth century, showed three separate brewhouse/bakehouse buildings, one each for the monks, for distinguished guests, and for paupers and pilgrims. Each of the breweries appears to have four furnaces/coppers and four fermenting vessels in one room, and a separate room alongside for wort cooling – *hic refrigeratum ceruisa* – which suggests a great deal of carrying hot liquids around in buckets. However, the plan is really only a sketch showing what the perfect monastery ought to have, and there is nothing to show that the layout and equipment in real monasteries was anything like this.

In aristocratic houses the brewer was one of the regular line-up of servants. He had to supply ale for the household's breakfast, where it would be drunk with bread and perhaps some cheese; for lunch, where the allowance would be one or two pints a head; and for supper, where it would again be two pints a person. Ale would be distributed from the door of the buttery, which would have a bar or barrier across it – the origin of our modern bar counter. When guests arrived, they would be served ale in their rooms after their journey, while their own servants were given ale at the buttery bar.

Commercial brewers, of course, had to accommodate paying customers rather than family, servants and guests. A description of an attempted kidnapping of a young woman living at the brewery of a man called Gilbert de Mordone in Crooked Lane, near London Bridge, in 1325 says the would-be kidnappers came into the public hall of the brewery, ordered four gallons of ale for eighteen men, and refused to go when asked because, they said, the house was open to the public – a 'public house'.

In Chester, where the brewsters included the wives of aldermen and mayors, these better-class ale-wives would sell their brews in the cellars of their houses, where, sometimes, fights would break out among the drinkers. Chester's brewers did not brew solely for retailing on their own account, however. In 1487, when the city authorities summonsed everyone in the drinks trade to have their measures 'sealed', or stamped as having the correct capacity, there were fifty-seven brewers and 101 other ale-sellers. This increase in non-brewing ale-sellers dates from the start of the fourteenth century: in Oxford in 1311 the majority of ale-sellers were said to be brewing, but by 1351 only a third were brewing their own. Winchester in 1417 had thirty-six drinking establishments run by brewers and twenty-seven other alehouses buying in their ale. (It also had ten wine taverns and nine inns: all for a population of around 5,000.)

By the fourteenth century, in the cities and large towns, pressures were growing for the professionalization, and the masculinization, of brewing. In the two centuries after Domesday Book was compiled in 1086, the population of England more than trebled, from an estimated two million to around six million. The rise in the big cities was even greater: London saw its inhabitants increase from just 14,000 in the late eleventh century to 40,000 by the end of the thirteenth.

The numbers of commercial brewers soared to meet this need. In the mid-twelfth century a survey of Winchester by the local bishop found more than a dozen breweries among 900 households, and that was very probably an understatement. Records from other cities, such as Oxford and Norwich, show that around the middle of the fourteenth century something like one household in fifteen brewed ale for sale. London in 1309 is said to have had 1,334 brewers, though there may be some confusion here between brewer, *brasiator* in Latin, and brasier, worker in copper and brass: both could be called *le braser*.

Outside the cities, it has been estimated that one peasant family in twenty-five brewed for sale at least occasionally. A trade list for St Albans from around 1360 contains the names of 168 individuals, eighty-one of whom were brewers. Of those, however, forty-four also had other trades, and the remaining thirty-seven probably primarily worked on the land as peasants, brewing only occasionally. All the seven named hostelers in the list also brewed, as did both the men surnamed 'Cooper': whatever the ordinary alehouse did, it is probable all of the more up-market hostelries in England brewed ale at this time except in the biggest centres, such as London.

From around the start of the fifteenth century, even in rural areas, the 'occasional' brewers-for-sale began to brew less frequently, and more and more specialized brewing operations began to take control of the business. In large centres such as London, the former dominance of the part-time brewster melted away and the full-time brewer took over. These professional brewers had a substantial amount of kit: in 1335 Richard, the son of Lawrence de Long, inherited a brewery in St Martin's Ludgate, London, that included a lead cistern, a boiler, a mash vat, a fining vat, an ale vat, tubs and other equipment. As brewing moved out of the semi-domestic context, equipment grew larger and more specialized. By 1293 vessels were big enough for one unfortunate woman in Chester to fall into a 'mascomb' – mash tun – filled with hot water and drown.

However, production on any substantial scale in England before the fifteenth century was unusual: in the 1390s, John Kep was the biggest brewer in Lynn, Norfolk, then an important port, but even he used only twenty-four quarters of grain a week to make around sixty to ninety barrels of ale, a tiny amount by later standards. In London around the same time brewing over five quarters a week, that is, twelve to fifteen barrels, made you a 'large' brewer (and liable to bigger fines for any offences).

Even so, an inventory of a brewery in London from 1442–3 included a furnace, a lead 'standing in the furnace' (a lead or 'lede', confusingly, was a large metal cauldron made of brass or copper, not lead, and normally permanently fixed into a masonry base or 'furnace'), a lead 'taptrough' (made of lead!) used to run liquor from one tun to another, a mash vat, a gyle (or fermentation) tun, a cleansing tun, four water vats, thirty-eight 'kemelyns', or tubs, a horse mill 'with all apparatus' and a substantial quantity of casks totalling almost 1,000 gallons of capacity. This was more than an alehouse brewing for itself. The equipment also included a lead tabard, which appears to mean a lid for the lead or brewing copper: lead tabards also appear in other brewery inventories in the fifteenth century, which raises the possibility that Chaucer's Tabard Inn in Southwark, where his pilgrims met before leaving for Canterbury, was named after an item of brewing equipment rather than a herald's coat. The Tabard, or another inn nearby with the same name, certainly brewed: the Rolls of Parliament show that among those who took part in Jack Cade's rebellion of 1450 was 'Joh'es Brewersman' of 'Le Tabbard, London'.

As well as the size of the operations, the raw ingredients were also changing: records at Chester's Dee mills between 1378 and 1485 show that until the 1440s the mills were grinding large amounts of oat malt, barley malt and wheat malt, with oat malt making half the total, which probably reflects the composition of the local brewers' mash tuns. After the 1440s, wheat malt fell away to nothing, being replaced by barley malt, which made up almost 75 per cent of the total in the 1480s.

Very little contemporary evidence survives on what herbs were used to flavour and preserve ale in the British Isles before the arrival of hops early in the fifteenth century. There is actually a strong argument for saying no herbs at all were used in much medieval English ale. In Norwich in March 1471 the 'common ale brewers of this citi', who by then were in competition with the beer brewers and evidently copying their habits, were ordered by the mayor and council not to brew 'nowther with hoppes nor gawle [sweet gale] nor noon other thing . . . upon peyne of grevous punysshment'. In 1483 the London ale brewers, again trying to maintain the difference between (unhopped) ale and (hopped) beer, persuaded the city authorities to rule that in order for ale to be brewed in 'the good and holesome manner of bruying of ale of old tyme used', no one should 'put in any ale or licour [water] whereof ale shal be made or in the wirkyng and bruying of any maner of ale any hoppes, herbes or other like thing but only licour, malt and yeste'. London and Norwich ale, then at least in the late fifteenth century, was herb-free. Even sixty years later, in 1542, the writer and physician Andrew Boorde agreed that ale was made of malt and water only, and anyone who added 'any other thynge' except 'yest, barme or godesgood [all synonyms for yeast] doth sofysticat theyr ale' – using 'sophisticate' in its original meaning of 'adulterate'.

Hopless ale, even without herbs, would not have been sweet, since most or all of the sugar would have fermented out to dryness, and as it aged the ale would have developed sharp, sour flavours, making it refreshing enough without the need to add herbs. However, there are enough medieval and later references to herbs and spices used in ales and beers in the British Isles to show that different flavourings were at least sometimes part of the pre-hop tradition with local brewers.

The 'gawle' or sweet gale banned by the Norwich authorities in 1471 was a common addition to beers on the continent, and it was also put into British ale on occasions: this heavily scented heathland shrub grew in wetlands throughout the British Isles. The Tudor cleric William Turner, in his book *A New Herball*, published in 1551, says of bog myrtle that 'it is tried by experience that it is good to be put into beare both by me and by diverse other in Summersetshyre'. However, the herbalist John Gerard was more wary: he wrote in 1597 that the fruit of bog myrtle 'is troublesome to the brain; being put into beere or aile while it is in boiling, it maketh the same heady, fit to make a man quickly drunk'.

Another herb popular with English brewers was ground ivy, which was given the alternative name alehoof because of its use in brewing and its hoofprint-shaped leaves. It imparts a bitter, very strong, tannic flavour to ale (described by the herbalist and brewer Stephen Harrod Buhner as like black tea), but more importantly it helps fine the drink, making it clear and transparent within hours. Ground ivy, with its small, purple-blue flowers, is a creeping plant common in woods and hedgerows all over the British Isles. The pre-Norman English culti-vated it, and another name for the plant, tunhoof, comes from tun meaning enclosure or garden rather than tun meaning cask. It was steeped in the hot liquor before mashing, and it seems to have been a widely used plant in brewing ale, even after the arrival of hops: John Gerard said that 'the women of our northern parts, especially Wales and Chesire, do turn Herbe-Alehoof into their ale'.

Brewers also used the spicy, clove-scented, bitter-tasting roots of wood avens or herb bennet, a common perennial plant whose yellow five-petalled flowers are found in woodlands and hedgerows around Britain. The plant has antiseptic qualities, useful in helping ale to keep. 'Auence' is mentioned as one of several ingredients in a number of East Anglian recipes for ale flavourings dated around 1430 from the Paston letters, a rare archive of letters and documents written between 1420 and 1504 by a well-to-do family from Norfolk.

The increasingly male-dominated professionalism of the brewing industry was reflected in the growing strength of the Brewers' Guild in London, which was founded at All Hallows' Church, London Wall, as a charitable and religious fraternity by a man, John Enfield, in 1342. When it received its first charter in the fourteenth century it was known as the Guild of St Mary and St Thomas the Martyr, in honour of the 'brewing saint' murdered in Canterbury Cathedral. Eventually the guild merged with the Mistery of Free Brewers, an overlapping non-religious trade organization, but in the early fifteenth century the brewers' records still differentiated between members, who were freemen of the mistery, and 'brethren', who were also members of the fraternity.

The brewers were important enough to send four representatives to the City's Common Council of 1376, putting them in the second rank of guilds, and by 1403 they had their own 'Brewers' Hall' in London, where business and social events could be held. Three years later, in 1406, the 'Mistery of Brewers' won the important concession from the city authorities that it could supervise all those who worked in the ale trade. These included not only brewers and brewsters but also the ale retailers, from hostelers to cooks and pie-bakers, and the 'hucksteres', women who bought ale from the brewers to sell to the public at stalls or booths around the city. The mistery also won the right to search every sack of barley coming into the city for sale to ensure that it was not 'broken nor mixed', and to enforce maximum wages on journeymen brewers employed by members of the mistery.

However, having the producers supervise the trade inevitably produced friction with the Mayor and Aldermen of the City, who still wanted to impose their ideas of suitable prices and measures for ale. There was a struggle in 1419, for example, between the brewers, who wanted to be able to charge 2d a gallon for ale sold outside their houses as well as within, and the aldermen, who insisted that ale sold 'outside their houses by retail' should cost no more than 1½d a gallon. The Mayor at this time was Richard 'Dick' Whittington, probably the most famous in the City's history, who had several battles with the brewers before his death in 1423.

The London brewers secured the goodwill of Whittington's successors with expensive 'gifts', presenting William Walderne, Mayor in 1422–3, with a boar priced at 20s and an ox priced at 17s; they gave the same to another mayor, John Michelle, 'so that he did no harm to the Brewers'. The brewers' guild had members who were wealthy enough to cover the costs of such gifts, and wealthy enough to entertain themselves well: the guild's election day feast in 1425, for example, cost the considerable sum of £38.

Although it was run solely by men, the brewers' guild was one of the very few in London that allowed women to be members, and certainly the only one where women were a considerable proportion of the membership. Records for the years 1418–25 show that around two out of five of those paying their dues and entitled to wear the livery of the guild (a hood or, for the more wealthy, a gown) were women. While most of those women were wives of male guild members, up to one in five were there as sole representative of their households, making them around one in ten of all brewing households represented in the guild. Even when men were members of the guild, many actually had other trades, and it was their wives who did the brewing.

The guild did not represent every brewer or brewster: a survey by the city authorities in 1419–20 found 290 households brewing commercially in London, of whom only 185 were connected with the Brewers' Guild. Many of those named by the city as brewing, but not in the guild, were women: while half London's brewsters were apparently not in the guild, only a quarter of its male brewers were not guild members.

As the fifteenth century advanced, women became less important in the guild's life: they had never been able to hold office, but when the guild won its second, royal charter from Henry VI in 1437 all the references in it are to the supervision of 'men' and 'workmen' by the Master and Wardens. Only at the end of the charter is there a reference to helping out 'the poor men and women' of the Mistery of Brewers. By the beginning of the sixteenth century in London widows of brewers were the only women being admitted to the guild, and in some years of the century there were no female guild members at all. (This is not to say women had stopped being commercial brewers, however: in 1544, when the guild had become the Brewers' Company, one member, Richard Pickering, told the Mayor and Aldermen he knew nothing about how much drink could be got from a given quantity of malt because 'he committeth the whole charge thereof to his wife', Joan, who was not a member of the guild.)

The disappearance of women from visible involvement with brewing in London is undoubtedly linked with the increased wealth possible to anyone brewing as a regular trade, thanks to the rise in the city's population: men were now willing to make full-time careers out of what had previously been only a way for women to supplement the household income. The 'masculinization' of brewing is also linked with the most important technological change in brewing since the move from beer-bread to ground malt. This was (its importance should be emphasized) the arrival of

HOPS.

An era had come to an end: we are now at the start of modern times.

CHAPTER FOUR

THE EARLY YEARS
OF BEER

---

how hops became hip

*See that ye keep a noble house for beef and beer,
that thereof may be praise given to God and to
your honour.*

Advice given to Leonard,
titular fifth Lord Dacre, in 1570

Hops have more uses than flavouring and preserving beer: the leaves, cones and sap were used to make dyes, the stems to make ropes, sacking and paper; hops can be used as a substitute for oak bark in tanning, and hop ash was used in the manufacture of Bohemian glass. This makes it difficult to say with any certainty when hops were first used by brewers.

Indeed, it is possible that the discovery by brewers of the bittering and preserving powers of hops in beer came some time after hop juices were first used to dye cloth. The preservative power of hops in beer comes from the bitter substances, called humulones, found in the resin glands of hop cones. These are not particularly soluble in their natural state, and they need boiling for between an hour and ninety minutes before they undergo a physical change, called isomerization, into the much more soluble (and more bitter) iso-humulones.

As well as giving bitterness to beer, isohumulones have a powerful antimicrobial action, killing or severely hampering the reproduction of the bugs that make ale go off. In addition, boiling the wort to bring about isomerization of the humulones also causes unwanted proteins to coagulate out of the wort, a process known to modern brewers as the 'hot break'. This has two bonuses: it removes substances that bacteria and other nasties might feed on, thus also helping to extend the life of the beer; and it produces a much clearer drink. As a minor bonus, beer brewed with hops also has a much better foamy head than unhopped ale.

However, unless you knew beforehand all this was going to happen, and why it would be a good thing, there would appear to be no reason to waste time and fuel boiling hops in your wort for ninety minutes. You can get the flavour of hops, if that is all you want, by putting the cones into a cask of cool, fermented ale for a couple of weeks or so. So the great unanswered question in the history of brewing is why someone first thought it would be a good idea to boil ale wort with hops for such a long time. Medieval ale brewers never seem to have boiled their worts at all, heating their liquor only once, to mash the grain. Before hops, flavouring herbs, when used, were added to the newly brewed ale, or steeped in the hot liquor before mashing, or laid in the mash tun or the running wort from the mash tun.

Perhaps it was a dyer somewhere in central Europe who boiled cloth with hop cones for an hour or more to dye some cloth deeply, and then accidentally tasted the cooled dye water, to be pleasantly surprised by its bitter flavour. If she decided to try the same with her ale, boiling hops in the wort for an hour before fermenting it, she would have got a second surprise when the finished drink remained potable far beyond the time when ale made with other herbs was sour and vile.

In whatever way the preserving effects of hops were discovered by brewers, it could not have happened much before the eleventh century, because hopped beer spread so rapidly across northern Europe from the twelfth century onwards: a long lag of several hundred years between the development of hopped beer and its triumph over the unhopped version is very unlikely, given the huge advantages boiling with hops brought to brewers in allowing them to brew weaker, cheaper beer (because hopped beer does not need lots of alcohol to keep the bugs out) which lasted much longer and could be sold to customers further away.

This is not to say that hops were never added to ale before AD1000:

William Shakespeare, as registered as a trademark by the Stratford upon Avon brewer Flower's. Ironically, Shakespeare preferred unhopped ale to the hopped beer Flower's made: every reference to 'the poor creature' beer in his plays is derogatory, but a quart of ale 'is a dish for a king'.

even unboiled hops will give flavour and aroma, which is why British brewers today 'dry hop' some of their finished beers, putting handfuls of hops in a cask to add to the taste of the beer. But if ale brewers in the first millennium did use hops, they were not employing them in the same way and with the same effect that beer brewers did later, to preserve and bitter their drink.

Hops have another advantage: unlike other herbs used in ale, they can be cultivated on an agricultural scale, thus ensuring regular supplies. Meadowsweet will keep unhopped ale drinkable for several months, but as a plant of damp woodlands and fens it cannot be farmed in fields. Ground ivy, another ale-preserving plant, was culti-vated as a garden herb, but could not be produced agriculturally on a commercial scale. Hops are certainly not easy to cultivate, but they can be (and are) grown on farms in considerable quantities.

Hops are not recorded by any ancient commentators (except in a passing reference by Pliny); indeed, the first mention of hops in connection with brewing comes as late as AD822, from Corvey, a Benedictine monastery on the Weser in Westphalia, Germany. A statute of Abbot Adalhard of Corvey lays down, among other regu-lations, details on the duties of the monastery's tenants, which included gathering firewood and hops – implying wild hops, rather than culti-vated ones. It goes on to say that a tithe (or tenth) of all the malt that came in should be given to the porter of the monastery, and the same with the hops. If this did not supply enough hops, he should take steps to get more from elsewhere to make sufficient beer for himself.

This is still not evidence that hops were being used to preserve rather than just flavour beer. For that we have to move 330 years into the future and 140 miles to the south-west – to another Benedictine establishment, at Rupertsberg, near Bingen, by the Rhine. Here, about 1150, Abbess Hildegard, mystical philosopher, healer, musician and writer, published a book called *Physica sacra*, which translates best as 'The Natural World'. Book I, chapter 61, 'Concerning the hop', says of the plant: 'as a result of its own bitterness it keeps some putrefactions from drinks, to which it may be added, so that they may last so much longer.' Even this, by itself, does not prove hops were used in beer. But in a later chapter, on the ash tree, the abbess wrote: 'If you also wish to make beer from oats without hops, but just with *grusz* [gruit], you should boil it after adding a very large number of ash leaves. That type of beer purges the stomach of the drinker, and renders his heart [literally 'chest' or 'breast'] light and joyous.' Clearly Hildegard knew about brewing beer with hops. (*Bier* in German or Dutch could mean the hopped or the unhopped drink.) The passage also suggests that she knew about boiling wort, without which just adding hops is not much help in keeping away 'putrefactions'.

Hildegard talks about the use of hops to keep putrefaction from drink in a way that suggests this was already a familiar practice. It seems certain that by now hops were being cultivated rather than just gathered wild: hop gardens are said to appear in records dating from the second half of the ninth century in and around Hallertau, in Bavaria, southern Germany, which is still the world's largest single hop-growing area. However, it was northern Germany where hops were first cultivated in quantity, in the twelfth century, around the time Hildegard was writing. Hopped beer became an important trading commodity in north Germany from the late thirteenth century onwards, and merchant beer brewers in north German cities eventually became rich enough to join the aristocracy (their British counterparts did not manage this until the eighteenth century).

By around 1325, imports of hopped north German beer to the Low Countries were considerable enough to encourage Netherlanders to begin brewing their own hopped beer. It was several decades before hopped beer is known to have crossed to England, but in 1361–2 James Dodynessone of Amsterdam paid a toll on beer at Great Yarmouth. Further mentions of beer imports followed, gradually increasing in frequency: at the end of the fourteenth century, Great Yarmouth was importing forty to eighty barrels of beer a month, while in 1397–8 Colchester imported 100 barrels of beer.

The drinkers of this imported hopped beer were mostly immigrant 'Dutch', a word that, until the end of the sixteenth century, covered German-speakers as well as natives of the Low Countries. And when, at some time during the first decade of the fifteenth century, beer brewing began in England, it was carried out in large part by 'Dutch' aliens, most of whom were probably supplying the immigrant market with the taste of home. One Bennet Tupton apparently started brewing beer in Shrewsbury in 1409; a female beer brewer, Agnes Smyth, 'Dutchman', was working in Colchester in 1412; and Florence Janson, beer brewer, became a freeman in York in 1416.

For the next 175 years beer brewing in England would be strongly associated with immigrants (even in 1585, half of London's beer brewers were 'aliens'). Ale brewing and beer brewing remained separate occupations for still longer, until at least the opening decades of the seventeenth century. There were English drinkers of beer in the early fifteenth century: Robert Waterton's household at Methley, near

Seventeenth-century brewing kit as pictured in the carved wooden panelling in the Stuart-era Brewers' Hall in London, rebuilt after the Fire of London and destroyed by bombing in the Second World War. The basket on the left would be pushed into the middle of the full mash tun, and sweet wort would then run into it and be ladled out; the copper, in the middle, holds a malt shovel, and a mashing fork for stirring the mash; the wooden-hooped cask on the right probably doubled as a final fermenting vessel.

Castleford, Yorkshire, consumed 5½ barrels of beer at 3s a barrel in 1416–17, while using almost 150 quarters of malt to make its (unhopped) ale (a quantity which would have produced around 650 barrels); Joan and Margaret, daughters of the Duchess of Clarence, were supplied with Holland beer at 4s a barrel while they were staying at Dartford Priory in 1419–21. But generally, for the early years of beer brewing in these islands, the natives seem to have stayed faithful to their traditional ale, leaving the hopped drink to immigrant Netherlanders and Germans.

Locally brewed beer was certainly being sold in London in 1424–5, when the capital's ale brewers complained about 'aliens nigh to the city dwelling,' probably in Southwark on the other side of the Thames, who 'brew beer and sell it to retail within the same city'. The beer brewers of London came under attack again in 1436, after the Duke of Burgundy changed sides in the Hundred Years War and besieged the English-held town of Calais in alliance with the French. The Duke's territories included Flanders, Holland and Zeeland, home to many of England's 'alien' beer brewers, and xenophobic rumours began to circulate in London that this Low Countries drink, 'beere', was harmful and unhealthy.

The beer brewers had powerful friends, however: an order came from the king himself, Henry VI, to the sheriffs of London in June 1436,

> to make proclamation for all brewers of *biere* within their baili-wick to continue to exercise their art as hitherto, notwithstanding the malevolent attempts that were being made to prevent natives of Holland and Seland and others who occupied themselves in brewing the drink called *biere* from continuing their trade, on the ground that such drink was poisonous and not fit to drink, and caused drunkenness, whereas it was a wholesome drink, especially in summer time. Such attacks had already caused many brewers to cease brewing, and would cause great mischief unless stopped.

Undoubtedly this protectiveness towards the beer brewers had its origins in the king's discovery that beer was much more useful than ale as part of the victuals for his troops and ships. Whenever a campaign started, the brewers and bakers were pressed to provide drink and food for the soldiers to take with them. Since ale would last only days, and beer's life could be measured in months, supplies of beer could be ordered and then stored until the commanders were ready to move. Henry did not want to lose the logistical freedom hopped beer gave his armed forces by having the beer brewers closed down just because they were foreigners.

The breweries of London made a special contribution to help pay the wages of the Calais garrison during the Duke of Burgundy's siege. Among the more than 200 brewers who chipped in were seven beer brewers, of whom six were aliens. Perhaps to emphasize their loyalty to England, perhaps because beer breweries were already bigger operations than ale breweries, the beer brewers gave much more on average to the Calais garrison fund than the English-born ale brewers.

As well as hops, the beer brewers also brought with them their measures and terminology. The beer barrel was thirty-six gallons, against the English ale barrel, which was thirty gallons up to the early sixteenth century and thirty-two gallons later. The inventory of a brewery in London from 1442–3 mentioned in chapter three includes several terms derived from pre-sixteenth-century Dutch, showing this was a beer brewer's establishment, not an ale brewery. They included gyle tun, or fermenting vessel, from medieval Dutch *ghijl*, related to *gijlen*, ferment; 'kyldekyn', the cask size kilderkin (eighteen gallons, or half a beer barrel), from Dutch *kinderkin*; and 'fferdekyn', or firkin, a nine gallon cask, from the Middle Dutch *vierdekijn*, that is, a fourth or quarter of a barrel.

The beer brewers seem not to have joined the ale brewers' guild, because a complaint was apparently made to the king that the brewers of hopped beer were not covered by any official regulatory arrangement. Henry's response, in January 1441, was to appoint two men, Richard Lounde and William Veysy, 'for life, for good service done to him', with powers of correction, search and survey over all 'les Berebrewers' of England. This suggests that beer brewers were much rarer and easier to keep track of than ale brewers, who were found everywhere. That the makers of beer were concentrated in a few places is confirmed by records showing 'alien' beer brewers (i.e. most of them) at the time living in just half a dozen or so large, mostly coastal, cities.

Lounde and Veysy apparently knew nothing about beer brewing (Veysy was a brickmaker), and their first job was to investigate the rules in force on the continent. The two presented a report in April 1443 which was bland enough, recommending that the malt and 'les hopps' the beer was made from should be 'perfect, sound and sweet', the malt 'pure barley and wheat' (clearly beer was still a mixed-grain drink, though oats were missing from the grain bill) and the hops neither rotten nor old. The beer should not leave the brewery for eight days 'after brewing' (whether this means eight days from the start of fermentation, which would be about the same time modern cask-conditioned British beer takes to be ready, or eight days after the end of fermentation is not clear). When it was ready to leave the brewery the beer should be tested by officials to see that it was sufficiently boiled (that is, presumably, long enough for isomerization of the alpha acids in the hops, and for proteins to coagulate out during the 'hot break' to leave a clear, haze-free beer), contained enough hops and 'is not sweet'.

However, there are serious doubts about how much expertise Lounde and Veysy had gathered. The two types of beer mentioned in their report were 'single coyt' and 'double coyt', which, they said, should be priced differently. Coyt or *koyt* was certainly a type of drink brewed in the Low Countries; unfortunately, municipal records from the Dutch town of Haarlem dated 1407 show that *koyt* was not a hopped beer, as Lounde and Veysy's report seems to assume, but a non-hopped gruit ale, made from barley malt, wheat malt and oat malt, and brewed with herbs such as sweet gale.

Nobody seems to have picked the pair up on their error (indeed, it may be that *koyt* had become a hopped beer by the 1440s), and Lounde and Veysy were given the right to take a halfpenny toll on every barrel of beer they or their deputies passed as good, with power to arrest and imprison 'all rebellious herein'. However, the two seem not to have been very successful in their attempt to tax the beer brewers, because in 1445 the king was being told that they 'had not received any profit' from their appointment.

After Lounde and Veysy's unsuccessful attempt to regulate the beer brewers, no other supervisory efforts were made for nearly twenty years, it seems; at any rate, it was in May 1464, when Edward IV was on the English throne, that the beer brewers of London went to the Mayor and Aldermen and asked for approval of a set of regulations for the 'goode folke of this famous Citee the which usen Berebruying within the same'. The problem was, the beer brewers said, that in the absence of such rules and ordinances, 'the people of the Citee myght be gretely disceyved as in mesure of Barelles Kilderkyns and Firkyns and in hoppes and in other Greynes the which to the said Mistiere apperteynen'. The mention of 'other Greynes' suggests that beer brewers were still adding herbs besides hops to their drink, though there is no clue as to what these might have been. The beer brewers went on to point out that 'the comon people for lacke of experience can not knowe the perfitnesse of Bere as wele as of Ale', suggesting that even after more than fifty years of beer brewing in England, the 'comon people' were still much more familiar with ale than beer.

A generation later, in 1483, the citizens of London were familiar enough with 'hoppes and other Greynes' going into their drink that the ale brewers were complaining to the Mayor about 'sotill and crafty means of foreyns' (meaning not foreigners from overseas, but those who were not freemen of London) who were 'bruing of ale within the said Citee' and who were 'occupying and puttyng of hoppes and other things in the ale, contrary to the good and holesome manner of bruying of ale of old tyme used'. However, the London ale brewers' protest was not an attack on hops as such, but a lament at the use of hops in English ale and an attempt to keep ale and beer as separate, clearly different drinks, an appeal which would be echoed around the country for the next sixty or so years.

The ale brewers persuaded the Mayor and Aldermen to rule that 'no maner of persone of what craft, condicion or degree he be, occupying the craft or fete of bruying of ale within the said Citee' should be allowed to 'put in any ale or licour whereof ale shalbe made or in the wirkyng and bruying of any maner of ale any hoppes, herbes or other like thing but only licour [water], malt and yeste'.

A year before the attack on hops in London ale, in 1482, the ale brewers of the capital had been granted a new set of ordinances by the City authorities which included the proviso that no ale should be put on sale or carried to customers after it was 'clensed and set on jeyst' until it had fully 'spourged' (that is, fermented and cleared), and had been tasted and viewed by the wardens of the craft or their deputy. At the same time they were also banned from maintaining a 'foreyn' (non-freeman) to sell their ale in the City; from hiring any servant who had not served his time as an apprentice and been appointed a freeman; and from having in their houses more than two or three apprentices 'at the most'. All apprentices, before they began, had to be presented to the wardens of the craft at Brewers' Hall and be publicly examined 'as to their birth, cleanliness of their bodies and other certain points'.

Even in crowded London brewers were still making their own malt, as is shown by the inventory of a beer brewery near St Mary Somerset church in Upper Thames Street in 1486. It included a 'steyping cestern', or steeping vat, of lead, for steeping the raw grain; a rake for raking the malt; a 'blacke haire [fine sieve of horsehair or similar material] for a kiln', on which the green malted grain would have lain to be dried; and a malt mill 'with all apparel'. The danger of fire that went with running a maltings kiln was recognized, for another item on the inventory was a 'fyrehoke' for pulling down burning timbers. However, the dangers of lead poisoning were clearly not recognized: as well as the lead 'steyping cestern' the brewery had a lead 'tappe trowe' or trough used for running the hot boiled wort into the cooler (a wooden version can still be seen in the Tudor brewhouse at Laycock Abbey) and 'two sesterns of ledde' for 'licoure', the word brewers still use (in its modern spelling) for water.

Other items in the inventory included a 'bruying ketyll of coper' (copper); a 'mash fatte with a lowse [or loose] botom', suggesting that false-bottomed mash tuns, which greatly assisted draining the wort off the grains, had already been invented; a 'wort fatte' and two 'kelers' or coolers for the hot wort; twenty little 'tubbes' for yeast; and a 'bere dray with two pair wheles' for getting the beer out to the customers.

In 1493, in the reign of Henry VII, the first Tudor monarch, the beer brewers of London finally came to the Mayor and Aldermen and successfully petitioned for official recognition as a City guild. They must already have had an unofficial organization, since their delegation was led by the 'Wardens' of the 'Art or Mistery of Berebruers'. The City authorities agreed to their request that the 'Wardens of the Fellowship' be officially sworn in the Court of the Guildhall 'to rule the Craft and see that its ordinances are observed'. They were given the right to search 'all manner of hops and other grain four times a year or more and taste and assay all beer', as well as to survey all vessels used for beer. They were also enjoined not to send any 'wheat, malt or other grain for brewing to the mill to be ground', a reminder that wheat was still an ingredient in London beer.

Hopped beer continued to have its outspoken enemies, one of the fiercest being the physician and former Carthusian monk Andrew Boorde, author of the medical self-help book *A Dyetary of Helth*, published in 1542. Boorde, who was fifty-two, declared firmly in his book: 'I do drinke . . . no manner of beere made with hoppes.' However, Boorde may have had a secret reason for being prejudiced against beer. A rival writer named Barnes said that when Boorde was studying in Montpelier he got so drunk at the house of 'a Duche man', presumably on the Dutchman's hopped beer, that he threw up in his beard just before he fell into bed. Barnes claimed that when

Boorde woke up the next morning, the smell under his nose was so bad he had to shave his beard off. For Boorde, the loss of his beard, during a period when a lengthily hirsute chin was the essential badge of every intellectual and scholar, must have been enormously embarrassing.

Boorde had his revenge on beer, if that is what it was, with a savage attack on the drink in his *Dyetary*, which he was writing during his time in Montpelier. He wrote that while 'Ale for an Englysshman is a naturall drynke', beer was 'a naturall drynke for a Dutche man' (by which he meant Germans), but 'of late days . . . much used in Englande to the detryment of many Englysshe men . . . for the drynke is a cold drynke; yet it doth make a man fat and doth inflate the bely, as it doth appear by the Dutche mens faces & belyes'. However, Boorde would have found increasingly fewer Englishmen, certainly in the south, to agree with him about beer. In the north, though, they still preferred unhopped ale: in 1543, when a planned invasion of Scotland was called off, the Duke of Suffolk reported to Henry VIII's Council that there were 100 tuns of beer (each tun containing 240 gallons) at Berwick on Tweed, which were no longer required for the English army and could not be sold, 'for here they care for no beer'. Instead, Suffolk said, the beer 'may serve for the King's ships when they come hither'. The Tudor navy calculated that a ship of 100 tons, carrying 200 men for two months, needed fifty-six tuns of beer (that is, around a gallon a man per day), 12,200 pounds of biscuit, three tons of 'flesh' and three tons of fish and cheese. Water would turn brackish and unhopped ale would go off: beer would last the tour.

The Tudor army certainly ran on beer. In July 1544, during an English invasion of Picardy, the commander of Henry VIII's forces complained that his army was so short of supplies they had drunk no beer 'these last ten days, which is strange for English men to do with so little grudging'. Relief arrived a couple of days later with 400–500 tuns of beer from Calais and ten of 'the king's brewhouses' (presumably mobile breweries) together with 'English brewers'.

The division between ale brewers and beer brewers lasted until at least the reign of James I, and in Henry VIII's day beer brewing, as opposed to ale brewing, continued to be a speciality of immigrants. An Act of 1530–1 said that 'strangers being brewers' should be among the very few aliens not covered by the penal statutes against foreigners 'exercising handicrafts within the realm'. John Pope, Henry VIII's personal beer brewer, was given special permission in 1542 to have as many as twelve 'persons born out of the King's Dominions' working in his household 'for the said feat of beer brewing', even though the law said no one should have more than four foreigners working for them. The size of Pope's workforce, enormous for the time, is understandable: Hampton Court Palace, Henry's main residence, consumed 600,000 gallons of ale and beer a year, more than 13,000 pints a day. Even the lowest officer of the household received four pints every evening; dukes were to get two gallons a day (presumably not all for themselves).

As well as a beer brewer, Henry VIII had an ale brewer, who had specific instructions not to forget which drink he was making: the regulations laid down by the Treasurer of the Household at Hampton Court in 1539 included a rule that the ale brewers 'put neither Hoppes nor Brimstone in their ale in the pipes [120 gallon casks], soe that it may be found good, wholesome and perfect stuff and worth the King's money'. The brimstone (sulphur), burnt in candles, would have been used to fumigate the casks.

The first beer brewers in England, early in the fifteenth century, would have used imported Flemish hops. It was another 100 years before the growing of hops got going in England, probably because so many of the country's beer brewers were originally from Flanders and adjoining provinces, and preferred to buy their hops from a source they knew grew good-quality produce. Although Kent (the county immediately opposite Flanders) was undoubtedly the first place in Britain where hops were cultivated seriously, and this almost certainly happened in the early sixteenth century, exactly where and when remains unknown.

One tradition says the first hop garden was established in 1520, in the parish of Westbere, near Canterbury. Most commentators date the earliest planting of hops in England to 1524, based on a couplet in *The Chronicles of the Kings of England* by the Kentish writer Sir Richard Baker, published in 1641. Referring to 1524, Baker wrote that 'Hops and Turkies, Carps and Beer / Came into England all in a year'.

Whenever English hop-growing started, and 'some time around 1520' seems a good bet, it was still needing help from continental experts thirty years later. Hops were strategically important enough for the Privy Council in 1549 to pay the expenses involved in bringing over hop setters, apparently from Flanders. The following year, and again in 1553, wages were paid in the name of the king to Peter de Wolf (whose name suggests he too came from the Low Countries) 'and certain workmen under him . . . for planting and setting of hops'. Royal involvement in encouraging hop planting in England was partly, probably, a question of reducing imports, and thus the amount of cash going out of the kingdom, but also because hopped beer was an important staple for the army and navy, almost as important as bread and meat, and reliable supplies of an essential raw ingredient in making beer for the forces had to be guaranteed in case of war.

By 1569 English hop cultivation was sufficiently advanced for one agricultural writer, the Sussex landowner Leonard Mascall (or Mascal), to claim that 'one pound of our hoppes dried and ordered will go as far as two poundes of the best hoppe that come from overseas'. Five years later, in 1574, the first book in English solely devoted to hop-growing was written by a thirty-six-year-old Kentish landowner called Reynolde (or Reginald) Scot. His *A Perfite Platform of a Hoppe Garden*, filled with woodcut illustrations to aid the less literate Elizabethan farmer, went to three editions in four years.

By 1577 hop cultivation had reached Herefordshire, where a 'hopp-yarde' was noted at Whitbourne, near Bromyard. The district around Hereford and Worcester was eventually to become the second most important hop-growing area in Britain, after Kent. Differences in terminology between the West Midlands and South-East England –

hop yard for hop garden, hop kiln for oast house, for example – suggest hop-growing was started independently in the two places.

By 1655 hops were being grown in at least fourteen English counties, including Somerset, though Kent accounted for a third of the total crop. However, although it was reckoned an acre of hops would bring in more profit than fifty acres of arable land in a good year, the hop farmer's life was more insecure than any other branch of agriculture. In 1799 John Banister of Horton Kirby in Kent, in a book called *Synopsis of Husbandry* wrote: 'There is no period of its growth when the hop is not subject to some one malady or another.' An old Kentish rhyme said of hops: 'First the flea, then the fly / Then the mould, then they die.'

The main beer styles of Elizabethan England seem to have been single beer and double beer. Double beer was made by running the wort back through the grain (or through fresh grain), while single beer was a single mash. The writer William Y-worth, in a book called *Cerevisiarii Comes or The New and True Art of Brewing*, published in London in 1692, gave a typical seventeenth-century pseudo-scientific explanation that the double wort 'doth . . . only extract the Sweet, Friendly, Balsamic Qualities' from the fresh malt, 'its Hunger being partly satisfied before'. He continued that double beer 'being thus brewed . . . may be transported to the Indies, remaining in its full Goodness . . . whereas the Single, if not well-brewed especially, soon corrupts, ropes and sours'. (Ropey beer has a bacterial infection which results in sticky 'ropes' appearing in the liquid.)

Recipes survive from the sixteenth century giving quantities of malt per barrel of beer, which means a stab can be made at guessing the strengths of the resulting brews. These can only be approximations: we can have no idea how efficiently Tudor brewers managed to extract fermentable materials from their malt, nor how well they made their malt in the first place. But it is probably fair to estimate that extraction rates were not much better than 70 per cent of today's values from the same amount of malt. Another problem is that the bushel and the quarter were measures of volume, not weight, and the weight of malt per bushel would have varied according to the density of the grain and the size of the grains. Finally, even if we could find the OG reasonably accurately, we do not know how efficient the fermentation process was, and thus how high the final alcohol content was.

Given these provisos, however, let us take a recipe for single beer printed by Richard Arnold in 1503. To make sixty barrels, the ingredients prescribed are ten quarters of barley malt, two quarters of wheat and two quarters of oats, plus forty pounds of hops. A modern-day brewing to this recipe by the home-brew expert Graham Wheeler, using modern yeast, modern malted barley (which would probably have given a higher extract than Arnold could have achieved), malted oats and Shredded Wheat, came out at 1065 OG and 6.7 per cent ABV. It is very unlikely that in 1503 it would have produced a beer of anything less than 1045 OG, or 4 per cent alcohol by volume, even allowing for the poorer extracts and fermenting efficiencies of the time.

Unfortunately, this guide to the strength of single beer is completely contradicted by a declaration from the authorities in London in 1552 regarding the amount of malt that should go into double and single beer. For 'doble beare', they said, a quarter of 'grayne' should produce 'fowre barrels and one fyrkin' of 'goode holesome drynke'. To make single beer, twice as much drink should be brewed from the same quantity of grain. This would have produced double beer with a strength of around 1047 OG at the bottom end, perhaps 1058 at most (barely 5 per cent ABV), while the single beer could not have been stronger than around 1025 OG, less than 2 per cent ABV.

Both these strengths seem far too low – indeed, they seem to use exactly half the malt one might expect, given Arnold's recipe for single beer, and evidence from other writers. (Recipes from the seventeenth century show beers of around 1035–1045 OG being described as 'small beer'.) Perhaps the London authorities in 1552 were deliberately trying to force the city's brewers to make weaker beers. Certainly there was a tendency among the country's ruling class to try to legislate against strong drinks. In around 1560, Queen Elizabeth I complained that the brewers had stopped brewing single beer, making instead 'a kynde of very strong bere calling the same doble-doble bere, which they do commonly utter and sell at a very grate and excessive pryce'. The Queen ordered the brewers to stop brewing double-double beer and to brew instead 'as much syngyl as doble beare and more'. In June 1588 the Corporation of St Albans, in Hertfordshire, hauled fourteen persons before the Mayor and charged them with brewing 'extraordinary strong ale', which they sold by retail 'against all good law and order'. Even in 1623 the Mayor of Woodstock, in Oxfordshire, was reporting that he had 'reformed the immoderate strength of beer' in the town.

In 1574 there were fifty-eight ale breweries in London and thirty-two beer breweries, but the ale brewers consumed an average of only twelve quarters of malt a week, while the beer brewers were on average consuming four times as much. Elizabethan commentators believed you could make twice as much beer from a quarter of malt as you could ale, because the hopped beer did not have to be as strong as ale to stop it going sour too quickly. The average London beer brewer's output in pints was thus probably on average eight times larger than the average ale brewer's production. Even the biggest London ale brewer was smaller, on this calculation, than the smallest of the capital's common beer brewers. The biggest Elizabethan London beer brewer consumed ninety quarters of malt a week, enough to make around 14,000 barrels of beer a year, very roughly, which would be a medium-sized brewery even in the eighteenth century.

It is difficult to be precise without knowing what proportion of grain went into single ale and beer, which used less malt per barrel, and what proportion went into double brews. But very roughly it looks as if, even though there were nearly twice as many ale breweries in the capital, by the 1570s Londoners were drinking four times as much beer from the common brewers as they were ale.

This beer was drunk, generally, from hooped wooden mugs: Jack Cade in Shakespeare's play *Henry VI*, promising his supporters great bounties when he is ruler of England, declared that as well as seven halfpenny loafs for a penny, 'the three-hooped pot shall have ten hoops'. The wealthy apparently used something grander than wood: the Frenchman Estienne Perlin, a visitor to London in the 1550s, wrote that the English drank beer 'not in glasses but in earthenware pots with silver handles and covers'.

Queen Elizabeth herself, like her father, had both a beer brewer, Henry Campion, who died in 1588, and ale brewers, two men called Peert and Yardley. (Campion's brewery, according to John Stow's 'Survey of London' in 1602, was in Hay Wharf Lane, at the side of All Hallows the Great church in Upper Thames Street, which puts it on the same site as the Calverts' later Hour Glass brewery.) She also had naval and military brewhouses in operation at Tower Hill, Dover, Portsmouth and, probably, Porchester by 1565, to supply the army and navy. The first royal beer brewery in Portsmouth was built by Henry VII in 1492, and its operations were enlarged by Henry VIII in 1512–13 at a cost of more than £2,600 to enable it to produce more than 500 barrels of beer a day.

The growing taste for beer meant beer brewers were starting to outnumber ale brewers in the provinces as well as the capital. Norwich in 1564 had five 'comon alebrewers' and nine 'comon berebrewars'. In St Albans in 1606, when the town council decided to restrict the number of brewers to try to halt a continuing rise in the price of fuelwood, they allowed four beer brewers to operate and just two ale brewers.

One of St Albans's 'permitted' brewers, John Moseley, kept the White Hart inn in the town. The White Hart appears to have been a former monastic guest-house, and came with brewing equipment when it was privately leased out by the Abbot of St Albans Abbey in 1535. But this is one of the very few links between monastic brewing, which was probably almost universal in religious houses in England before the dissolution of the monasteries between 1536 and 1540, and secular brewing afterwards. The redundant monastic brewers seem to have vanished, their breweries to have gone unused. A few echoes remain. Morgan's brewery in King Street, Norwich, which ran under several names until 1985, has been identified by some optimistic historians as the site of an Augustinian friary founded in 1360. The Blue Anchor at Helston, Cornwall, today one of the last remaining 'old' home-brew pubs still operating, is said to be a monastic rest-house dating from a century later. The brewery at Mortlake, Surrey, now known as the Stag brewery and leased to Anheuser-Busch to produce Budweiser, is sometimes said to derive from the monastery brewery at the Manor House owned by the Archbishops of Canterbury and to date back to the fifteenth century. However, commercial brewing does not appear to have started until the Manor House was pulled down in the eighteenth century. These slight ghosts apart, links between monastery breweries and later commercial brewers are remarkable by their absence.

By the sixteenth century, another change besides the use of hops was altering the taste of English drink: commercial brewers in the South-East had largely ceased putting oats in the mash. When the English navy was offered West Country-brewed oat beer in 1513, the sailors refused to drink it. The grain bill for English ale and beer still included wheat, however: in 1568 the brewers of Oxford were banned from having their 'wheate malte' ground anywhere except at the 'Castell Milles'. London's brewers, at least, used wheat only in their strong beer, according to a report from the Lord Mayor to the Privy Council in 1574. He went on to indicate that wheat was used one-to-ten with barley malt to make 'stronge bere'. Two years later, in an attempt to keep the price of grain down, the brewers of London, Kent, Essex and Middlesex were banned from brewing 'any extraor-dinary beare with wheate or wheate meale commonlye called March beere'.

The practice of brewing strong beer in March, the last month before the spring and summer temperatures made brewing dangerously unpredictable, had evidently become common throughout England. March beer would stay wholesome in cask for two years or more, and the gentry and nobility were starting to take pride in the age of their beers. William Harrison, a parson from Essex, writing in 1577, said the March beer served at noblemen's tables 'in their fixed and standing houses is commonly of a year old' and sometimes 'of two years' tunning or more', though 'this is not general'. Indeed, Harrison said, nobles vied with each other to serve the oldest beer.

Unhopped ale, Harrison said, was more 'thick' and 'fulsome' than beer (since it was 'sodden', or boiled, 'not at all or very little' before fermentation and thus, although Harrison did not know this, contained more suspended proteins). It was regarded by many as an 'old or sick men's drink', Harrison said. However, ale still had its important supporters, even at the end of the sixteenth century. In the plays of William Shakespeare, every reference to beer is derogatory, from Prince Hal in *Henry IV Part II* condemning 'the poor creature, small beer' to the villain Horner in *Henry VI Part II*, who loses a fight after getting drunk on strong double beer. A quart of ale, however, 'is a dish for a king', Autolycus sings in *A Winter's Tale*; and for Launce in *Two Gentlemen of Verona* it is an important virtue of the woman he loves that 'she brews good ale'. One attraction of ale must have been its cheapness: 1½d a gallon wholesale in St Albans in 1598, against 2½d a gallon for even the weaker sort of beer.

The distinction between ale and beer was slowly eroding, however. Gervase Markham, in his book *The English Huswife*, published in 1615, wrote that

> the general use is by no means to put any hops into ale, making that the difference between it and beere . . . but the wiser huswives do find an error in that opinion, and say the utter want of hops is the reason why ale lasteth so little a time, but either dyeth or soureth, and therefore they will to every barrel of the best ale allow halfe a pound of good hops.

The rise of beer over ale was matched by the decline in the tradition known as the 'ale'. This was a local celebration designed to raise funds for a particular purpose. The longest-lasting was probably the 'church ale', organized by the churchwardens, the profit from which – from the brewing and selling of drink, and the consumption of food to go with it – was used for the maintenance of the local church, and for improvements such as a ring of bells or a new loft. Often the 'ale' was held in a building called the church-house. Other 'ales' were held for municipal purposes. Lyme in Dorset held regular 'cobb ales' in the early seventeenth century to pay for keeping up the town's harbour: the one in 1601 raised £20 14s 10d. But the more Puritan-minded Tudor clergy were appalled by church-ales, with one in 1570 claiming they were occasions for 'bul-beatings, beare-beatings, bowl-ings, dycing, cardyng, dauncynges, drunkenness and whoredom'. Largely suppressed under the Protestant Edward VI in the late 1540s, church ales had sprung back up under his Catholic sister Queen Mary in the 1550s right across the south and west of England. But from the 1570s, under pressure from Protestant clergy and local magistrates, church-ale celebrations began to disappear from many counties, including all of East Anglia, Kent and Sussex, and to diminish sharply in number elsewhere. By the end of Elizabeth's reign they were confined mostly to parishes in the West Country and the Thames Valley.

Tax first began to be a concern for brewers in the seventeenth century, as the government started to look at the growing revenues of the common brewers for a source of income. Previously the dubious weapon of 'requests' for 'loans' had been used: a petition made in 1600 to Queen Elizabeth by a London beer brewer called John Vanhulst, born in the Duchy of Cleves, on the Dutch–German border, asks that he be let off lending Her Majesty £500 for six months as his stock is 'so wasted by bad debts' he had been forced to 'give over' the trade of brewing 'and cannot lend money as heretofore'.

James I used scarcely less subtle methods around 1614 to impose a royal levy of 4d a quarter on all the malt used by the London brewers, in return for giving up the 'right' to send his officers in to appropriate beer for the king's household. But one problem about trying to tax brewing was that in most parts of the country outside the South-East of England, almost all of the ale and beer sold was still produced by thousands of alehouse and inn brewers, whose production would be difficult to monitor. James I found a harsh solution in 1620, proposing to ban all 'victuallers' from brewing and force them to buy their drink from the common brewers, who would be licensed by the king. The country brewers fought off this plan only by agreeing to accept the same fourpence a quarter levy on malt, roughly a penny a barrel, that the London brewers paid. However, in 1624 the levy had to be scrapped when Parliament declared all money-raising 'patents' issued by royal prerogative illegal.

Thirteen years after Parliament squashed James's attempt to give common brewers a monopoly of supply, in 1637 his son Charles I came back with a similar proclamation that banned all innkeepers, alehouse keepers, taverners, cooks and victuallers in England and Wales from being brewers, introduced a scheme of royal grants to specula-tors to set up brewing corporations with exclusive rights of supply, and imposed a levy on barley at the maltings and malt in the mash-tun. The tax lasted only two years before Parliament again declared it illegal. However, since only a quarter of the estimated £6,000 a year the tax was meant to bring in had actually been gathered, it looks as if avoidance was widespread.

In 1642 the tension between Parliament and Crown exploded into war, and the need of both sides for reliable sources of income to pay for their forces became desperate. In May 1643 the Parliamentarian leader John Pym introduced the excise, a tax on consumables, which included 2s a barrel on all strong beer worth 6s a barrel or more (just over a halfpenny a pint), and 6d a barrel on all weaker beer worth less than 6s a barrel. The tax covered both domestic and commercial brewers. Three years later Charles I issued a proclamation in Oxford saying the Royalists would levy the same taxes.

Domestic brewers were exempted from the excise on beer in 1653, though the tax on commercially brewed strong beer went up to 2s 6d a barrel in 1657. The revenue from beer excise was running at £500,000 a year, or more than 40 per cent of the entire annual excise revenue of £1.2 million. But the commercial brewers were hopeful when the monarchy was restored in 1660 that they, too, would be allowed to brew without the attentions of the excise men. In May

1660, the same month Charles II returned to England from exile, the Brewers' Company in London petitioned Parliament to be given 'freedom from the illegal and intolerable burden of Excise, burdensome to the poor to whom ale and beer, next to bread, are the chief stay and ruinous to us both in itself and in the tyrannical and arbitrary practices of the farmers [that is, the men given the commission to gather the tax] who collect it'.

Charles's new Parliament cut back the list of articles subject to the excise to a small range of beverages, including the newly fashionable coffee as well as tea and chocolate. However, the levy on beer and ale remained, at the same levels; indeed, it stayed for another 170 years, rising generally during periods when Britain was at war.

The Brewers' Company in London, despite taking the lead in campaigning against the excise on beer and ale, was slowly losing influence in the capital's brewing industry. It had survived a dangerous period in 1538 when Henry VIII – having his own problems with the Church, and wanting no reminders of clerics who had defied kings – declared the brewers' patron saint, Thomas Becket, to have been a traitor. Thomas's shrine at Canterbury was destroyed, his name was removed from the service books, and all churches dedicated to St Thomas had to be renamed. The next year, the City of London took an image of the saint off its official seal. The brewers hung on a little longer, but eventually, in 1543–4, decided it would be smart politics to take Thomas's arms from theirs and acquire a new set.

However, the brewers still managed to sneak in a subtle reference to the saint in their new arms. To this day the crest of the Brewers' Company shows a dark-skinned woman with fair hair, a nod to the (inaccurate) tradition that St Thomas's mother was a Saracen who had followed his father Gilbert home from the Crusades. It is lucky the king never realized what the brewers and the heralds were up to, maintaining a link to a banned saint: Henry VIII is estimated to have had 75,000 people killed during his reign, and a few cheeky brewers added to the list would not have worried him.

Despite charters granted by Elizabeth I and Charles I extending its jurisdiction first to two, then to four miles outside the City, the Brewers' Company was not one of the twelve great livery companies of the City, from whom Lord Mayors and Aldermen were traditionally chosen, and a politically ambitious London brewer would be a member of one of the big twelve companies as well as the Brewers': Isaac Pennington of Southwark, for example, an alderman in the 1640s, joined the Fishmongers.

Thus increasing numbers of brewers, especially in London's growing suburbs, refused to join the Brewers' Company, particularly after the Great Fire of London in 1666, when Brewers' Hall was one of forty-four livery company halls to be destroyed. They saw no advantage in joining a small livery company, only cost. The brewers rebuilt their hall in 1673, and in 1685 James II granted the company a charter that extended its powers to eight miles around London. But power in the brewing industry increasingly resided with individual wealthy brewers rather than in Brewers' Hall. The Great Fire of 1666 also destroyed sixteen brewhouses; when the owners petitioned for a rebate of some of the £4,000 excise money they had pre-paid on beer lost in the fire they did it as a group, rather than through the Brewers' Society.

The seventeenth century saw the start of brewing concerns in the south of England that would continue to operate for hundreds of years, often in the same family's ownership. Thomas Cole, for example, was brewing in Twickenham, Middlesex, from at least 1635, to be followed by seven more generations of the Cole family. The business was finally sold in 1892 to Brandon's of Putney, further down the Thames, which closed the Twickenham brewery in 1906. In Ramsgate, Kent, also in 1635, a deed recorded the sale by Robert Sampson of a dwelling house, malthouse, brewhouse and other property. The brewhouse was bought by Thomas Tomson about 1680. The Tomsons, who were joined in partnership by the Wooton family in 1867, amalgamated with a rival Kentish brewer, Gardner & Co. of Ash, in 1951, but the Ramsgate brewery stayed open until the amalgamated company, Combined Breweries Holdings, was acquired by Whitbread in 1968. In Hertfordshire, once again in 1635, Thomas Searancke, whose family had come to England from Flanders the previous century, was running the Chequers Inn in Fore Street, Hatfield. His descendants developed this into a successful brewery business which passed out of the family in the nineteenth century, growing to be the second biggest brewer in the county under the name Pryor Reid. It finally closed in 1920, taken over by Hertfordshire's biggest brewer, Benskin's of Watford. These three concerns thus ran from 1635 for, respectively, 271 years, 333 years and 285 years. No industry except brewing so regularly produced commercial enterprises that lasted so many generations.

London, having the biggest, longest-established brewing industry, led the way in long-lasting brewing enterprises. By the end of the seventeenth century there were in the capital at least five well-established breweries that would be good for another quarter of a millennium of brewing. The Red Lion brewery, Lower East Smithfield, Wapping, which became famous under the Parsons and, later, the Hoares, was on the site of a fifteenth-century brewhouse supposedly once owned by Robert, Earl of Leicester; it brewed its last beers in 1934. Edmund Halsey was running Child's Anchor brewery in Deadman's Place, Southwark, founded by James Monger around 1616 next door to the Globe Theatre. It was later to become Thrale's brewery, then Barclay Perkins; it closed, under the flag of Courage, in 1960. Joseph Truman had been brewing in Black Eagle Street, Spitalfields for more than twenty years, in a brewery built in 1666. Truman's brewery shut only in 1989. The Greenes were brewing at the Stag brewery, Pimlico (later Watney's), where they had brewed since before the Civil War. The Stag brewery ceased brewing in 1959. And the Campion family had been at the Hour Glass brewery in Thames Street (acquired by Sir William Calvert in 1730) since at least the 1580s: this had bounced back after the Great Fire, and as the City of London Brewery Company it finally stopped brewing in 1922.

However, the size of London's breweries was an exception even in the south-east. The city's 194 common brewers, who served some

500,000 people, produced more than 962,000 barrels of strong beer and ale and 690,000 barrels of small beer in 1699, while those inns and alehouses in London that still brewed their own managed only 6,000 barrels of strong brew and 6,700 barrels of small between them: not even 1 per cent of the capital's beer. In 1701, the 190 common brewers in London produced almost twice as much as the 574 common brewers elsewhere in the kingdom, making a London brewery, on average, six times larger than a provincial one.

Outside London, common brewers were considerably less important than the 41,000 'brewing victuallers' (inns and alehouses still with their own brewhouses attached), who together produced more than 2.8 million barrels of beer and ale in 1701. It has been estimated that around two-thirds of all alehouses across the country brewed at least part of the time even at the end of the seventeenth century, with the proportion considerably higher outside the southeast. Their production may have been only, on average, 1¼ barrels a week, against the country common brewers' thirty barrels a week (and the London brewers' 175 barrels a week), but the inn and alehouse brewers outnumbered the common brewers 70: 1. Brewers of all kinds were an important part of the nation's economy: the economist Gregory King estimated that in 1695 expenditure on beer and ale made up 28 per cent of annual per capita spending.

The situation was summed up by the anonymous author of the *Guide to Gentlemen and Farmers for Brewing the Finest Malt Liquors*, published in 1703, at the start of Queen Anne's reign. 'In most (if not all) of the Northern counties there are few or no common brewers,' the author wrote,

> The Inn-keepers and Publick Ale Houses brewing what they retail in their own houses. And Private Families for themselves. In the West of England they have some common brewers, but not in proportion to the East and South. In the Southern counties, abounding in common brewers, almost all the Inhabitants of cities and great towns there, and the meaner people of their

neighbourhood, take their drink of the common brewers, which few or none of all the Inhabitants of the Northern towns do.

The *Guide to Gentlemen and Farmers* revealed that West Country beer was still liable to be rejected by outsiders, as Tudor sailors had refused West Country oat beer: 'In most parts of the West, their malt is so stenched with the smoak of the wood with which 'tis dried, that no stranger can endure it, though the Inhabitants, who are familiarized to it, can swallow it as the Hollanders do their thick black Beer brewed with Buck Wheat.'

The author also showed that beer was now being kept to mature for even longer than in William Harrison's time: 'Many country gentlemen talk of, and magnify their stale Beer of 5, 10 or more years old . . . I always broach mine at about nine months' end, that is, my March beer at Christmas and my October beer at midsummer, at which times it is generally at the best. But will keep very well in Bottles a year or two more.'

The *Guide* recommended using eleven bushels of malt to make a hogshead of strong March or October ale from the first mash, which would have given an enormous OG, somewhere up in the 1130s or 1140s, and which explains why it would keep so long. For 'Ordinary Brewings, where you design not very strong Drink, six or seven Bushells of Malt will make one Hogshead of good strong, and another of small Beer.' Here the OG for the strong beer was still probably around 1080 or more.

It also revealed that any difference between ale and beer was now one of degree of hoppiness: 'All good Ale is now made with some small mixture of Hops, tho' not in so great Quantity as Strong Beer, design'd for longer keeping.' The *Guide* recommended two pounds of hops to a hogshead of March or October beer, one pound of hops to a hogshead of 'ordinary Strong Beer to be soon Drank out' and half a pound of hops to a hogshead of strong ale. This is still a far smaller proportion than later brewers would use. A hogshead is one and a half barrels: for comparison, a nineteenth-century barley wine, which would be about halfway between the Guide's 'ordinary Strong beer' and its October beer in strength, might be brewed with six to seven pounds of hops per hogshead.

Bottled ale, mentioned briefly in the *Guide*, was increasingly available, despite the introduction of a tax on glass in 1645. Samuel Pepys recorded drinking 'several bottles of Hull ale' with friends at an inn called the Bell in London in November 1660. The household accounts of the Cecil family, Earls of Salisbury, in 1634 suggest the nobility and gentry, who brewed their own ale and beer on their country estates for themselves and their households, would drink strong bottled beer when they came to London. This was probably bottled in the country and brought up to the capital when necessary: Wheatley Hall, Doncaster, home of the Cooke family, had a bottle room in 1683, Holkham Hall in Norfolk in 1671 had two bottled beer stores leading off the 'small beer cellar' (that is, cellar for small beer), and in 1676 the Earl of Bedford's household accounts show the purchase from a brewer near the family seat at Woburn of ale 'to bottle for my lord's drinking'.

The brewing of strong beer by gentry and nobility was given a considerable boost as a result of developments that followed the signing by the diplomat John Methuen of a trade agreement between Britain and Portugal in 1703. The treaty's provisions included an agreement that Portugal would open its doors to English cloth. In return the Portuguese were given hugely preferential rates of duty by the British on their wine exports to the United Kingdom: £7 a tun, against the £55 a tun, almost eight times as much, that was imposed on French wine. Since rough Portuguese wines did not appeal to wealthy English wine-drinkers, the English began to turn to smugglers for their French claret and burgundy, while the Portuguese were making their wines smoother and sweeter by adding brandy, to make a drink that by 1691 the British were calling port. But those drinkers who did not want to deal with smugglers or port merchants had a home-made option: the extremely strong, sweet, well-hopped old beers described in the *Guide to Gentlemen and Farmers*, published the same year as the Methuen Treaty. In the halls of the gentry and aristocracy a fashion spread after 1703 for drinking tiny glasses of powerful, aged, sticky beer, in quantities of three to four fluid ounces, less than a quarter of a pint.

These strong beers were made from expensive pale malt, dried with coke rather than charwood, which made them lighter in colour than the more common alehouse brown beers, and although they were well-hopped beers they were known, euphoniously, as pale ales. This was about the last step on the road that led ale and beer to become synonyms rather than words meaning different drinks. The little ale glasses themselves were decorated with wheel-cut engravings of hops and barley, or, in the case of glasses for honeyed or buttered ales, bees and butterflies. These strong ales were to influence several developments in brewing in the decades that followed the death of Queen Anne in 1714.

CHAPTER FIVE

BLACK IS BEAUTIFUL

the eighteenth century

Whig and Tory, opposite
In all things else, do both unite
In praise of nappy ale

John Gay (1685–1732)

Early in the reign of George I two anonymous rhyming 'good pub guides' to London were published. The *Vade Mecum for Malt Worms* (malt worm being an old slang expression for a drinker) came out about 1716–18, and the *Guide for Malt Worms* was written in or soon after 1720 (since it mentions the South Sea Bubble, the great stock exchange boom-and-slump of that year). The two books, probably composed by the London tavern keeper and poet Edward 'Ned' Ward, covered between them more than 200 of the 5,000 or so inns, alehouses and taverns in and around the capital.

Almost thirty different types of beer were mentioned, the commonest being twopenny pale ale (the most expensive regular beer in London), and mild and stale. These last two were the 'fresh', or newly brewed, and 'mature', or older and more tart versions of the staple brown beer of the capital's working class in the early eighteenth century. Mild and stale were frequently mentioned together in the two guides, suggesting they were drunk half-and-half, the way mid-twentieth-century drinkers drank mild-and-bitter. Other popular beers mentioned in the guides were stout, amber beer, Oxford ale and Derby ale. There was a host of others, including Burton ale, cherry beer, Dorchester, Dr Butler's Ale (a medicinal beer), York pale ale, Nottingham ale, oat ale, Stingo, Welsh ale, pale Hocky and three-threads.

The guides also name-checked six brewers out of the 190 or so operating in the city at the time: Calvert, of the Hour Glass brewery in Upper Thames Street; Halsey of the Anchor brewery in Southwark; 'Horwood', presumably Harwood of the Shoreditch High Street brewery; Nicholson, another Spitalfields brewer; Tate; and Feast of the Peacock brewery in Whitecross Street. Already drinkers were being asked to seek out pubs because of the excellence of the brewer supplying the house with beer. Some of these relationships proved to be extremely long-lasting: the Flying Horse off Moorfields was serving beer from the Anchor brewery in Southwark in 1720, for example, and was still serving beer from the same brewery 240 years later.

The beer that does not seem to be mentioned in the two guides, however, is eighteenth-century London's great gift to world brewing: porter, otherwise known (to brewers) as entire. There is one reference in the *Vade Mecum*, under the Bull's Head, Leadenhall Street, to 'Tom Man's Entire' – 'for so the Belch is called that sets his Face on Fire'; but porter is not named at all, with the possible exception of a single comment in the *Guide* that a tavern in Shoe Lane is 'filled / with folks that are in Porter's liquors skilled'.

Porters as pub customers, however, are mentioned in the two guide-books more often than any other trade. These men, whose role in London's life and economy has been almost forgotten today, were not 'market porters' but that considerable mass of the working-class population in London – perhaps 11,000 in the 1750s – who made their living from 'porterage': carrying assorted goods about the streets, in and out of cellars and warehouses, and on and off boats and ships in the Thames.

The porters' hot, hard work fuelled the desire for a sharp, filling, refreshing, nutritious beer: it has been estimated that eighteenth-century manual workers were getting 2,000 calories a day from beer, the equivalent of an uneatable quantity of bread. As a result they were great frequenters of pubs, both on duty and off. A writer in the *Penny Magazine* in 1841, describing a former public house called the Triumphant Chariot near Hyde Park Corner, in the 1770s said that outside the pub, by the kerb-stone, was a bench for the porters and a board [that is, table] over it 'for depositing their loads' while they stopped for 'deep draughts of stout . . . such as are idealised in Hogarth's Beer Street'. Similar resting-places for porters outside pubs, the *Penny Magazine* said, 'were once universal'.

Ned Ward's two pub guides seem to have come out just at the moment when the beer drunk by the working classes of London, including the many thousands of porters, was changing into something new. There is a traditional, 'heroic' account of the development of porter or entire, which claims it was first made in 1722 by a brewer named Ralph Harwood at his brewhouse in Shoreditch High Street, on the eastern edge of the City of London. Though this story is regularly repeated whenever porter is discussed, sadly, it is almost entirely inaccurate.

The legend asserts that Harwood made the first porter as a taste-alike replacement for a popular drink of the period called three-threads, which required the publican to mix three different types of beer from three different casks, a laborious job. Harwood called his new, single-operation beer 'entire', or 'entire butt', to distinguish it from the blended three-threads – one meaning of 'entire' is 'unmixed'. (Another meaning of 'entire' is 'stallion', a pun probably not lost on Georgian drinkers.)

This traditional story first became established at the beginning of the nineteenth century, eighty years after the events it supposedly describes. It has been repeated by dozens, perhaps hundreds of writers. Unfortunately there is scarcely a 'fact' in it which is not doubtful or demonstrably wrong in some way, from the year porter first appeared (it was certainly before 1722) through the origin of the name entire, its alleged invention as a replacement for three-threads, and on to Ralph Harwood's involvement in porter's invention.

It is probable porter was never 'invented' as such, so much as developed out of London's existing style of brown beer. Even in 1744 a brewer in Yorkshire was referring to 'the very best sort of brown Strong Beer, commonly called London Porter', implying that porter was then regarded as the head of the family of brown beers, rather than a completely new sort of beer.

This strong brown beer, also known as 'Stitch', was brewed at 1¼ barrels from a quarter of malt, according to a brewers' manual of the mid-1730s, which would have given it an original gravity of perhaps 1070 or 1075, depending on the extraction rate (which was probably quite low). It was the same strength as pale or amber ale, rather weaker than 'Stout-beer' at one barrel to the quarter (1080 or 1090 OG), and stronger than common brown ale at 1065 OG or so. The weakest was 'intire small' at five or six barrels from a quarter of malt, around 1040 or 1035 OG (the strength of a 'standard' lager or bitter today).

Ralph Harwood was certainly a brewer in Shoreditch from at least 1703, when he is recorded as a brewer leasing four cottages in nearby Hoxton. Kent's *Directory and Alphabetical List of Trades in London* for 1736 shows Ralph and James Harwood in partnership as brewers in Shoreditch. Ralph Harwood was an important enough operator to be a trustee of the Lea Navigation in the 1740s. The Lea river was vital to London's brewers, as it was the route the malt barges used to bring their supplies from the great malting town of Ware, in Hertfordshire, which produced up to 60 per cent of the malt consumed in the capital's beer. To ensure this supply route operated efficiently, London's bigger brewers always took a great interest in keeping the navigation running.

But the Harwoods' brewery in Shoreditch was never among the very biggest concerns; nor was it particularly successful. In August 1747 the *Gentleman's Magazine* recorded the bankruptcy of Ralph and James Harwood of Shoreditch, 'brewers and partners'. Despite this setback, the Shoreditch rate books show that Ralph and James were still together at the brewery in 1748. But Ralph died in September 1749, and James Harwood was on his own at the Shoreditch brewery in 1750; by 1752 it was in the hands of Andrew Pankeman and Co., who ran it until Thomas Proctor took over in 1773. All the same, when James Harwood died in 1762, his obituary notice described him as 'an eminent brewer in Shoreditch, and the first that brought porter to perfection'. Thus it was James Harwood, rather than Ralph, who was first identified with porter; but as the man who perfected it, rather than its inventor.

Porter certainly needed perfecting. The only eye-witness report of the birth of this new style of beer was made around forty years after the event, by an elderly 'outdoor clerk' (or brewery rep) at one of the London breweries, writing in the *London Chronicle* in November 1760 under the pseudonym Obadiah Poundage. He told the *Chronicle's* readers that when 'Porter or Entire Butt' was first brewed, 'it was far from being in the perfection which since we have had it. I well remember for many years it was not expected, nor was it thought possible, for it to be made fine and bright, and four and five months was deemed to be sufficient age for it to be drunk at'.

Poundage does not say who first discovered that porter was much better left to mature for at least twelve months. Tying up capital in beer and casks for a year or more without any cashflow (or with negative cashflow) until the matured porter went out to the pubs must have badly hurt the pockets of the first brewer to experiment with elongated ageing. If it was James Harwood who perfected the making of porter, and if it meant the Shoreditch brewery suffered a cashflow crash while the first 'long maturation' butts of porter were slumbering in cellars for many months, perhaps this explains why the Harwoods went bankrupt in 1747.

Poundage, who claimed to be eighty-six, and who said he had worked in the brewing industry for seventy years, wrote that porter had first been brewed 'about the year 1722'. But he did not name anybody as the first porter brewer. It was not until nearly thirty years after Poundage's account appeared that Ralph Harwood was put forward as the great originator. In 'A Short Description of Shoreditch Parish' by 'A Parishioner', published in the *Gentleman's Magazine* on

14 October 1788, the anonymous author wrote: 'on the east side of the High Street is Proctor's brewhouse, formerly Ralph Harwood's, who, *it is said* [italics added], was the first brewer of porter-beer, which he made there.' The article then quoted a song by 'poet Gutteridge, a native of Shoreditch':

> *Harwood my townsman, he invented first*
> *Porter, to rival wine, and quench the thirst;*
> *Porter, which spreads its fame half the world o'er,*
> *Whose reputation rises more and more,*
> *As long as porter shall preserve its fame*
> *Let all with gratitude our parish name.*

It was thus around seventy years after porter arrived that Ralph Harwood was first claimed as its inventor, and by a fellow resident of Shoreditch – hardly an unbiased witness.

Fourteen years later, in 1802, the account appeared which was to be the core of the 'heroic' narrative of the birth of porter. In his guide-book *The Picture of London*, John Feltham wrote three pages on 'The Porter Brewery' (using 'brewery' in the eighteenth-century sense of 'brewing industry'). Feltham said that porter 'obtained its name about the year 1730 [*sic*], from the following circumstances, which, not having yet been printed, we think them proper to record in this work'. He continued:

Prior to the above-mentioned period the malt liquors in general use were ale, beer and twopenny . . . In course of time it . . . became the practice to call for a pint or tankard of three-threads, meaning a third [each] of ale, beer and twopenny; and thus the publican had the trouble to go to three casks and turn three cocks for a pint of liquor. To avoid this trouble and waste a brewer by the name of Harwood conceived the idea of making a liquor which should partake of the united flavours of ale, beer and twopenny. He did so and called it Entire or Entire-butt, meaning that it was served entirely from one cask; and as it was a very hearty nourishing liquor it was very suitable for porters and other working people. Hence it obtained the name porter.

Feltham's version of history has been repeated by almost every writer since 1802, sometimes altering his date of 1730 to Poundage's 1722, often using exactly the same phrases. Even in 1909, Frederick Hackwood's book *Ales and Drinking Customs of Old England* was still using whole sentences originally written by Feltham in his own account of the birth of porter a century before (though Hackwood was wildly wrong with the year porter first arrived, suggesting it was 'about 1750').

This repetition over two centuries has reinforced the apprehension that entire, alias porter, was invented to save publicans the bother of mixing a pot of 'three-threads' from three separate casks, and was called entire because it was 'entirely' from one cask. However, the

The street or ticket porter from William Hogarth's engraving Beer Street, made in 1751: he is wearing the tin or pewter badge or 'ticket' bearing the arms of the City of London that identifies his trade, and he is draining a quart pot of his eponymous drink after putting down the load he was carrying.

surviving contemporary accounts suggest overwhelmingly that neither of these two statements is true.

Certainly London's drinkers liked to have their beers mixed to achieve the flavour they wanted, a habit that lasted centuries. Mixed drinks such as mild-and-bitter, Burton-and-bitter or brown-and-mild continued to be popular until the 1960s (and even in the late 1990s mixed drinks such as 'lager and light' were occasionally asked for in London's pubs). Three-threads is probably a corruption of 'three-thirds': it is not unlike the name given in East Anglia until recently to a mixture of mild and bitter, a 'pint of twos'. (The name cannot, incidentally, be derived from taps or spigots 'threaded' or screwed into the separate casks, as some modern writers have asserted, since the spigots were never screwed but always hammered into a hole bored not quite all the way through the end of the cask.)

Ward's *Vade Mecum* from 1716–18 gives about the only contemporary clue to the nature of three-threads. Under the Hole in the Wall, Hatton Garden, the guide says:

> *Joyous and glad, thy trade increasing see*
> *and daily broach full casks of Threads call'd*
> *Three.*

This suggests that if three-threads was indeed a mixed drink, it came to the publican ready-blended in full casks for dispensing straight away, rather than having to be mixed by the alehouse keeper or potboy in the tankard from three separate casks. However, it is possible the drink was called three-threads not because it was blended from three different beers but because it was, in fact, an 'entire' in the sense that it was one beer made from three mashes blended together. It is also at least possible that a replacement for three-threads was called entire butt, meaning unmixed beer, if three-threads was, by contrast, 'mixed butt', full casks of ready-blended pale ale, mild beer and stale beer. The fact that three-threads gets only one mention, while other beers such as mild and stale get several, suggests it was not as popular as later writers claim, another blow to the idea that porter was invented as a replacement for a popular but difficult-to-serve three-threads.

Looking at later evidence, Obadiah Poundage in 1760 said that before porter, in the years of Queen Anne (1702–14), the regular drinks in London were ale, which was still sweet and heavy, and beer, which was much more hopped and thus more bitter. However, Londoners found the beer too bitter, and 'in general' the ale and beer were mixed together and bought by customers from the 'Ale draper' (or alehouse keeper) at 'twopence halfpenny and twopence three farthings the quart'.

Meanwhile, Poundage wrote, the country gentry, 'residing in London more than they had in former times', had brought with them to town around the start of Queen Anne's reign a taste for the strong pale ales they brewed back home on their estates. Pale malt for pale ale cost more than the brown malt the London brewers used for their regular brown beers, not least because pale malt required better-quality barley, and more expensive fuel to dry it; as a result pale ale retailed at 45 per cent more than regular brown beer: 4d the quart, or 2d a pint, which gave it the name twopenny.

London's brown beer brewers, prompted by loss of sales to the pale ale brewers, began trying to win back customers by adding more hops to their mild (or new) beer, Poundage said, while the habit also grew of allowing the brown beer to age or 'stale'. This would have given it the sort of tart, vinous qualities found today in a Belgian or Dutch 'oud bruin' brown ale. The maturing was done by third-party entrepreneurs who would buy fresh, mild beer, keep it until it was matured or 'stale', and then sell it to the publicans, an arrangement which saved both brewers and publicans cashflow difficulties, though it denied the brewers profits that went to the middlemen.

Some drinkers now liked to order 'mild beer and stale mixed', said Poundage; others 'ale, mild beer and stale blended together at three pence per quart, but many used all stale at fourpence per pot'. Notice, incidentally, that Poundage's recipe for the three-drink mixture, ale, mild beer and stale beer, is different from Feltham's version of three-threads forty-two years later – ale, beer and twopenny; and notice, too, that he says the mixture was 'blended together', not 'mixed in the pot'. Another writer, the brewer John Tuck, writing in 1822, agrees with Poundage that three-threads was stale, mild and pale ale mixed, but says it cost 4d a quart.

Poundage wrote in 1760 that the invention of entire butt was deliberate, that 'about the year 1722' the brown beer brewers of London 'conceived there was a method to be found' which would do away with the middlemen who were storing beer until it was mature and selling it back to publicans as 'stale' at a higher price, and also do away with the subsequent need to mix beers to match the public's taste. Poundage said the London brewers decided that 'beer well brewed, kept its proper time, became racy and mellow, that is neither new nor stale, such would recommend itself to the public'. This improved brew sold at 3d a quart, the same price as three-threads and less than stale beer, and although 'at first it was slow in making its way . . . in the end the experiment succeeded beyond expectation'.

As for the name of the new beer, Poundage said, when 'the labouring people, porters etc. experienced its wholesomeness and utility, they assumed to themselves the use thereof, from whence it was called Porter or Entire Butt.' This is slightly confused, like much of Poundage's narrative, but it does confirm that at the beginning porter and entire butt were the same beer, something that has been doubted by some writers. It also confirms that the beer was nicknamed porter because it was consumed by porters.

The best explanation for the name entire butt links it to contemporary brewing practice, rather than Feltham's idea that it was called 'entire' because it was drawn from only one cask. Butt-beer was a synonym for porter, according to *The London and Country Brewer*, a brewing manual first published in the 1730s. Entire, or 'intire', was an expression used by brewers to indicate a beer where the first, second and third mashes had been mixed and fermented together to make one grade of beer, rather than brewed separately to produce three beers of different strengths: the 1735 edition of *The London and Country Brewer*, for example, mentions 'intire small beer', brewed from a complete set of mashes, rather than just the last, weak mash, the normal source for small beer. Entire butt got its name because, as eighteenth-century recipes make clear, it was butt-beer made from an entire set of mashings, unlike stout butt beer, another brew mentioned in *The London and Country Brewer*, which would have been a strong (or stout) beer made from the first, strongest mash only. It was then matured in butts, 108 gallon casks, the equivalent of the medieval pipe.

Poundage's claim that the brewers 'conceived' the idea of entire butt supposes that they knew enough to be able to design a beer that they could be confident would capture public taste. Poundage was a propagandist for the brewers (his letter to the *Chronicle* was a long argument against higher beer taxes) and would want to make them appear skilled operators. It seems quite possible, however, that the first entire butt was a lucky accident. The sole ingredient of the earliest porters, apart from hops and water, was 'high brown', 'blown' or 'snapped' malt, which had been dried very quickly at high temperature. The result was that the husks of the malt grains burst like heated popcorn, and the malt became very dark in colour. It is hard to see the first 'blown' malt being made deliberately: there would have been no ready market for apparently ruined grain. It is easy to imagine, however, that one day in the early years of the eighteenth century a Hertfordshire brown malt maker accidentally left a batch of malt too long in the kiln, and had to sell the popped, almost charred result cheaply to one of his London customers who brewed brown beer.

The brewer (perhaps it was Ralph Harwood; it probably wasn't one of the leading brewers, who would have no need to buy cheap, damaged materials) made a beer out of this 'damaged' malt which turned out to be qualitatively different from the brown beers then being made by London brewers from 'ordinary' brown malt, which was kilned at a temperature 5–10° Fahrenheit lower than 'high brown' malt. The new beer sold well to the city's drinkers, and the brewer went back to the maltster to ask for some more of this new kind of malt. The city's 'labouring class', among them those thousands of porters, soon came to prefer the new beer to any other brew.

This is entirely speculation, however, and all the evidence from brewers suggests that porter was a slow development, not an invention. A hundred years after the arrival of porter, the brewer John Tuck, author of *The Private Brewer's Guide to the Art of Brewing Ale and Porter*, published in 1822, said porter came about because the London brewers, spurred by increasing sales of pale ales, 'began to improve' the 'heavy and glutinous' brown beer that existed about 1720. Tuck said that the 'improved' brown beer 'was started, well hopped, into

Interior of a brewery around the end of the eighteenth century, from *A Practical Treatise on Brewing the Various Sorts of Malt Liquor*, by Alexander Morrice. On the lower floor, by the under-back, casks full of still-fermenting beer have been placed over troughs which will catch the excess yeast as it flows out.

butts, and was kept a considerable time to grow mellow. Being the beverage of labouring men, it obtained the name of PORTER and was called INTIRE BUTT BEER'. Porter or entire butt, according to this version of history, was simply a hoppier, more aged interpretation of London brown beer, matured in butts, brewed using an entire mash, which caught on with the portering classes. Tuck's narrative agrees with comments made by the brewer Michael Combrune in 1762 in a book called *Theory and Practice of Brewing*, which make it clear that the original London brown ale, brewed at two barrels from a quarter, was 'heavy, thick, foggy and therefore justly grown in disuse . . . especially since porter or brown beer has been brought to a greater perfection'.

The earliest specific mention of porter by name comes in a pamphlet by the Whig political journalist and poet Nicholas Amhurst dated 22 May 1721, which talks about dining at a cook's shop 'upon beef, cabbage and porter' as being preferable to the life of a galley slave. Five years later, in November 1726, the twenty-one-year-old Swiss traveller César de Saussure, writing home from lodgings in East Sheen, on the edge of the capital, said about England that 'nothing but beer is drunk and it is made in several qualities. Small beer is what everyone drinks when thirsty; it is used even in the best houses and costs only a penny a pot. Another kind of beer is called porter . . . because the greater quantity of this beer is consumed by the working classes. It is a thick and strong beverage, and the effect it produces if drunk in excess, is the same as that of wine; this porter costs 3d the pot. In London there are a number of houses where nothing but this sort of beer is sold'.

Several fanciful stories have been needlessly invented to try to explain the name porter, when the simplest answer is the one given by contemporary sources: it was called porter because porters drank it. The important place of porters in the economic history of London has now been generally forgotten, but for several hundred years they were a large, thriving and hugely necessary part of the capital's commercial life.

London had thousands of registered porters in the eighteenth century, under the ostensible regulation of the City of London guilds, the two main groups being the 'fellowship porters', who mostly unloaded 'measurable' goods (such as corn, coal and salt) from ships on the river; and the 'ticket porters'. The ticket porters, who wore a pewter 'ticket' or badge stamped with the arms of the City of London, were themselves two separate groups, 'uptown porters', concerned with carrying goods about the city, who wore a white apron as well as the 'ticket', and 'waterside porters', who worked on the city's wharves and quays doing the portering jobs the fellowship porters did not touch. Thousands more men combined unofficial, casual portering with other unskilled jobs such as 'chairman', or sedan chair operative. Brewers of the time were big hirers of porters, with Barclay Perkins's Thames-side brewery taking on up to 140 fellowship porters at a time to unload malt barges.

The ticket porters, originally known as street porters, were supposed to have the monopoly of all land porterage, though they also acted as messengers and express letter carriers. They were hefty, stroppy fellows, capable of carrying loads of any sort of up to three hundred-weight (which required a team of four porters with poles and chains), and, like the taxi drivers of a later London, they waited to be hired for work at stands around the city: there were nearly 100 official stands in use by porters in the 1770s. A ticket porter, wearing his ticket, appears on the extreme right of William Hogarth's 1750s engraving 'Beer Street' (p.95), draining a quart pot of what was, undoubtedly, his eponymous drink.

There were at least two public houses called the Ticket Porter in London, one in Moorfields and the other (closed and demolished around 1970) in Arthur Street, near London Bridge. Charles Dickens invented a riverside pub called the Six Jolly Fellowship Porters in his novel *Our Mutual Friend*. The fellowship porters are said in fact to have used the Ship, in Gate Street, just to the north of Lincoln's Inn, where new members were initiated. A description of the rite written in the 1920s says that a quart of strong ale was ordered, and the novitiate's badge of office was dropped into the mug. The would-be porter then had to extract the badge with his teeth without spilling any ale.

Hogarth's 'Beer Street', with its porter-drinking porter and jolly, healthy beer-topers, was drawn in 1751 to contrast with its companion piece, 'Gin Lane', a picture of degradation and death, where only the pawnbroker thrived. While porter was the drink of the working classes from around 1720 onwards, gin had become the solace of the non-working classes. It was an eighteenth-century urban myth, dating from at least as far back as 1736, that gin-shops set up signs outside 'inviting people,' in the words of Tobias Smollett, 'to be drunk for the small expense of one penny . . . dead drunk for twopence and have straw for nothing'. But with gin retailing at distillery strength for a penny a quartern, or quarter-pint, it was certainly a cheaper and speedier way of getting drunk than porter at 3d a pot, and a quick way to oblivion if you wanted to forget you were living in the foetid slums.

The government introduced three different Acts between 1729 and 1743 to try to put a brake on the selling and drinking of gin. Each failed: gin consumption rose, according to one estimate, from 6.65 million gallons in 1730 to 11.33 million gallons in 1751. Only at the end of the latter year did the government introduced legislation that did turn back the gin tide; thereafter consumption of spirits dropped away, to 7.5 million gallons in 1752 and 3.66 million gallons by 1767/8.

The gin crisis, while it had terrible effects on the poorest parts of London, where contemporaries claimed one building in four was a dram-shop, seems not to have held the porter brewers back much. While sales of the rival drink were at their highest, London's biggest brewhouse owners were reaping incomes that bracketed them with the wealthiest industrialists and landowners in Britain. Profits at Benjamin Truman's brewery in Brick Lane, Shoreditch between 1742 and 1751 averaged £6,600 a year, and were probably much the same at the four or five other biggest London breweries, such as the Calverts, Thrale of the Anchor brewery in Southwark and Parsons of the Red Lion brewery near the Tower. This was a huge leap from fifty years earlier, when, during the 1690s, profits at the Anchor brewery, then owned by Edmund Halsey, were no more than £800 a year. By the last quarter of the eighteenth century the biggest London brewers saw profits often topping £20,000 a year, while the country's 400 great landowners had yearly incomes starting at just £10,000.

All the biggest brewers were specialist porter brewers, and most were old-established concerns, which had had time to build up plenty of capital. Porter-brewing needed capital in all directions: to buy raw materials; to build the huge vats that, by the middle of the century, were regarded as essential for producing the best porter; to finance the long wait while the beer matured; and to pay for casks and horses and drays to convey the beer to publicans (a big brewery would have a cooperage bill of £1,000 a year, and a stable containing sixty or more drayhorses, worth together another £1,000). A publication called *The London Tradesman* estimated in 1747 that more capital was needed to set up as a porter brewer than in any other business except banking.

Only one man broke into the top five without inheriting or acquiring an already solid business. Samuel Whitbread had come to London from Bedfordshire aged fourteen in 1734, and two years later paid £300 for the privilege of starting an apprenticeship with John Wightman, then Master of the Brewers' Company. At twenty-two he left Wightman's brewery in Gilport Street to go into business with the Shewell brothers, Thomas and George, owners of the Goat brewhouse on the corner of Old Street and Whitecross Street – not far from John Calvert's Peacock brewhouse, one of the largest porter breweries in London.

The Whitbread–Shewell partnership produced porter at the Goat brewhouse and pale and amber ales at another small brewhouse diagonally across Old Street in Brick Lane (now Central Street). However, the Goat site was too small to compete properly with the giants of London porter brewing; so in 1750 Whitbread persuaded Thomas Shewell to join him in buying the King's Head brewhouse and the adjoining row of houses in Chiswell Street, a short walk down Whitecross Street. There, as Shewell and Whitbread, they built a new porter brewery which grew, in just eight years, to be the biggest in London (and therefore in Britain). By 1758 it was producing 64,600 barrels a year, ahead of its near neighbour the Peacock brewhouse on 61,800 barrels and Ben Truman's Black Eagle brewhouse in Brick Lane, Spitalfields on 55,500 barrels.

Until this time the name 'porter' seems to have been regarded by London's brewers as a colloquialism, a word used by customers when ordering the drink in the alehouse but not to be used officially in the brewery. The surviving business records of big porter brewers from the 1740s do not contain the word porter and list only vast stocks of 'mild beer', meaning unmatured porter, alongside smaller quantities of stale (that is, matured) beer, amber, brown ale and pale ale, the other important styles. The first appearance of the word in Whitbread's records comes with the opening of a 'New Porter Tun Room' at the Chiswell Street brewery in 1760, while the same year Sir William Calvert of the Hour Glass brewery and Edward Burnaby Greene of the Stag brewery in Pimlico each insured a porter brewery and an ale brewery. However, even when the porter brewers finally accepted the word 'porter', they continued to use the older word 'entire' when advertising its availability on the outside of pubs and alehouses, right through to the end of the nineteenth century.

The money porter brewing brought in bought influence, and co-option into the ruling class. Brewers, most especially London brewers, became Members of Parliament, with Southwark, stuffed as it was with breweries, regularly returning one or two brewer MPs throughout the eighteenth century. (It was an old tradition: among Southwark's MPs in 1323 was 'Willielmus le Brewere', and Richard Tuffneale, brewer of Southwark, was an MP in the early seventeenth century.) London brewers who became knights or baronets included Sir Felix Feast of the Peacock brewhouse in Whitecross Street, near the Barbican, described early in the eighteenth century as 'the greatest brewer in England', Sir John Parsons of the Red Lion brewhouse by St Katharine's, and Sir Benjamin Truman.

No English brewer actually entered the peerage in the eighteenth century, though Edmund Halsey of the Anchor brewhouse in Southwark married his daughter to the man who became Viscount Cobham, who inherited the concern when Halsey died in 1729. Control of the brewery passed to a nephew of Halsey, Ralph Thrale, because, as Samuel Johnson, a friend of Thrale's son, said, it was 'not fit that a peer should continue the business'. In Ireland, however, one brewing family did acquire a title, though only after leaving the trade. Joseph Leeson ran a brewery on the south side of St Stephen's Green, Dublin, begun by his father, Hugh, a former sergeant in the army of Charles II. Joseph built up a fortune by investing the brewery profits (and his heiress wife's money) in real estate; when he died in 1741 he left his son Joseph II an estate of £50,000 and an income of £6,000 a year. Joseph II immediately quit the brewery trade, leasing the St Stephen's Green brewery to Patrick Sweetman, and bought a large property in Wicklow. There he built what remains today one of Ireland's finest stately homes, Russborough, and filled it with artworks and antiques brought back from his Grand Tour to Italy. Four years after being made a baron in 1751, Leeson became Viscount Russborough; and in 1763 he was made Earl of Milltown, the village near Dublin where the family had bought considerable amounts of land.

The Leesons were an early example of the dictum coined by Dr Samuel Johnson at the sale of the Anchor brewery in 1781, that what was on offer was not 'a parcel of boilers and vats, but the opportunity to grow rich beyond the dreams of avarice'. Johnson was probably not thinking of the Earl of Milltown, or even of his friends the Thrales, owners of the Anchor brewery, when he said this, but of the Thrales' 21-year-old nephew, Sir John Lade. The young man had inherited his own brewery-derived fortune from his great-great-uncle, the first Sir John Lade. The young Sir John's riches enabled him to indulge in hugely expensive pastimes including, as well as horse-racing and gambling, the Georgette-Heyer-sounding Four-Horse Club, a group of young aristocrats who enjoyed racing four-horse coaches as quickly as possible on public highways, spreading fear and panic among other road users. Through this hard-drinking, fast-living set, Lade became a regular companion of the raffish Prince of Wales, and acted as his coachman when the Prince went by six-horse barouche from his Pavilion at Brighton to the local races. Eventually the huge fortune Lade had inherited ran out, and in 1819 he was locked up for debt in the King's Bench prison in Southwark (not far, ironically, from the site of the brewhouse that had originally provided the Lade fortune).

Lade was a spectacular exception: for the most part, London's wealthy brewers lived unostentatious lives, though in luxurious surroundings. They served as Lord Mayor; and they bought estates – generally in Hertfordshire for those whose breweries were north of the Thames, and Surrey for those whose brewhouses were in Southwark or Bermondsey. Benjamin Truman, for example, moved into Pope's Manor, near Hatfield, Hertfordshire, in 1757, and lived there until he died: he, his son and wife are all buried in the church-yard of St Mary's in Hertingfordbury. From 1765 Truman's close neighbour was Samuel Whitbread, who bought Bedwell Park, near Essendon, for £8,000. Ralph Thrale of the Anchor brewery, Southwark, another 'top five' brewhouse, built Streatham Place, set in 100 acres of parkland bought from the Duke of Bedford near to Streatham. (At that time Streatham was becoming a fashionable village for the wealthy wishing to escape London.)

Sir John Parsons of the Red Lion Brewery, St Katharine's, near the Tower of London, bought an estate near Reigate. His son and heir, Humphrey, was one of the few 'flashy' London brewers: his stable of horses was described as 'brilliant'. There is an apocryphal story that he won the exclusive right to export porter to France duty-free by presenting the French king, Louis XV, with a particularly fine steed the monarch had admired when Parsons rode it one day while hunting with the French court.

By the latter years of the eighteenth century, technological advances were helping the big brewers to generate even more profit. It was known that getting the right temperature for the water in the mash tun was hugely important. Until past the middle of the century, however, the only ways the brewer had of judging the temperature of his mashing liquor were laughably unscientific. (Liquor was the universal brewer's word for water used in brewing, and it was 'sixpence forfeit in the London brewhouse if the word water is used' one writer revealed in the 1730s.) Apprentice brewers were told that if they could rotate their hands in the liquor for the mash tun only once or twice, the water was too hot: if they could just bear to do it three times, the temperature was right for mashing. (In fact, this level was probably on the low side, depending on how much pain you could take: the human skin finds a temperature of 50° Centigrade (122° Fahrenheit) very hot and 55° Centigrade (131° Fahrenheit) unbearable. A text of 1911 said that for stouts and black beers 'generally, a mashing temperature of 148° to 150° Fahrenheit [around 65° Centigrade] is most usual; for pale or stock ales, 150° to 154° Fahrenheit'). Another method was to wait until the boiled water had cooled enough for the steam to clear and 'you can see your face in the liquor', as Richard Bradley, professor of botany at Cambridge University, told readers of his *Guide to Gentleman Farmers and Housekeepers for Brewing the Finest Malt Liquors* in 1727.

In 1758 the London brewer Michael Combrune published a book called *Essay on Brewing* which was the first technical text to recommend the thermometer, rather than the hand, for gauging the temperature of the mash liquor. The mercury thermometer had been invented in Amsterdam by Daniel Fahrenheit in 1714, but even after Combrune's endorsement it was slow in becoming accepted as an essential tool for the brewer, who was generally conservative by disposition. James Baverstock, who helped run the family brewery in Alton, Hampshire in the late 1700s, wrote that he had to hide his thermometer from his father, who declared his opposition to 'experimental innovations'. At last, in the early 1790s, thirty years after Combrune, John Richardson, a brewer from Hull, could write in *Philosophical Principles of the Science of Brewing* that the thermometer was arriving at general use in 'the brewery'. Many brewers, though, used what was called a 'blind' thermometer, with no numbers, and no scale other than marks at the brewer's preferred temperatures for mashing, fermenting and so on. This way he kept his trade secrets from 'the impertinent pryings of those about him' as one brewery manual said in 1822. (Even in the 1880s Watney's brewery in Pimlico, London still used a thermometer marked with letters, not numbers, to hide the true reading from those without the code.)

An even more important technical advance was the saccharometer or hydrometer. The device was simple: drop it in the wort that had run off from the mash and it sat there like a fisherman's float; the height it rose out of the water told you how much fermentable material the wort contained. For the first time brewers could accurately gauge the amount of fermentable sugar they wrested from different types of malt, bought from different maltsters, mashed at different temperatures for different times. Distillers and excisemen were using the hydrometer before 1750, to measure the amount of alcohol in spirits. The first real suggestion for using it in a brewery came in 1760 in *A Practical Treatise on Brewing* by W. Reddington, one of a growing number of guides to brewing. It was another ten years before a leading London brewer, Henry Thrale, began using a hydrometer in his brewhouse, encouraged by the experiments of the same James Baverstock of Alton whose father objected to his using a thermometer. When Baverstock tried to persuade Samuel Whitbread to use a hydrometer, however, the country's biggest brewer told him to 'go home, and not engage in such visionary pursuits'.

It was not until John Richardson (who wrote several of the earliest truly technical books on brewing) published a study in 1784 under the title of *Statical* [sic] *Estimates of the Materials for Brewing or, a Treatise on the Application and Use of the Saccharometer*, that the simple apparatus began to be taken up. Its adoption was helped by the introduction for excise purposes in 1782 of a new 'intermediate' category of beer, taxed halfway between strong and small beer, which made it more important for the brewer to know the strength of his brews, and an 80 per cent rise the same year in the tax on malt, which made it more important that he ensured he was buying the raw material that gave the best fermentable extract. Within seven years the Burton upon Trent brewer Benjamin Wilson could say that 'almost every brewer' used a hydrometer to measure his wort. (However, a traveller to Ireland in 1812 claimed no brewer he met there had even heard of the saccharometer.)

Richardson's book on the saccharometer shows us how strong eighteenth-century beer was. He found that five different samples of porter had an average original gravity (before fermentation) of 1071, and a final gravity (after fermentation) of 1018. For comparison, strong ale had original and final gravities of 1110 and 1052, common ale of 1075 and 1025, and table beer 1040 and 1004. The approximate alcohol content for the four beers would have been 7.1 per cent for porter, 7.8 per cent for strong ale, 6.7 per cent for common ale and 4.8 per cent for table beer. Today 4.8 per cent alcohol would be regarded as strong, and 7.8 per cent as thumping.

Richardson's hugely influential publication also introduced the idea of 'brewers' pounds', meaning the weight of sugar dissolved in pure water needed to give a particular reading on a hydrometer. British brewers continued to use brewers' pounds as a measurement of wort strength for the next 170 years or more, until it was replaced by original gravity, or OG.

All beers were now hoppier than they had been. Daniel Defoe noted in 1725 that even in the more conservative north, brewers 'use hops in the brewing their ale much more than they did before'. Partly this was changing taste, but in 1710 the use of hop alternatives such as broom and wormwood had been banned by Parliament to ensure brewers did not try to avoid the new hop tax of a penny a pound.

This tax had an unexpected benefit: it gave hop growers the information to set up a clever 'hedging' operation to try to ensure that they still made money when there was a glut of hops. Annual yields swung wildly: 1.57 million pounds of hops in 1726, for example, 20.39 million pounds the following year. Demand was regular, and dealers in hops would bet on the size of the crop, as revealed in the annual excise returns, to smooth out their incomes. Odds were quoted at every inn in the hop-growing and hop-marketing areas, and newspapers carried reports of the yields. If a dealer feared a glut, and low prices, he could bet on a high yield and still see a profit. The sums staked could be enormous: in Sittingbourne in 1821 there was claimed to be £130,000 riding on that year's hop yield.

The hop dealers met the sellers at regular fairs: Stourbridge fair, just south of Cambridge, was the biggest hop mart in England in the late seventeenth and early eighteenth centuries, with hops following on in October after the sale of cloth and wool in August and September. By the late eighteenth century Stourbridge had been largely replaced as the great hop-dealing hub by Southwark, in London, which was handily placed on the road up from Canterbury, and which remained the country's most important hop centre. (When 'three-letter' telephone exchange names were introduced in London before the First World War, Southwark's was HOP.) Other big fairs took place at Weyhill in Surrey, where the fine hops of the Farnham vale (particularly liked for brewing pale ales) were sold, and Worcester, where a hop mart was started in 1703 to deal in Severn Valley produce.

In 1774 an Act of Parliament required the hop 'pockets' in which the dried, compressed hops were packed to carry the hop grower's name and parish, and the year of production. Commentators were now identifying 'many' different types of hop, with a writer in 1799 mentioning 'the Flemish, the Canterbury, the Goldings, the Farnham etc.'. Goldings is still regarded as one of the great English hops, though it now comes in several varieties: it was supposedly propagated from an especially fine plant spotted by a Kentish grower called Golding, who was still alive in 1798.

For at least forty years, from around 1720 to 1760, the price of porter remained at a constant 3d a quart pot, with the brewers bearing the impact of fluctuating grain and hop prices. In 1761, however, the rate of duty on strong beer went up 60 per cent, to 8s a barrel, while the tax on malt rose 72 per cent, to the awkward-sounding ninepence-farthing and two-twenty-firsts of a penny a bushel, to help pay the costs of the Seven Years War against France. The big brewers told the publicans to raise the price of beer by a halfpenny a pot, to cover the higher taxes, although under legislation going back to the thirteenth century and before, price rises for beer and ale (and bread) without formal permission of the authorities were illegal. There were riots in Norwich, and several publicans in London were brought before Westminster magistrates for raising their prices. Eventually an Act was passed in 1762 cancelling more than five hundred years of legalized price control, and brewers and publicans were free to put prices up whenever they liked.

Higher taxes and the search for economies led the big porter brewers to invest in more new technology: steam engines. Until the 1780s all rotary power for grinding and pumping in even the biggest breweries came from horses plodding round and round while attached to the horsewheel. Old, often blind horses were used for this job, but they still needed feeding, at £40 a head per year, stabling and, regularly, replacing. By getting rid of mill horses, a big brewer axed £400 a year or more from his expenses. Their replacement, the steam engine, might cost £750 to buy and install and £90 a year for running and repairs, plus £100 a year on coal, but, unlike a horse, it could run for fourteen hours a day and would last for decades. (Some brewery steam engines remained in service for a century or more.)

The first brewer to install one of James Watt's steam engines was Henry Goodwyn of the Red Lion brewhouse at St Katharine's, Wapping. The new machine arrived in the summer of 1784, during the closed season for brewing (when the porter brewers often went on holiday to Cromer, so they could take a look at the Norfolk barley and judge how good the harvest might be). This was the first steam engine in London, let alone in brewing. When Samuel Whitbread saw how successfully Goodwyn's four-horsepower engine was working, he ordered a ten-horsepower model for the Chiswell Street brewery; it was installed and running by the spring of 1785.

One after another, most of the other big London porter brewers bought steam engines from Boulton & Watt: Felix Calvert at the Hourglass brewery in October 1785; Barclay Perkins, the new owners of Thrale's brewery, in 1786; John Calvert of Whitecross Street and the Gyfford partnership in Long Acre, both in 1787; John Stephenson at the Horseshoe brewery, St Giles, in 1789. Truman's stood back, after cancelling a provisional order in 1788 because the partners could not find a free spot to erect the enginehouse on the brewery site. (It was nearly twenty years before the Black Eagle brewery finally had a steam engine to replace its mill horses.)

The next major advance was to be attemperation, both cooling the wort more quickly after it left the mash tun (which reduced the possibility of wort infection) and regulating the temperature of the fermenting wort after the yeast had been added or 'pitched' (which would mean fewer 'off' ferments and a brewing season that could end later in the hot summer months and begin sooner in the autumn). A man called John Long, of Longville, County Dublin, approached the Commissioners of Victualling for the Navy in 1791 with a proposal that they test his patented idea for cooling fermenting vessels in one of the naval breweries, which regularly needed to try to brew during the dangerous months from June to September, when a fleet turned up unexpectedly and required supplying with beer. His scheme consisted of coiled copper pipes to be placed in the mash tun and the fermenting vat, through which water at a set temperature, hot or cold, could be circulated to regulate the heat of mashing or fermentation. Unfortunately, when the Commissioners asked the leading London brewers for their opinion, Whitbread said he doubted if it would work, Calvert refused to comment and Barclays said the £1,200 expense of a year's trial could not be justified. Temperature control in the brewery had to wait until the next century.

Throughout the eighteenth century the big porter brewers dominated the brewing scene, with the top twelve London brewers in 1786 providing half the capital's beer production, leaving another 150 brewers to supply the rest. These twelve brewers were supplying almost one pint in five of national beer production, not counting the still considerable amount of private brewing.

It was generally porter brewers trained in the capital who disseminated the techniques of the London brewers to other parts of the

British Isles. In the earliest known reference to porter brewing in Scotland, an Edinburgh brewer, Thomas Cleghorn, told the Town Council in December 1752 that he had 'engaged a London expert' for an experiment in producing porter 'equal to that made in London with Thames Water', and asking for permission to run a pipe from a well at the West Port to his brewery in Kingstables, for which he was willing to pay two guineas yearly. The success of his venture into porter brewing 'will foster home trade and hinder import', he told the council.

Bringing in outside experts could be tricky, however. When the Glasgow brewers Murdoch, Warren & Co. of the Anderston brewery decided they had to brew the best porter in the city, they hired a London porter brewer, Nathaniel Chivers, who arrived in October 1775 to teach them how to make it. Chivers had spent less than a year at the Anderston brewery when his new employers felt they had learned enough to dispense with his services, and gave him his fare back to London.

In Chivers' contract with Murdoch, Warren forbade him to reveal the secrets of porter brewing to any other brewer in or around Glasgow. However, instead of returning south, Chivers hopped over to a rival Glasgow brewer, John Struthers in the Gallowgate, where he began teaching the brewers how to make London-style porter. Understandably, when Murdoch, Warren found out they went to the Court of Session to get an interdict banning Chivers from spreading his knowledge to their rivals.

Dublin was brewing porter by 1763 (Glasgow had actually begun around the same time); porter was being made in Bristol by 1780, in Norwich by at least 1791 and in Liverpool by 1799. All these efforts at replicating the capital's favourite beer were prompted by the local brewers' loss of beer sales to the London porter brewers as drinkers in the regions took up the dark and bitter brew. In the first couple of decades of the nineteenth century the pupils began to show how well they had learned their lesson: by 1812 porter was being exported to England from Ireland.

But the local brew was still always compared against the original, and a link with the home of porter was almost a necessity. Kavanagh

& Brett of the Anchor Street brewery in Dublin had to underline in 1798 that they were brewing porter 'under the direction of Mr Chas Page of London'. Similarly in 1806, when the Edinburgh brewers A. C. & W. Younger announced in the city's evening newspaper that they had 'commenced brewers of Porter', they took care to say that 'a London brewer of great professional ability' had been engaged to make it, and he had 'succeeded in producing porter that will vie in every respect with the best that can be imported from London'.

By the end of century the common brewers were gaining ground against the brewing victuallers, or pub brewers. The numbers of publican brewers had risen from 41,800 in 1701 to 48,000 in 1751, but then fallen to 23,690 in 1799, a drop of 77 per cent over the century. The figures mean that between the middle and the end of the eighteenth century, publican brewers were stopping brewing at a rate of ten a week. What evidence that has been gathered suggests that the total number of alehouses in the United Kingdom fell during the period, although the population doubled. But most of the alehouses that stopped brewing must have stayed open to take their beer from the rising number of common brewers.

The decline of public house brewing meant the slow end of at least one local speciality: Devon White Ale, mentioned by William Ellis in *The London and Country Brewer* in 1735. Ellis said that 'the Plymouth people . . . are so attach'd to their white thick Ale, that many have undone themselves by drinking it'. Ellis said white ale started as a clear wort made from pale malt, but fermented with a mixture called 'ripening', made from malt flour, yeast and egg whites. Ripening was mixed and sold by two or three specialist vendors to 'many' of the local publicans, who then added it to their raw wort. White ale was drunk while it was still fermenting in earthenware jars, Ellis said, 'in such a thick manner as resembles butter'd Ale', and sold for 'Twopence Halfpenny the full Quart'. It was clearly regarded as a healthy brew, being 'often prescribed by Physicians to be drank by wet Nurses for the encrease of their Milk, and also as a prevalent Medicine for the Colick and Gravel'.

This is obviously the same drink described in Andrew Boorde's *Dyetary of Helth* from 1542, 200 years earlier, who said Cornish ale, made across the Tamar from Plymouth, was 'whyte & thycke, as pygges had wrasteled in it, smoky and ropey, and neuer a good sope'. John Bickerdyke, writing in 1889, said that 'a considerable quantity' of white ale was still being made in and around Tavistock, but by then it consisted 'simply of common ale with eggs and flour added'. George Saintsbury, however, could only say in 1920 that white ale, or 'lober agol', used to exist in Devonshire and Cornwall 'within the memory of man', but that he had sought it in vain half a century earlier.

The number of common brewers rose from 764 in the whole United Kingdom (including Ireland) in 1701 to 995 in 1751, a 30 per cent rise over fifty years, and to 1,382 in 1799, an increase of 80 per cent over the century. Allowing for the inevitable closures, throughout the eighteenth century an average of at least seven or eight new common breweries must have been opening every year. The evidence we have today from known brewery foundation dates backs up this inference, and suggests that while in the years 1700–49 the increase in common brewers was mostly a south of England phenomenon, with some activity in Scotland, from 1750 the north of England had joined in.

Quite a number of the new brewers were Quakers, members of the Religious Society of Friends. It was part of a general involvement by Quakers in commerce: most professions were barred to them because of their beliefs, and an objection to tithes, the tax on farmers imposed by the Church of England, drove them away from agriculture. Once in business their integrity, and their willingness to help each other through difficult times, helped them prosper.

By the end of the century two of the biggest breweries in London (and, therefore, the world), Truman's and the Anchor brewhouse in Southwark, were being run by Quakers. Sampson Hanbury, from a Quaker banking dynasty, bought a share in Truman's and began running the brewery in 1789. Eight years earlier, after the death of Henry Thrale, owner of the Anchor brewery in Southwark, what his widow Hester called 'a knot of rich Quakers' had bought the brewery at auction for £135,000, spread over four years. The legend is that the Quaker banker David Barclay spotted the 'For Sale' notices on the brewery wall as he was walking across one of the Thames bridges, and decided on the spot this was just the career for his half-nephew Robert, just back from America. However, since Henry Thrale's brewery manager, John Perkins, was also a Quaker, it seems very likely Perkins had mentioned the brewery sale to Barclay. At any rate, Perkins became a partner in the new set-up with Robert Barclay, David Barclay and David's banking partner Silvanus Bevan, and once all payments had been completed in 1785, the brewery became Barclay Perkins.

Some eighteen or twenty other Quaker-run breweries are known; however, by the nineteenth century the strains of being both a Quaker, naturally inclined to temperance, and a brewer, whose products sometimes led people to be very intemperate, were making business difficult for many members of the Friends. William Lucas of Hitchin wrote in his diary in 1843, the day after one of the brewery's tenants died of 'an entire breaking up of the constitution' caused by drink, that 'the evil consequences to the tenants of our Public Houses is the most trying circumstance attending our business, and makes one wish at times to be in some less objectionable line of trade . . . I cannot say I wish my sons to engage in it'.

During the first half of the eighteenth century the proportion of beer sold by the common brewers, as against publican brewers, fell slightly from 48 per cent in 1701 to 45 per cent in 1751; but it then rose to 66 per cent in 1799 as they gained the custom of more and more formerly brewing alehouses. Total beer consumption, including private brewing, rose over the century just 6 per cent, it is estimated, while private brewing as a percentage of total brewing had fallen from around 65 per cent of all beer drunk in 1701 to 54 per cent in 1799.

The increase in common brewers was still most noticeable in the East Midlands, East Anglia and the South-East of England, while in the North, the West Midlands, the West Country and Wales the publican-brewer continued to thrive. Yorkshire in particular was very slow to establish independent breweries. The first common brewers here opened in Sheffield only in 1744, in Leeds in 1756, and in Bradford in 1757. Overall, around half of all alehouses and inns must have still brewed their own beer at the end of the eighteenth century, varying from perhaps two-thirds or more in Yorkshire to less than a quarter in the Home Counties.

The pressures that led to the decline of the alehouse brewer were considerable. He had to pay the excise duty on the ale he brewed before it could be sold, a much greater strain on cashflow for a small concern than for a large brewer with dozens or hundreds of clients. He was not permitted the same allowance for waste and leakage – the equivalent of three barrels in every thirty-six free of duty – by the excise authorities that the large brewers were granted. (This allowance was a deliberate attempt by the authorities to give extra advantages to large concerns and put small ones out of business, on the grounds that a few large concerns were much easier to monitor than shoals of small ones.) He could not enjoy all the economies of scale available to a large brewer, from better deals buying raw materials to greater output per employee.

A consequence of the decline in alehouse brewing was the rise of the tied house. To some extent this was proactive, with common brewers deliberately seeking to buy licensed houses to guarantee themselves outlets for their beer. Much, however, was reactive: licensees got into debt to brewers for the beer they had bought, until eventually the only way for the brewer to be guaranteed the money he was owed was to be given a mortgage on the alehouse or inn, or its lease. The licensee failed to clear the debt, the brewer foreclosed the mortgage, and found himself owner or senior lessee of the pub. Even in 1686 the Commissioners of Excise said most London publicans were 'in debt to the Brewers and living on their Stocks'.

Unsurprisingly, given the early rise of common brewers in the Home Counties, the earliest references to brewery tied houses are mostly in this region as well. Common brewers in Deal, Kent, had publican tenants before 1734. In Hatfield, Hertfordshire, John Searancke's brewery was acquiring tied houses from 1728. Among the big London brewers, Samuel Whitbread had thirteen public houses, all close to his brewery, on the rent-books in 1746, and twenty-four ten years later. Benjamin Truman listed twelve public houses in the lease valuations of 1741 and twenty-six in 1747. By 1776 one writer could say of Canterbury that there 'is scarce a public house but is either by purchase or lease in the hands of the brewers'.

◇

CHAPTER SIX

PALE AND INTERESTING

the nineteenth century, part one

Genial and gladdening is the power of good ale,
the true and proper drink of Englishmen.

George Borrow
(1803–81), Lavengro

The start of the nineteenth century saw the London porter brewers still dominating the capital's beer market. There were ninety-eight common brewers in London in 1815, but the twelve 'principal' porter brewers now made 75 per cent or more of the city's beer. Rival types of beer struggled: the combined output of all the seven biggest ale brewers in London for the twelve months from 5 July 1813 to 5 July 1814 totalled 85,000 barrels: the same as one porter brewer, Barclay Perkins, could produce on its own in just four months.

However, porter itself was changing. The arrival of the saccharometer in British breweries had a big impact on London's favourite beer: now that brewers could measure the amount of fermentable extract they were getting from their malt, they could see what poor value the brown, high-dried malts they used for making porter were in comparison to pale malts. A good pale malt produced an extract of eighty-two pounds per quarter; Ware brown malt from Hertfordshire, the sort used by London porter brewers, might give only fifty-six pounds of extract per quarter – nearly a third less. Brown malt gave porter its colour and flavour, but compared to pale malt it was poor value for producing alcohol.

Prices of all raw materials rose at the end of the eighteenth century, and the tax on malt shot up more than threefold, from 1s 4¼d a bushel in 1800 to 4s 5¾d in 1804. The increase was to help pay for Britain's efforts against Napoleon, and the malt tax stayed at that level until his final defeat in 1815. Prices, meanwhile, remained steady, at 3½d for a quart of porter from 1760 to 1799, rising only under the impact of war taxes, to 5d a quart in 1803. Apart from minor and temporary bulges to 6d in 1804 (for a week), 1813 and 1817, retail prices remained more or less the same until 1830.

With beer prices so stable, meaning the real price of a pot of porter fell by a third compared to the rising cost of other goods in the last four decades of the eighteenth century, the big porter brewers had a strong cost incentive to use the malt that gave the highest proportion of fermentable extract. Many thus stopped using 100 per cent high-dried brown malts, and added lighter-cured malts to their porter mashes, in varying proportions depending on the individual brewer's preference.

But using paler malt, in whatever proportion, would lighten the vital dark colour porter drinkers expected. What the brewers needed was a colouring agent that enabled them to brew with pale malt and still produce a dark beer. One possibility was liquorice, used either 'straight' or in the form of 'Spanish juice' or 'Spanish liquorice' (liquorice boiled in water which was then evaporated); but not everybody wanted the flavour of liquorice in porter. Many professional porter brewers used instead burnt sugar, known as 'essentia binae'. This was made by boiling muscovado sugar in an iron pot and then briefly setting fire to it. However, essentia binae had been illegal since at least 1713, when it was one of several 'unwholesome' ingredients banned from use in beer. Another colouring agent, wort evaporated until it became the colour of treacle, and equally viscous, was promoted from 1802 by Matthew Wood, a member of a firm of London hop merchants and wholesale druggists. However, it was caught in a popular drive against 'adulteration' of beer, despite being made from malt, and the excise authorities prosecuted several brewers who used Wood's colouring.

In 1811 porter brewers were finally allowed to use colouring made from muscovado sugar, after much pressure on Parliament (and to the anger of the ale brewers, who also wanted to use colouring). However, the Act granting this permission was in existence for just five years. After accusations that other adulterants were being sneaked into beer under cover of the measure, in 1816 anything other than brown malt was again banned as a beer colouring.

The following year a man called Daniel Wheeler, who had previously made sugar colouring, came to the porter brewers' aid with a patented method of roasting malt at 400° Fahrenheit or more for up to two hours in an apparatus very similar to a coffee roaster. The resultant black malt, or 'patent malt', gave 'extractive matter of a deep brown colour, ready soluble in hot or cold water . . . A small quantity of malt thus prepared will suffice for the purpose of colouring beer or porter'. The excise authorities could not object, since the colouring was made from malt upon which tax had been paid, though they did insist that the roasting house must be at least a mile from the malthouse, and malt roasters must have a special licence. The big London porter brewers all took up Wheeler's patent malt: Whitbread in 1817, Barclay Perkins in 1820, Truman by 1826. In Dublin two roasting houses were set up by members of the Plunkett family to supply that city's porter brewers.

The introduction of patent malt must have made a considerable difference to the taste of porter, and to its colour, since it could now be made as black as night, even with a huge proportion of pale malt in the mash. In 1822 John Tuck was lamenting that 'the real taste of porter, as originally drank, is completely lost; and this by pale malts being introduced . . . Our ancestors brewed porter entirely with high dried malt; while in the present day, in many houses, high dried or blown malts are entirely omitted'. However, Tuck acknowledged that 'to say the truth, there is little of porter left but the name . . . the taste of the public is so changed, that very few would be found to fancy its original flavour'.

The London brewers continued to use brown malt in their porter mashes, with Whitbread, for example, in 1850, brewing to a recipe that was 80 per cent pale malt, 15 per cent brown malt and 5 per cent black malt. But in Ireland, within a few years of the invention of patent malt, brewers were abandoning brown malt entirely: Guinness, for example, which had been using between 25 per cent and 47 per cent brown malt in its porter up to 1815, was using only pale malt and patent malt probably by 1824, and certainly by 1828. The result was a divergence in flavour between Irish porter (and stout) and London porter (and stout), with the former now drier and more bitter.

In Ireland by this time the practice had grown up of adding two gallons of unfermented or partially fermented wort into barrels of porter as it left the brewery. This 'gyling', as it was called, from the original meaning of the word 'gyle' – wort in process of fermentation – caused a second fermentation in the cask which meant that by the time it reached the publican the beer was lively and sparkling. This was known as the 'high' cask, and it was delivered together with another containing maturer, less lively, flatter beer, called the 'low' cask. Publicans would fill glasses three-quarters full from the 'high' cask, then top them up with flat beer from the 'low' cask. The 'high' and 'low' cask system was in use for Irish stout and porter until at least the 1960s.

The lack of price competition early in the nineteenth century made many drinkers suspicious that the eleven or twelve 'first' or 'principal' London porter brewers, who brewed three pots in every four of the capital's beer, were operating a cartel at the expense of the public. The public, and the legislators, were also worried about adulteration, including the use of bittering agents other than hops (to avoid the hop tax) and drugs to increase the intoxicating effect of the beer (thus saving on malt and the malt tax). A cartoon published in 1806 showed the leading London brewers hailing Quassia, the South American negro who had discovered the bitter properties of the tree later named after him: one pound of quassia was supposed to be equivalent to sixteen pounds of hops in terms of the bitterness it gave to beer.

Naturally, the big London breweries insisted that whatever lesser brewers did, the leading firms used only malt and hops in their beer. But they did meet together from at least 1795 as the Committee of Porter Brewers at Brewers' Hall in Addle Street, London, and one of the committee's objectives was to agree a common policy on pricing. Common prices encourage new entrants who believe they can sell the same quality of product more cheaply and still make a profit. In 1804 two men, William Brown and Joseph Parry, announced that they would be starting a concern to be called the 'Genuine Beer Brewery', using Michael Combrune's old premises in Golden Lane, off Old Street. They would brew porter and sell it to publicans at a wholesale price per barrel the equivalent of a halfpenny a pot cheaper than the old-established big brewers charged.

The brewery was in the heart of the 'brewers' quarter' of London north of the Thames, bounded by Old Street, Aldersgate Street, London Wall and City Road/Moorgate. This square half-mile was already home to three of the biggest porter brewers – Whitbread in Chiswell Street, John Calvert at the Peacock brewery in Whitecross Street and Cox & Co. just south of the City Road/Old Street junction – as well as one of London's biggest ale brewers, Hale & Co. of Redcross Street. To raise the money necessary to brew on a big enough scale to challenge the top firms, Brown and Parry signed up 600 'copartners', including 120 publicans, who subscribed in total more than £250,000. The first beer went out in October 1805; production hit a peak of 131,600 barrels in 1808, when only Barclay Perkins, at 184,000 barrels, and Meux Reid, at 190,000, brewed more. It was an astonishing and unparalleled achievement for a company which was only three years old.

That year, however, Brown and Parry were fighting an attempt by the excise authorities to deny them the allowance of three barrels in every thirty-six free of duty that was given to all common brewers, but not to licensed victualler pub brewers. The excise argued that because the Golden Lane concern had 120 publicans as partners, it was not a common brewer but an enormous pub brewer, and not entitled to the allowance. Brown and Parry, who would have to pay up to £6,000 a year extra duty if the excise won its case, naturally suspected the other big porter brewers of encouraging the firm's prosecution. Brown pointed out that, as owners of managed houses, most big common brewers were also technically 'victuallers'.

The firm lost the first hearing but won on appeal. The next year it was back in court, this time being prosecuted for using isinglass finings. Since isinglass, made from fish membranes, had been in universal use in London breweries from at least the early 1740s to clarify beer and porter, and was mentioned in most technical books on brewing from the fourth edition of the *London and Country Brewer*, published in 1742, onwards, Brown and Parry probably wondered why they were being picked on again. Once again they won their case, and the excise retreated.

The Golden Lane brewery's real problem lay outside the courts. Between 1807 and 1813, the price of malt rose by more than 30 per cent, and the brewery's managing partners were forced to brew a weaker beer to continue to keep their porter a halfpenny a quart cheaper than their rivals. Unlike the old-established porter brewers, the Golden Lane concern did not have rich partners or a network of banking associates to supply extra credit when it was needed in the short term. Customers began to turn back to the richer brewers who had not lowered the standard of their beer as raw materials rose in price, and the Golden Lane brewery's production began to decline. In 1827, by which time production was down to 16,100 barrels a year, the brewery closed and its buildings were pulled down.

All England's porter brewers, meanwhile, were having to cope with changes in public taste away from the sour, aged beers of the eighteenth century. Charles Barclay of Barclay Perkins had admitted in 1818 that the demand was for a milder, fresher beer, and porter was not kept for as long as it had been. Porter was, in fact, now being served as a mixture or old and new beer, just like the mild and stale of a hundred years earlier. Rees's *Cyclopaedia*, published in 1819–20, described the method:

> All the London porter is professed to be 'entire butt', as indeed it was at first, but the system is now altered and it is very generally compounded of two kinds, or rather the same liquor in two different stages, the due admixture of which is palatable, though neither is good alone. One is mild and the other stale porter; the former is that which has a slightly bitter flavour from having lately been brewed; the latter has been kept longer. This mixture the publican adapts to the palates of his several customers and effects the mixture very readily by means of a machine containing small pumps worked by handle.

The 'machine' contained four beer pumps and only three spouts, the *Cyclopaedia* said, because two pumps threw out at the same spout, which could draw on mild or stale at will.

The *Cyclopaedia*'s comments showed that there was already confusion over what 'entire butt' actually meant. Thinking that 'entire butt' meant 'all from one cask', it declared: 'An indifferent observer supposes that since it all comes from one spout it is entire butt beer, as the publican professes over the door.' However, although 'entire butt beer' originally meant 'butt beer brewed from the entire mash', entire had indeed come to mean something different from what it meant in the 1730s. The big London brewers were now mixing in old beer with maturing porter at the brewery, calling the mixture stale porter or entire, and sending it out alongside mild porter to the pubs and taverns for landlords to mix again to their customers' requirements when serving. Charles Barclay of Barclay Perkins described the system to a House of Commons committee investigating the alleged adulteration of beer in the capital in 1818. The committee called several of the capital's brewers to give evidence, and Barclay was asked by a committee member: 'Is sour or stale beer used in your vats to your knowledge?' He replied:

> Every publican has two sorts of beer sent to him, and he orders a proportion of each as he wants them; the one is called mild beer, which is beer brewed and sent out exactly as it is brewed; the other is called entire, and that beer consists of some brewed expressly for the purpose of keeping: it likewise contains a proportion of returns from publicans . . . a proportion of beer from the bottoms of vats [and] beer that is drawn off from the pipes which convey the beer from one vat to another . . . it also contains a proportion of brown stout, which is twenty shillings a barrel dearer than common beer: it also contains some bottling beer, which is ten shillings a barrel dearer . . . Now all these beers united are put into vats; when it becomes bright it is sent out to the publicans for their entire beer, and there is sometimes a small quantity of mild beer mixed with it.

Asked what proportion of the total number of barrels sent out 'would those remnants form', Barclay replied: 'We send out about one tenth of entire, but that is not consisting of remnants, because, I believe I stated before, part of it is beer brewed and kept for that purpose.' To the question from a committee member: 'Is it absolutely necessary that a publican should have some of these remnants to mix it for the taste of his customers?', Barclay said: 'I should think so. It has been the constant practice for as long as I have known the trade; and in former years they used to draw more of that entire than they do now . . . I do not see how the publican could well please his customers unless he had the means of making his beer either stale or mild as they wish for it.'

We can now draw a number of conclusions about porter as it was at the start of the nineteenth century, and how it differed from porter in the early years of George I's reign, when the style first evolved.

Most porter (90 per cent) was now sent out to publicans 'mild', that is, unaged. The remaining 10 per cent, which was known as 'stale' or, using the old word for porter, 'entire', was aged for two years, helped on its way to maturity with the addition of everything from returns from pubs to unsold brown stout to ullage from the bottom of the brewery vessels. Entire had thus become more than the brewing of one full mash; it now had an 'entire' range of old brown beer tipped in, partly to use up beer that would otherwise be poured away, partly to help it age and acquire the wanted flavour more quickly. These two beers, mild porter and entire, or stale porter, were then drawn by the publican to the individual customer's requirements.

While we might be dubious today at the idea of adding returns to maturing beer, the public clearly continued to enjoy the taste, and the practice gave the great porter breweries two economic advantages, speeding up the maturation process, while also cutting costs. Barclay told the House of Commons committee that his own brewery recycled 20,000 barrels a year in this way, around 5 or 6 per cent of total production, and 'the price of beer must be considerably higher' if all that beer had to be thrown away.

Entire porter was still matured in huge vats. But a trend towards building bigger and bigger vessels to store the ageing beer in, with each big porter brewer trying to have a larger vat than his rivals, had ended after a tragedy in 1814 at Henry Meux's brewery in Bainbridge Street, off Tottenham Court Road. On the afternoon of Monday 17 October, one of the huge iron hoops on a twenty-two-foot-high vat at the brewery fell off without warning. George Crick, a storehouse clerk at the brewery who was in charge that day, was not particularly alarmed, as he had seen hoops fall off vats before without any serious consequence. He wrote a letter detailing the occurrence, which he was going to have delivered by hand to one of the partners, Florance Thomas Young, who was also the brewery's vat-builder (and brother to the man who founded the Young & Co. brewing dynasty in Wandsworth). At 5.30 p.m., Crick was standing near the vat in question, with the letter in his hand, ready to send it to Young, when suddenly the vat, filled with some 3,550 barrels of ten-months-old porter, burst apart, releasing a black tsunami of more than a million pints of beer, weighing around thirty-eight tons. The huge wave of porter demolished the east wall of the storehouse and flooded out into the surrounding slums of St Giles.

The houses of the district, one of London's poorest, were all in

GREAT VAT

A giant beer vat at Barclay Perkins's brewery in Southwark, London, some twenty feet high, of the kind that broke with devastating results at Henry Meux's brewery, off Tottenham Court Road, London in October 1814.

multiple occupation, and families living in the cellars of the adjacent streets had to scramble on to tables and cupboards to avoid being drowned in beer. A women and her four-year-old daughter sitting at their tea in a first-floor room were swept out of the window by the tide of porter: the girl was killed and the mother badly injured. Eight people died in total, all women or children, and five were injured, including two workers in the brewery, while four houses were partially demolished.

The collapsing staves of the broken vat had knocked the cock from another giant and smashed a pipe running to a third, which added most of their contents to the flood. In all, more than 5,100 barrels of beer were lost, worth at retail more than £15,000. Meux and his partners in the brewery had to get a special Act of Parliament passed the following year to claim a refund on the £6,700 in malt and hop tax they had paid on the raw materials used in the lost beer. The giant vat that had burst was replaced by seven smaller ones.

In 1823 porter output in London hit 1.8 million barrels after a continual rise over fifty years. But this was a peak that would never be surpassed: by 1830 porter production would be down 20 per cent on its 1823 level. The porter brewers reacted to falling sales by turning to brewing actual mild ales, made for quick consumption – still dark, still with an OG of around 1050, made with some higher-dried malt, but unaged and therefore sweeter, less acid than porter. A House of Commons select committee on the sale of beer in 1833 was told that the London drinker 'will have nothing but what is mild, and that has caused a considerable revolution in the trade, so much so that Barclay and Perkins, and other great houses, finding that there is a decrease in the consumption of porter, and an increase in the consumption of ale, have gone into the ale trade; nearly all the new trade is composed of mild ale.'

By this time one of the most popular drinks, particularly in London, was 'half and half': half ale and half porter. Whitbread, then the third or fourth biggest brewer in London, having produced only porter up to 1834, started brewing mild ale in 1835. Ale quickly rose from nowhere to more than 10 per cent of Whitbread's production by 1839, and more than 20 per cent by 1859, when Whitbread's porter sales had dropped by almost 30 per cent from those of twenty-five years earlier. At Truman's, then fighting with Barclay Perkins to be London's biggest brewer, the swing from porter was stronger still, with ale making up 30 per cent of production by 1859.

The change in taste was a boost to London's traditional ale brewers, such as Charrington in the Mile End Road and Courage at Horsleydown on the south bank of the Thames, almost opposite the Tower. Charrington's trade increased by almost 250 per cent between 1831 and 1851, for example; and by 1889 its output had risen to more than 500,000 barrels a year, level with Barclay Perkins.

One of the most successful London ale brewers was Goding's Cannon brewery on the north side of Knightsbridge, backing on to Hyde Park. Building work began in 1804, and by 1807 the brewery was producing 8,500 barrels of ale a year, making it the third biggest ale brewery in London. Production of 'fine XXX ale' and other brews had doubled by 1814, after an extension was built in 1812, and the brewery was enlarged twice more in 1818 and 1836. However, the brewery's 'eternal smoke' got literally up the noses of Knightsbridge's residents, especially the novelist and socialite Lady Morgan, and she and the builder Thomas Cubitt plotted its removal. They proposed a new entrance to Hyde Park, to be named Albert Gate, which would mean the demolition of the Cannon brewery. Down it duly came in 1841, with Albert Gate opened in 1845 on the site of the former brewery tap, the White Hart.

While the working and labouring classes were drinking mild ale, however, the middle classes were turning to what has been called 'the new high-fashion beer of the 1830s and 1840s', pale ale. The classiest of these fashionable beers was India Pale Ale, London's second great gift to brewing after porter, though IPA eventually found its acme on the banks of the Trent rather than the Thames.

Greed and luck were the parents of India Pale Ale. It was born from the desire of officers commanding the East Indiamen sailing ships to make a fortune supplying home comforts to nostalgic expatriate Britons working for the East India Company in eighteenth-century India. The Company, founded in 1600, grew in the eighteenth century to be the most powerful economic and political force in India. Although for a long time it had a monopoly on British–Indian trade, it allowed the independent ships' commanders who carried its goods back from India to conduct private trade on their own accounts. This private trading could be hugely valuable: a ship's commander might well make up to £12,000 a year from private business, selling English goods in India, generally to the company's 'civil servants' in the trading posts known as 'factories', and bringing Indian goods back to Britain. By 1784 it was customary, although illegal, for an East Indiaman captain to sell his command to his successor for between 4,000 and 7,000 guineas.

There were seventy ships in regular service in the East India trade, and the goods their commanders and officers brought out from London in their holds ranged from clothes, perfume, china and glass to hams, cheese, cider, wine and beer. It was a stroke of luck all round that one of the beers they shipped turned out to improve amazingly on the long journey from England to the East, creating a style that is still a world classic.

The East India Company's docks were at Blackwall, on the north bank of the Thames east of the City and just to the west of the mouth of the Lea. When the commanders and captains of the East Indiamen went to buy beer to sell out in India, they turned to a brewer close by the docks, George Hodgson, just up the Lea at Bow. Hodgson, who had begun brewing near St Mary le Bow church in October 1752, was one of the smaller London brewers, making an average of just 11,200 barrels a year for the first sixteen years of the brewery's existence. But his beer could be got down to Blackwall easily by barge for loading on to the East Indiamen, and Hodgson gave the commanders and captains lengthy credit of up to eighteen months. Thus they took their supplies from him rather than one of the bigger, better-known London brewers.

The beers the East Indiamen officers bought from the Bow brewery included porter (Hodgson was still shipping porter out to India even in 1823) and October beer. This was the strong, pale, well-hopped, autumn-brewed stock beer popular among eighteenth-century country gentry, a class whose sons probably made up a good number of the East India Company's 'servants', as it called its staff. October ale was a powerful product, with an OG of 1140 or more. According to George Watkins, a brewer in the 1760s, October beer would be ready for bottling after twelve months, and should be kept in bottle for a further year, making it two years old before it was fit to drink.

The October beer the East Indiamen officers bought from Hodgson spent four to six months or more at sea on its long journey to India. The voyage was rough: an East Indiaman would make only four or five round trips before being broken up or sold off. But the slow, regular temperature changes and the rocking the beer received in its oak casks as the East Indiamen ploughed the waves had a magical maturing effect. By the time the beer arrived in Bombay, Madras or Calcutta, having gone via Madeira, Rio de Janeiro, St Helena, Cape Town and the stormy Mozambique Channel, it was as ripe as a brew six times its age that had slumbered unmoving in an English cellar. The expatriate British loved it, and by the beginning of the nineteenth century Hodgson's was 'the beer in almost universal use' in India. (In India it was called 'beer', rather than 'pale ale'.)

There is no evidence at all that George Hodgson knew October beer would be particularly well suited to the rigours of a journey out to the East by sailing ship, or that he brewed a special beer to sell to the East Indiamen officers. He was not especially entrepreneurial: he just happened to be in the right place at the right time with the right product.

Pale ale, 'light and excellent', was being sold in India alongside cider and London porter by at least 1784, as an advertisement in the *Calcutta Gazette* for April that year shows. Pale ale, porter, 'small ale' and strong ale continued to be advertised in the *Gazette* for the next fifteen or so years, but the brewer remained unnamed. In January 1801 the *Gazette* at last carried an advertisement for the arrival of 'beer from Hodgson . . . just landed and now exposed for sale for ready money only'. The Bow brewery's reputation was established in India, its name now a guarantee of quality: in 1809 the *Gazette* was trumpeting 'Hodgson's select Pale Ale, warranted of superior excellence'.

The identification of India Pale Ale with an October-brewed seasonal or stock beer is confirmed from several sources. An advertisement in the *Calcutta Gazette* from 20 January 1822 describing the 'select investment of prime London goods just landed from the HC [Honourable Company] ship *Sir David Scott*' included 'Hodgson's warranted prime picked pale ale of the genuine October brewing . . . fully equal, if not superior, to any ever before received in the settlement'.

Three decades later the beer was still an autumn speciality: in the *Leeds Intelligencer* of 18 October 1856, Tetley's brewery announced to its customers: 'East India Pale Ale – This Season's Brewings are now being delivered.' By the second half of the nineteenth century the advance of refrigeration meant that brewers could brew all year round, and the original justification for strong March and October stock beers, that they would last the months when the heat made brewing impossible, was being lost. But even in 1898 Waltham Brothers' brewery in Stockwell, south London, could say of its own India Pale Ale: 'This Ale is heavily hopped with the very best Kent hops, and nearly resembles the fine Farmhouse *Stock-Beer* of olden times.'

By 1811 George Hodgson's son Mark was running the Bow brewery. Within a couple of years, in 1813, some 4,000 barrels of Hodgson's beer a year were being shipped to the East, four times as many as in 1801. Four years later the brewery had moved 230 yards east, to Bow Bridge, and in 1821, by which time it was being run by Frederick Hodgson and Thomas Drane, it was rebuilt. About the same time a public house opened alongside the brewery called the Bombay Grap or Bombay Grab; the name almost certainly comes from the two-masted Eastern coasting-vessel known in Arabic as a *gurab*, or galley, and celebrates the brewery's Indian trade.

With the brewery rebuilt, Hodgson and Drane were now ready for a coup: they would cut out the East Indiamen's officers and ship their own beer to India, retailing it themselves once it arrived, and thus gathering all the profit of the Indian beer trade. Shipping charges for the eastward voyage were kept low to encourage trade, and the cost of shipping a barrel of beer to the East, even for an outside trader, was no more than the cost of shipping one to Edinburgh. The partners opened an office in Cornhill in the City of London and set up as shippers. At the same time they ended the long-standing arrangement of giving twelve or eighteen months' credit on the beer they sold to the East India Company's employees, raised the price by 20 per cent and refused to sell on any terms but cash.

Naturally, the East Indiaman officers were furious: Hodgson's beer had previously 'formed one of the principal articles in their investments', as one commentator wrote. Hodgson and Drane also deeply upset the merchants in Calcutta and Madras, who also found themselves cut out from the local beer trade. Whenever the Indian merchants tried to import someone else's beer, Hodgson and Drane dropped their prices. They were confident, moreover, that even if the East Indiamen's commanders did find regular supplies of beer elsewhere, their own product had such a reputation in India that no one else could compete.

They could not have been more wrong. Powerful men in the shipping business were determined Hodgson and Drane should not be allowed to wreck with impunity a trading arrangement that had help make their ships' officers wealthy. Early in 1822 Campbell Marjoribanks, who represented the shipping interest on the East India Company's court of directors, invited the Burton upon Trent brewer Samuel Allsopp to dinner at his London town house. The Russian government had just imposed a huge tariff on English ale imports and Allsopp was suffering, like the other Burton brewers, from the subsequent loss of trade to what was then their main market. Marjoribanks persuaded Allsopp that the Indian market could easily replace the Russian one, telling him that seven and a half thousand barrels of

English beer were exported to India every year, and 'we are all now dependent upon Hodgson, who has given offence to most of our merchants in India'.

Allsopp went back to Burton to try to replicate 'Hodgson's India beer', which was paler and more bitter than the ales the Burton brewers were used to brewing for the Baltic marketplace. Burton beer of the sort exported to Russia had been traditionally nut-brown and sweet, using dark malt, and the first step towards replicating Hodgson's beer was for Allsopp's maltster to make a suitably pale 'East India' malt. What Hodgson and Drane probably did not know, and even the Burton brewers scarcely realized, is that the well water of Burton, rich in calcium sulphate, naturally produces a much better pale, bitter ale than London water, rich in calcium carbonate, which is more suited to dark beers such as porter. Until London brewers learned how to treat, or 'Burtonize', their water late in the nineteenth century, a Burton brewer was always going to make a superior pale beer, because his type of hard water made for better conversion of starch into sugar when pale malt was used in the mash tun. The beer could also be made paler, since the sulphate-rich water extracted less colour from the malt that London water did.

After experiments, it was said later, with a brew made in a teapot, the first consignments of Allsopp's new pale ale went out to India in 1823. Within a year the Burton brewer was receiving letters from the subcontinent telling him that his beer 'is almost universally preferred by all old Indians [that is, Europeans in India] to Hodgson's'. A correspondent in 1828 informed Allsopp that in the hot season his beer was 'always cooled with saltpetre [potassium nitrate] before it is drank: we can make it by this article as cold as ice'. The letter is one of the earliest references in English to the delights of a cold beer: the technique of cooling containers by placing them in a solution of water and potassium nitrate was an ancient one, though in India it was normally used to make ice-cream and sorbets rather than solely to chill pale ale.

Allsopp's success in finding a new market could not be kept a secret, and two other Burton brewers, Bass & Ratcliff and Salt, began to brew pale ale in 1823. Figures for the growth of the Burton brewers' Indian trade are missing for the 1820s, but by 1832/3 Bass had 43 per cent of a yearly trade of 12,000 barrels, Hodgson and Drane just 28 per cent and Allsopp 12 per cent. Slowly the firm that had once been synonymous with the Indian market faded into obscurity. The Bow brewery was demolished in 1933 to make way for London County Council flats.

The popularity of India Pale Ale at home in England was ascribed in a guidebook issued by Bass in 1902 to a shipwreck in the Irish Channel in 1827. Some hogsheads of IPA salvaged from the wreck, the guidebook said, were sold off in Liverpool by the underwriters. The beer supposedly proved very acceptable to those who tried it and, according to this story, demand for the novel pale bitter beer subsequently spread 'in a remarkably rapid manner' throughout the country.

No verified details of this incident are known, and the story has one big narrative difficulty: if it had got only as far as the Irish Sea this must have been 'raw', unmatured India Pale Ale, still young, that had not yet had the long sea journey and the south-then-north passage across the equator which gave IPA its reputedly unsurpassable flavour. Did someone have the sense to store these hogsheads for several months before broaching them? Even then, how did a beer that matured best on a long sea voyage through tropical oceans become popular at home without, apparently, lengthy warm maturation? Was the IPA sold in Britain actually a different beer from the one exported to India, and if so how different?

An idea of what early IPAs tasted like comes from a book written in 1843 by Jonathan Pereira and called, in the windy style of the times, *A treatise on food and diet: with observations on the dietetical regimen suited for disordered states of the digestive organs*. Pereira said that 'the Pale Ale prepared for the India market, and, therefore, commonly known as the Indian Pale Ale, is . . . carefully fermented, so as to be devoid of all sweetness, or, in other words, to be dry; and it contains double the usual quantity of hops; it forms, therefore, a most valuable restorative beverage for invalids and convalescents'.

There is some evidence that while pale ales for export were, as Pereira indicates, massively hopped, at six pounds per barrel or more, 'domestic' IPAs were hopped at something like half that rate. This would reduce the time it took them to become drinkable. The brewer Michael Combrune suggested in the 1760s that hops should be used at the rate of one pound to the quarter of malt for every month that a beer was to keep. If early IPA brewers were looking for their beers to mature over as long as eighteen months to two years, and followed Combrune's advice, they were probably hopping at around six pounds to the barrel, which would have made for a very bitter beer, and that would take about a year and a half to round down.

However, the Victorian brewer George Amsinck, who included several recipes for 'East India Pale Ale' in his book *Practical Brewing*, published in 1868, seemed to think that even a well-hopped six pounds to the barrel IPA was 'fit to deliver to the trade' after just two months. Amsinck also included recipes for IPA with hop rates of three-and-a-half pounds to the barrel, still high by modern rates, which was probably the norm for IPAs meant for 'home' consumption. The strengths, at least, of early Burton IPAs seem to be much the same as later nineteenth-century versions, at around 1065–1075 OG.

In any case, the real growth of Burton pale ale in Britain looks to come a decade or more later than 1827. Pale ale production began rising noticeably only in 1831, after the passing of the Beer House Act increased considerably the number of licensed retailers in England and Wales, and leaped dramatically from 1839, the year the railway first arrived in Burton, when it rose nearly 50 per cent in twelve months, to just under 17,000 barrels. By 1849 Bass's pale ale production had risen to 56,000 barrels a year, of which only around 10 or 12 per cent was exported to India.

The railway allowed Burton's brewers to meet what was obviously a growing demand for pale bitter beers. India Pale Ale was the king of them, but it was expensive; Burton pale ale sold in Britain for 8d a quart retail, twice as much as either porter or lesser pale beers. By the middle of the 1840s, at the latest, other brewers were starting to brew a cheaper 'East India Pale Ale' or 'India Pale Ale' to compete with the Burton brewers' product. One of the first was J. W. Baker of the Castle brewery, Leamington, Warwickshire, which was advertising East India Pale Ale at 1s 4d a gallon in 1846, the equivalent of 6d a quart pot retail. Most brewers outside Burton sold their IPA or EIPA at 1s 6d a gallon wholesale, or 7d a pot retail, implying, again, an OG of around 1065–1075. While porter, mild and other styles of beer were sold at different strengths, IPA almost never appeared in brewers' price lists at anything other than one strength and one price. (One Newcastle upon Tyne bottler, however, was advertising in 1854 'Pale India Beer' at 2s 6d for a dozen quarts and 'best High-Hopped India Pale Ale' at 4s a dozen – brewer, sadly, unknown.)

Attempts to imitate Burton pale ale were hampered by the need to brew with similar hard, sulphate-impregnated water, which could be found in only a few places. As pale ale sales grew, so did the number of breweries in Burton, opening to take advantage of the local water. By 1834 there were nine; in 1851 there were fifteen. The total output of the Burton brewers more than quadrupled in the 1840s, from 70,000 barrels a year to 300,000. This was still less than just one of the big London brewers would produce on its own, but the Burton brewers were catching up. In the 1850s Burton's output more than tripled, to 971,000 barrels a year; and at the end of the 1860s the town's output had risen to 1.75 million barrels a year, from twenty-six active breweries. Two decades later, in 1888, thirty-one breweries produced three million barrels of beer a year. Bass, which now had three separate breweries in the town, had become the biggest brewing company in the world, and Burton was the biggest brewing-dominated town in Britain. Average production of the Burton brewers was now more than double that of their London rivals.

Several London brewers had set up branch breweries in Burton to try to brew the pale ales they could not make properly with London water. Ind Coope of Romford was the first, arriving in 1856. By the end of the 1860s the pressure on London brewers to produce Burton-style ales was obviously growing, because the early years of the next decade saw a rush to the banks of the Trent. The East London ale brewer Charrington & Co. bought a brewery in Abbey Street, Burton in 1872, while their East London rivals Truman, Hanbury & Buxton acquired the Phillips brewery in Derby Street the following year. A third big East London brewer, Mann, Crossman & Paulin, built a completely new brewery in Shobnall Street, Burton in 1874, 'constructed according to the most approved model of modern times'.

Regional brewers also came to Burton: Henry Boddington of Manchester acquired the Bridge brewery in 1869 to brew the pale ales his Strangeways brewery could not, selling it only in 1912. Andrew Walker of Warrington and his brother Peter Walker junior, who had a brewery in Wrexham, north Wales, opened branch breweries in the town in 1877 and 1880 respectively, while the Leicester brewery Everard & Co. took over the Trent Bridge brewery in 1885.

Ironically, while outside brewers were rushing to Burton, a chemist called C. W. Vincent was discovering how to reproduce Burton water everywhere. Brewers knew that it was the minerals, particularly gypsum, or calcium sulphate, dissolved in Burton well water that gave pale ales brewed in the town a drier, more bitter flavour and a brighter appearance than ales from areas without Burton's mineral advantages. Vincent's invention was a method of artificially altering the mineral composition of water in areas such as London so that it would emulate north Staffordshire's finest wells: no need, now, to move to Burton; just 'Burtonize' your own brewing liquor.

Vincent's work on brewing water was part of the new scientific approach to brewing, which reached its apotheosis in the work of the Frenchman Louis Pasteur. In the 1830s chemists in France and Germany were finally proving that yeast was a living organism and produced alcohol when it came into contact with sugar. One experimenter, Theodor Schwann, named brewer's yeast the 'sugar fungus', *saccharomyces* in Latin, which eventually became its official appellation. However, many scientists refused to believe that fermentation was anything else than essentially a chemical reaction. It was Pasteur who first defined the anaerobic life of yeast in both beer wort and wine, when it produces alcohol from sugar. He was also the first to tell the world, in his book *Etudes sur la Bière*, published in 1876, that frets and failings in beers were caused by disease organisms, which could be seen if a sample of the yeast from an unsatisfactory brew was examined under a microscope.

As part of his research into beer, Pasteur had travelled to London in 1871, where he visited several breweries, including Whitbread's in Chiswell Street. There he startled the brewers by identifying through his microscope infected yeast from a batch of beer he correctly said must be giving them problems. Whitbread's brewers knew the beer was bad, but until Pasteur showed them they had not known why. Within a week the brewery partners had bought a microscope, costing a substantial £27 15s, for use at Chiswell Street.

Pasteur was not preaching to the entirely ignorant. Truman, Hanbury & Buxton in London had a chemist working for it – Robert Warrington, who was eminent enough to be elected to the Royal Society in 1864. Burton brewers had been employing chemists as advisers since the 1840s, and at least one, Dr Horace Brown, had a laboratory at Worthington's brewery in 1871, where he was trying to apply Pasteur's earlier findings on the fermentation of wine, published in 1860, to the brewing industry.

Some lucky brewers lived in towns that did have similar water to Burton, and took advantage of it: in 1854 Flower's in Stratford upon Avon, where the well water also contained quantities of gypsum, was selling a 'Pale India Ale' at 1s 8d the gallon, 8d a pot retail, the same price as Burton pale ale. Flower's IPA won such a reputation that in 1872, the year Charrington opened in Burton, the London mild ale brewer Courage & Co. signed an agreement for the Stratford company to supply it with pale ale for its houses. Eventually, in 1903, Courage took over a brewer called G. & E. Hall in another town with a reputation for Burton-like brewing water, Alton in Hampshire. Brewing in Alton has lasted through to the twenty-first century, though

Director's, the pale ale that was originally supposed to be brewed for the Alton brewery boardroom, is no longer made there.

In Yorkshire, Tadcaster, which had five breweries in 1890, also had a reputation for sulphate springs and fine pale ales. When the journalist Alfred Barnard visited the largest Tadcaster brewer, John Smith's, in 1890 he found the 'great cellar' filled with casks of IPA stacked two deep. Barnard also visited the Edinburgh firm William Younger & Co., brewer of a 'justly celebrated India pale ale'. Younger had been brewing IPA at its Abbey brewery since at least 1854, later transferring production to the newer Holyrood brewery next door. All the successful Edinburgh brewers took their brewing liquor from the same underground ring of water-bearing sandstone known as the 'charmed circle', which, like Burton water, was rich in gypsum. Younger's had also copied one of Burton's great innovations in the brewing of pale ales – the union cask system of fermentation.

A perennial problem facing brewers was what to do with the excess yeast the brewing process generated. If the yeast was left in the beer it would make for a cloudy pint, with the danger that the yeast would 'autolyse', or dissolve through its own enzymes, giving a yeast-bitten flavour to the beer. The solution was to 'cleanse' the beer as it fermented. The simplest, though messiest, method was to run the wort into the 'carriage casks', the barrels, firkins and hogsheads in which the beer went out to publicans, letting the excess yeast fob off out of the bunghole in the top of the cask and down the sides into troughs underneath the casks. This primitive system, common in the eighteenth century, and used by Guinness until 1834, was still being employed by at least one commercial brewer, Bateman's of Wainfleet, until the firm finally installed proper fermenting vessels in 1953.

The 'carriage cask' method had several disadvantages, but the biggest was that as the yeast flowed out under the pressure of the carbon dioxide produced in the brewing process it took beer with it, and the casks had to be topped up at the height of fermentation every two hours, day and night, by a man with a can. Around the beginning of the 1830s Robert Dickinson, of the Albany brewery in Camberwell, south-east London, had worked out a method of topping up the casks automatically, by having the overflowing yeast rise up out of the bung-hole through a pipe into a tub filled with fresh wort. The yeast displaced the wort in the tub, which ran back down into the cask.

The next step was to eliminate the need for 'top-up' wort and arrange for the beer that came up with the excess yeast to drain back into the cask, thus saving money as well as labour. The man who patented a system to do this, in 1838, was a Liverpool brewer called Peter Walker (father to the Alexander and Peter Junior mentioned above). Walker's system had banks of casks arranged in double rows, called unions. Each had a swan-neck pipe in the top of the cask through which the excess yeast foamed, before dropping into a trough placed above the twin rows of casks. The yeast and beer separated out in the troughs, and the beer flowed back down into the casks.

Walker's patent system was taken up by brewers around the country, from Edinburgh to London (Watney's Stag brewery in Pimlico still had union fermenters in the years between the First and Second World Wars). Walker himself moved his brewing operations to Warrington in 1846, and the operation there was still using unions in 1890. However, it was the brewers of Burton upon Trent who took most eagerly to this method of brewing, which consequently became known as the Burton union system. When Alfred Barnard visited Burton he found all the brewers he saw using the union system to finish off their pale ales.

The reason why the Burton brewers employed unions for the production of their pale ales is intimately connected with the yeast they used, which thrived best in Burton's high-sulphate water under the union system. Which came first – the use of the union system, which then bred a yeast that fitted in perfectly with a life spent surging up out of casks into troughs, or a yeast already in use, waiting for the union system to arrive – is not clear. The yeast used in Burton unions gave excellent flavour and good stability, just what pale ale brewers wanted. Its disadvantage under normal circumstances was that it formed a poor 'head' on a conventional fermenting vessel and did not 'flocculate' or form into clumps at the end of fermentation for easy removal from the finished beer. This did not matter under the union system, which automatically removed the yeast from the beer and which gave a good quantity of yeast for pitching into the next batch of wort.

Other ways of removing the excess yeast from the fermenting beer included skimming it off with wooden boards, as practised by Guinness in Dublin from at least 1865 (though Guinness used the Burton union system as well until 1886), and the 'dropping' method, where the finished beer is drained out of the fermenting vessel into another back, or vessel below, leaving the yeast and dregs behind. Late in the eighteenth century a brewer from Huddersfield, Timothy Bentley, invented, or perfected, another arrangement that became known as the 'Yorkshire square' system. The beer fermented in the lower part of a two-storey square vessel made of slate, and the excess yeast foamed up out of a manhole into the top part of the fermenting vessel, where it stayed while the beer it had carried up with it ran back down through pipes. The method produced full-bodied beers with a high degree of carbonation, and, as the name implies, it was very popular with brewers in Yorkshire; however, it failed to catch on further south.

At least one author, writing anonymously in 1884, regarded the development of Burton IPA as the invention of bitter beer in general. Certainly IPA's spread in Britain coincides with the growth in what was called variously in the 1840s and 1850s 'bitter ale', 'pale ale' and 'bitter beer'. Pale ale and bitter are effectively the same drink, pale ale being the brewer's designation, bitter what the customer called it in the pub. Even today, Young & Co. of Wandsworth sends its Ordinary bitter out in casks marked PA, for pale ale, and its Special bitter in casks marked SPA, special pale ale. In 1952 Marston's of Burton named its best pale ale Pedigree Pale Ale, though no drinker today thinks of Pedigree as anything except a bitter. Since pump clips were not in general use until after the Second World War, there was nothing at the bar to tell the customer he should be asking for pale

ale, and so he called for 'bitter', to indicate he did not want the sweeter, generally less hopped mild. With bottled beer, however, the brewer supplied his own description on the label. This is why pale ale is thought of today as mostly a bottled beer category, because the name was seen mostly on bottles.

However, while all pale ales are part of the bitter family, not all bitter was 'pale ale'. Brewers outside Burton, particularly in London and the south of England, had an older style of bitter beer than pale ale, more lightly hopped, which they indicated with a K designation. The letter X, in different quantities, seems to have been generally reserved for mild and dark beers. K beers, however, were always bitter, and amber or lighter in colour. Brewers frequently offered a range of K beer which ran in strength from K or AK (the cheapest and weakest, at fourpence a quart retail and an OG of around 1045) through KK and KKK up to KKKK, which was a stock beer at a higher strength of around 1090 OG or more.

The most commonly found member of the K family in Victorian brewers' advertisements is AK. There is evidence that AK was less heavily hopped than other bitter beers: Crowley's brewery in Croydon High Street in 1900 described its AK in one of its advertisements as 'a Bitter Ale of sound quality with a delicate Hop flavour', and the frequent description of AK as 'for family use' suggests a light, not-too-bitter beer. Alfred Barnard in 1889 gave almost identical tasting notes to Crowley's for the 'AK shilling ale' brewed by W. J. Rogers at the Jacob Street brewery in Bristol: 'most pleasant to the palate . . . a bright sparkling beverage of a rich golden colour and possesses a nice delicate hop flavour'. (Rogers actually used the letters AK as its company trademark.)

It is also clear from old advertisements that AK came near the bottom of the table in terms of price, and thus of strength. AK was almost always one shilling a gallon wholesale, the cheapest or second-cheapest beer, no matter who brewed it. This is borne out by the mention of 'AK bitter' by Professor Charles Graham in his talk to the Society of Chemical Industry in 1881. The professor gave the original gravity of AK as 1045, with an alcohol-by-weight percentage of 4.3. This may look high by today's standards, but, at that time the average OG of British beers was 1057.

As a light bitter, the beer was kept in storage for a period halfway between IPAs and milds before it was ready to serve. In 1898 Dr Edmund Moritz, describing beer types to a parliamentary committee on beer, spoke of light pale ales, or AK, kept two to three weeks before delivery, and mild ale, X or XX, kept four to ten days before delivery. The stronger varieties of K bitter beers could be kept as long as IPAs, however. Mann, Crossman & Paulin in the East End of London brewed a KKKK ale, and Alfred Barnard drank some in 1888. It was, he said, 'two years old, of a rich brown colour and with a Madeira odour, a good generous drink for those who can stand a full-bodied beer'. Barnard also revealed that Mann's brewed a London stock ale it called KKK, while a Mann's advert from 1898 also shows KK medium bitter ale at 10s 6d a firkin and K light bitter ale at 9s 6d a firkin.

None of this explains why a K was used to identify this kind of beer. Here we must open the door to speculation. There is evidence that the K designation was more common in the south than elsewhere in England. Few brewers north of Newark, in the East Midlands, seem to have used Ks in their beers' names. In 1898 the *Brewers' Journal* said the X mark was 'almost universal in provincial towns, the alternative K being equally common in the London district'.

It was a commonplace in the seventeenth century that while the City drank beer, the country drank ale. Is this city/country split between K and X as a designator for beer strength a hangover from a time when Xs would have been used only for different strengths of the countryside favourite, unhopped (or less-hopped) ale, while the strength of London's preferred drink, hopped beer, was indicated by different numbers of Ks?

The answer may lie in the popular medieval Dutch beer called *koyt*, which came in two different strengths, single *koyt* and double *koyt*. Single *koyt* to its original brewers would be *ankel koyt*, *ankel* being the Old Flemish for 'single'. We can easily suppose that casks of *ankel koyt* would be marked with a chalked 'K', or even 'AK', while casks of *dubbel koyt* would be marked with two Ks, 'KK'. Like Xs, Ks are easy for even the illiterate to write. When Flemish brewers settled in the south of England from the fifteenth century, bringing hopped beer with them, they may also have brought a habit of marking casks of weak beer 'AK' and casks of stronger beer 'KK', just as they brought so many other brewing words, from gyle to kilderkin. It certainly seems likely their numbers included the occasional *koytbrouwer*, and they brought *koyt* brewing with them.

The major problem with this theory is that municipal records from the Dutch town of Haarlem dated 1407 show that *koyt* was a gruit beer, flavoured with herbs such as sweet gale, not hops. However, when Lounde and Veysy were charged by Henry VI in 1441 to find out what regulations were imposed on beer brewers on the continent, as the first step to regulating beer brewers in England, the only brews their subsequent report talked about were 'single coyt' and 'double coyt'. The implication here is that Lounde and Veysy believed *koyt* to be a hopped beer, and perhaps by the middle of the fifteenth century it was.

Until a better story is found, this seems a more likely explanation for the K designation than most. It has the advantage, not only of going back 550 or 600 years to the origin of bitter beers in Britain, but of giving a root for AK that describes exactly what it was: weaker-than-standard, cheap, everyday beer.

Almost as universally as K meant pale bitter beer, around the country X on its own meant mild. This is not always true: some brewers made bitters with X in their name, such as XX light bitter from the old Starkey, Knight & Ford Brewery in Tiverton, and 6X bitter from Wadworth's of Devizes in Wiltshire. These are rare exceptions, however: mostly X was reserved for milds and dark beers. As late as 1937 the Northampton Brewery Company was selling four different grades of mild ale, designated from X at 9s 6d a pin (4½ gallons) to XXXX, almost twice as expensive at 18s 9d. (Confusingly, a number of brewers mixed the systems, brewing beers they called XK, as well as making XX: however, XK, like all K beers, was always a bitter ale.)

The X is derived from medieval monastic brewers' Latin names for the beers they brewed. The weakest sort was 'single beer', *birra simplex* in medieval Latin, the stronger sort *birra duplex*, 'double beer': *birra duplex* occurs in a document from 1480. *Simplex* and *duplex* sound like 'single X' and 'double X' in English, and casks would thus be marked with a punning single X if they contained *birra simplex* and a double X if they contained *duplex*. The habit passed over to commercial brewers after the dissolution of the monasteries in 1536, and by the end of the eighteenth century the Burton brewer Benjamin Wilson, for one, was using 'Xth' in his letters to customers as shorthand for 'strength'.

In at least one part of the country, Durham and Northumberland, the taste had always been for sweet mild ale, known specifically as Newcastle mild or Newcastle sweet ale. This was a very sweet, dark ale with what Victorian observers called a 'sub-acid' flavour. The beer was sweet and dark because that was the sort the local 'indifferent' water supply made best, and in 1890 Alfred Barnard was told the Durham and Northumberland pitmen held it in high repute and 'prefer it to any other'. However, although Newcastle mild was said to be the only beer brewed in the town in 1863, by 1890 it was disappearing from Newcastle itself and the larger towns of the region. Its place was being taken by ales from the brewers of Edinburgh and Burton.

CHAPTER SEVEN

MAKE MINE MILD

the nineteenth century, part two

Come one and all, both great and small,
With voices loud and clear
And let us sing 'Bless Billy the King',
Who bated the tax upon beer.

Anonymous, nineteenth century

While Burton was famous for pale ales, it also had another style that was widely imitated: Burton ale, a rather darker, sweeter beer closer to the brews exported to the Baltic in the eighteenth century. Today Burton ale is effectively forgotten, a type of beer popular for a century and a half and obsolete within a couple of decades after the Second World War. Just a handful of beers are still brewed in the Old Burton mode, such as Young's Winter Warmer, and none of those bears the name Burton.

A book on *The Brewer's Art* published by Whitbread in 1948 said Burton was one of the 'four chief types of beer' in Britain, along with pale ale, mild ale and stout. Burton, it said,

is a strong ale of the pale ale type, but made with a proportion of highly dried or slightly roasted malts; it is consequently darker in colour and with a fuller flavour than the pale ales. Essentially a draught beer, it is usually given a prolonged cellar treatment, in the course of which those special flavours develop which are associated with maturity in beer. Although not necessarily made in Burton, it is based on the types of strong beer made famous by that centre of pale ale brewing.

When the Russian government suddenly and unexpectedly imposed a deliberately prohibitive tariff on beer imports in 1822, to the shock and concern of the Burton brewers, Samuel Allsopp for one found himself with large amounts of newly brewed but unexportable beer. He tried selling it to customers in England, with some success. But 'those who admired its flavour and its purity, and who wished to drink more of it,' according to the journalist John Stevenson Bushnan, writing in 1853, 'found it too heady, too sweet, and too glutinous, if not too strong. Indeed it was so rich and luscious that if a little were spilled on a table the glass would stick to it'.

The original Burton ale as was described by Bushnan must have been very similar to the recipe for a Burton ale in an anonymously written book from 1824, *The Young Brewer's Monitor*. This gave a beer with an OG of a thumping 1140, using pale malt and 4½ pounds of hops to the barrel, which needed maturing for at least eighteen months. But this sticky brew was already being superseded by a new style of Burton ale.

When the October 1822 brewing season opened, Bushnan wrote, Allsopp brewed 'the first specimen of the improved Burton ale now so universally drank and admired', making it less sweet and more bitter than the original Russian version. The first casks of the new beer were sold to customers in Liverpool. They were not an instant success: after complaints, Allsopp had to visit each publican to persuade them to let the beer mature, promising to take back any that was unsaleable. The beer was found to improve considerably with age, and eventually none of that first brew was returned unsold. It was a busy time for Allsopp: the following year he sent his new India Pale Ale out east in another endeavour to find a market to replace the Baltic trade. But while IPA also succeeded eventually in the British market, it always sold alongside Burton ale. By the early 1840s Burton ale was popular across the country: a traveller for the Edinburgh brewer William Younger reported in 1843 that 'in Newcastle Burton Ale seems to be as fashionable as porter in Aberdeen,' while in London 'Burton ale is taking the lead everywhere'.

The Victorian brewer George Amsinck gave a recipe for Burton ale which used hard Burton water, pale malt and Kentish hops at a rate of (again) around 4½ pounds to the barrel to produce a beer with 6 per cent alcohol by volume. Amsinck used the same recipe, with slightly different mash temperatures and soft water, to make a 'London XXXX' of the same strength. Both were to be stored for six weeks to mature before being tapped.

The beer was honoured by royalty: when King Edward VII visited Bass's brewery in Burton upon Trent in February 1902, the brew he started during his visit, and which was later bottled as King's Ale, was actually Bass No. 1 Burton ale. A bottle of King's Ale opened in 1932 was found to have a present gravity of 1043, according to the writer Andrew Campbell, implying an original gravity above 1125. King's Ale was still being drunk in 2002, when it was 100 years old, though the brewers had taken the precaution of opening the bottles and decanting the beer off its lees (sediment or dregs) every ten years.

Bass's red diamond trade mark for its Burton ales distinguished it from the famous red triangle used on Bass India Pale Ale – the first British trade mark ever to be registered and still number one in the UK listings. (The firm registered the red diamond as trade mark number two on January 1 1876; it was used for Burton ale from 1857, two years after the firm first put the red triangle on its pale ale labels.) Bass brewed half a dozen different strengths of Burton ale in 1880. They ranged from the powerful No. 1, at over 1110 OG (still brewed today) down through Nos. 2, 3, 4 and 5 to No. 6 at around 1050 OG.

Just as other brewers copied Burton's India Pale Ales, so they reproduced Burton ale. By the early 1890s brewers far from Staffordshire were producing a beer called Burton: Alfred Barnard found Burton ales being brewed at the Tyne Brewery in Newcastle, by John Smith's in Tadcaster and by Eldridge Pope in Dorchester. Page & Overton's Shirley brewery in Croydon, Surrey, was brewing XXX Burton at 13s 6d a firkin in 1898, implying a retail price of threepence-halfpenny a pint, while its rival Croydon brewery Crowley's sold Burton Ale at fifteen shillings a firkin. The Scots had their own version, known as Scotch Ale, of which Younger's No. 3 was the most widely distributed brand.

Victorian brewers recognized five or six unofficial price bands for their beers, with original gravities rising from 1035 or less for the table beers and harvest beers to 1090 for the 'Imperials', Christmas ales and the like, and even higher for the strongest Burton ales. Generally, every brewer would sell a table beer and then each of the main national beer styles – mild, pale bitter ale and porter/stout – at three different strengths, making nine or ten different beers on the price list, with prices rising from 10d to 2s a gallon. Not all the beers sold were actually brewed separately. For many brewers, the middle-strength beer in any style would be a blend of the highest- and lowest-strength beers. Occasionally brewers would produce beers even stronger than the Imperials, No. 1s and XXXXXs: Allsopp's Arctic Ale, for example, which was specially brewed (as the name suggests) for Arctic expeditions, had an OG of 1130. The popularity of mild, at 4d a quart, with the working or labouring classes led to the public bar, where they drank, being known as the four-ale bar. The clerks and other middle-class pub goers drank pale ale or bitter in the saloon. Prices (and strengths) for all the Burton brewers' pale beers were generally higher, with Bass, for example, starting at 24s a kilderkin for its No. 6 Burton Ale and rising to 45s for the No. 1.

In Scotland the nomenclature was different, with the Scottish equivalent of bitter known as heavy and mild as light (regardless of colour), and strength indicated by the wholesale price per barrel: 30/-, or thirty-shilling, was thus the equivalent in strength of X, K or table ale, 54/- was as strong as KKK, double stout or IPA, and so on.

In England and Wales, Victorian beer styles fell into two families, brown and pale, each family dividing into two main sub-groups depending on their underlying sweetness or lack of acidity. Thus the sweeter XX mild brown ale had its more acid/bitter equivalent in porter; the XXX mild in single stout; the XXXX mild in double stout; and the XXXXX strong in Imperial stout. No. 6 Burton pale ale, a mid-strength beer of OG 1065, had its more bitter equivalent pale ale in KKK, IPA; and so on.

Few country brewers sold beers much above a gravity of 1080, leaving this territory to the Burton brewers. In the early twentieth century, ales with an OG of 1080 and above became known generically as 'barley wine', although this blanket classification cut across a wide variety of beer styles. This means that today 'barley wine' can have any of the very different characteristics of a sweet dark ale, a super-strong stout, a strong Burton ale or a strong bitter ale.

Although porter made up three-quarters of London beer sales even in 1863, the tide was running against it with increasing speed. The rising clerical classes – the 'nobby' clerks, often ridiculed in contemporary newspapers for aping the 'nobs', their social superiors – were preferring Burton-style pale ales, which were seen as having more cachet, while the manual classes were turning completely away from the aged, stale beer their fathers drank. In 1872 the last porter-only brewery in London, Meux & Co., off Tottenham Court Road, gave up its exclusivity and began brewing ales as well. Around the middle of the 1870s both Whitbread and Truman (and, undoubtedly, the other historically big London porter brewers also) began selling more ale than porter. By 1887 porter was down to only 30 per cent of the London trade.

For smaller brewers the fall was even greater: at Young & Co. of Wandsworth, porter had made up 70 per cent of production in 1835; in 1880 the figure was just 16 per cent. One result was the disappearance from big breweries of the huge porter vats that had been the fascination of visitors. 'The fickle public,' wrote Alfred Barnard, 'has got tired of the vinous-flavoured vatted porter and transferred its affections to the new and luscious "mild ale" . . . Our old friend porter, with its sombre hue and foaming head, is no longer the pet of fashion, but a bright and sparkling bitter, the colour of sherry and the condition of champagne, carries off the palm.'

Barnard's observations did not apply across the Irish Sea, however, where porter was still hugely popular. When James J. Murphy's Lady's Well brewery was founded in Cork in 1856 it tried brewing Lady's Well ale alongside porter for the first five years, but stopped ale production when its then head brewer left, and made nothing but porter until stout was introduced in 1889.

One problem in England and Scotland was that as sales of porter fell, brewers began to abandon proper porter brewing methods. The *Scottish Wine, Spirits and Beer Trades' Review* complained in September 1887 that

> far too much of the stout brewed in ale brewings might well be described as coloured mild ale; indeed, we know of a case where porter is made from the same mash as mild ale, adding to the last copper a large quantity of sugar to raise the gravity, and enough black malt to impart the requisite colour. Little surprise can be felt that the article thus produced did not give satisfaction to the customer.

The decline of porter matched the decline of the men from whom it took its name. Through the nineteenth century, with the railway companies and new docks employing their own men, the ticket porters and fellowship porters lost their economic power, and dwindled in numbers and importance. By the late 1870s the ticket porters had vanished, and the fellowship porters had fallen to fewer than 100 men earning their living from the trade. An Act of Parliament abolished the fellowship on Midsummer Day 1894, giving each former porter compensation for the disappearance of his job.

As porter sales fell, brewers stopped mentioning it in their advertising. By the 1890s ale (meaning pale ale and mild ale) and stout (meaning the stronger version of porter) were generally the only styles promoted. Stout as an adjective originally meant 'proud' or 'brave'; only later (around the fourteenth century) did it gain the meaning 'strong'. The first recorded mention of its application to beer comes in the 1630s, when Robert Herrick wrote a poem about the Harvest Home supper which included the lines: 'If smirking wine be wanted here / There's that which drowns all care, stout beer.' The *Vade Mecum for Malt Worms*, the rhyming guide to London pubs written around 1716–18, mentions stout several times. Stout was still seen as a rather common expression when used on its own as the name of a beer, however: Samuel Johnson, in his *Dictionary of the English Language*, published in 1755, wrote that stout was 'a cant [that is, slang] name for strong beer'.

When stout was first applied to beer, the drink could be any colour, as long as it was strong. Truman's brewery in East London had both brown and pale stout in stock in 1741. Whitbread was selling pale stout in 1767 for a price a third more per barrel than regular porter. The opposite word to stout was 'slender'. In 1796, when wartime restrictions were forcing brewers to make their beers weaker, Thomas Greenall of St Helens was telling a customer that he would no longer send out larger casks, because the 'slender ale' that was all he could brew would turn sour before an innkeeper could empty a big cask.

'Stout' was still being used as an adjective in 1810, when Guinness in Dublin decided 'to try whether the publicans will encourage a stouter kind of porter'. (This was Superior Porter, the forerunner of Extra Superior Porter, which eventually became today's bottled Guinness, Extra Stout). Single and double survived as descriptions of beer, but only in reference to degrees of stoutness. Barclay Perkins, for example, brewed a 'strong double-brown stout' in 1802. It was still necessary to say 'brown stout', to distinguish it from pale stout (Guinness labels referred to 'brown stout' as late as the 1950s): brown stout was brewed using the same methods as porter but to an OG of around 1060, against porter's 1045 to 1050.

Gradually, the porter brewers appropriated the word 'stout' for themselves, so that it became a word associated by the drinking public solely with strong dark beer, rather than strong beer of any colour: to Queen Victoria's earliest subjects 'pale stout' would probably have seemed an oxymoron. Though stout lingered on as an adjective – in May 1854, Flower & Sons' brewery in Stratford upon Avon still listed 'stout porter' at a price equal to other people's double stout – it came to be generally used in breweries on its own, as the name of a stronger version of porter. The almost universal names for black beers by the middle of the nineteenth century were, in ascending order of strength: porter; stout or single stout; double stout or extra stout; and Imperial stout.

By the end of the nineteenth century stout had won a reputation for its supposed restorative qualities, with doctors recommending it as a pick-me-up for patients, particularly females, who had lost their appetites. Victorian and Edwardian brewers played up to the image. In 1887 the Richmond brewery in Surrey was advertising 'Ladies' Stout' and 'Double Stout (Invalids)', while its near neighbour across the Thames, William Gomm of the Beehive brewery, Brentford, sold 'Double Stout (for nursing)'. The same year Waltham Brothers' brewery in Stockwell, south-west London, was calling its SN stout an 'alimental tonic', 'particularly suited for invalids, ladies nursing or anyone requiring a good sound strengthening beverage', while warning that its Double Stout was 'Highly nutritious, but too strong for some invalids'. Nurses appear in several advertisements for stout from the 1890s and 1900s, with Ind Coope of Romford actually listing the more than twenty hospitals where its beer was used.

Oatmeal stout, a variant that appeared around the end of the nineteenth century, was promoted as even better than ordinary stout for the enfeebled: the Rochdale and Manor Brewery in Lancashire in 1909, for example, advertised its Oatmeal Nourishing Stout as 'Refreshing and strengthening', while Walker and Homfray's of Salford in 1904 declared its own Oatmeal Stout was 'particularly suitable for invalids'.

At the opposite end of the scale to stout was dinner ale. With beer the national drink of England and Wales (though not of Scotland and Ireland), it was always the beverage of choice for drinking with meals. When Victoria came to the throne in 1837, 'Beer was universally taken with dinner,' Sir Walter Besant wrote fifty years later, and 'even at great dinner parties some of the guests would call for beer. In the restaurants every man would call for bitter ale, or stout, or half-and-half [ale and porter mixed] with his dinner, as a matter of course'.

The custom of drinking beer with dinner persisted throughout Victoria's reign, surviving even though in the early 1860s William Gladstone, as Chancellor of the Exchequer, had cut duties on French wines, especially table wines, in part to encourage wine-drinking with meals. Thirty years later, in 1894, Baedeker's guide to London still told visitors from abroad that if they wished to dine out, 'beer, on draught or in bottle, is supplied at almost all the restaurants,' and 'is the beverage most frequently drunk'.

The cask of ale at home, delivered by the brewery roundsman, was still common, and many small concerns advertised themselves specifically as 'family brewers'. Young's of Hertford, for example, ran ads in the local paper in the 1870s promoting its 'superior pale bitter ales, brewed expressly for the supply of Private Families and delivered in 9 or 18 gallon casks . . . AK for family use, 10d per gallon'. Richard Reeve's West Ham brewery in what was, in 1900, still Essex, had a huge sign across the front of its Romford Road premises declaring that its beers, including Nursing Stout and Pale Dinner Ale, were 'brewed expressly for private families from English malt and hops only'.

But by the 1880s, while a pint of beer with dinner or supper was still popular, there was less demand for a whole cask – 4½ gallons – of dinner ale to be delivered to the family home. Overall beer consumption was falling, and the chances of the beer turning sour before it was used were too great. Some brewers had started selling their beers in one or two gallon screwtop stoneware jars, with brass taps: Healey's of Watford would let you have a gallon jar of its 'family bitter ale' for 1s 2d, 'jars and stoppers charged and allowed for when returned'. But even a gallon was too much for many families.

Fortunately the hour brought forward its hero: Henry Barrett. Bottled beers had been available for centuries, and Whitbread had started a considerable bottling operation in 1870. But these were corked bottles, which meant brewers needed an army of workers to knock home the corks with a leather 'flogger'. They were also inconvenient for the drinker: a corkscrew was always required, and bottles could not be easily resealed. In 1879 Barrett invented the screw-top beer bottle, a cheap, convenient, reusable container that meant little or no waste for the man desiring his lunchtime or suppertime pint. Four years later Barrett started his own brewery in Wandsworth, south London, Barrett's Brewing and Bottling Co. His early advertisements contrasted the ease with which a screw-top bottle could be opened against the potentially gory disaster of trying to open a corked bottle, with broken glass, blood and beer everywhere.

The screw-top caught on rapidly (Whitbread started using them in 1886), ushering in thirty years when almost every brewery had to have a bottled dinner ale or its equivalent. Half a crown – 2s 6d – for a dozen pints was the standard price (Barrett's actually used the brand name 'Half-Crown Ale'). The other favourite way to buy bottled beer was in wooden crates containing four screw-topped quart bottles, retailing at 1s 4d.

All these early bottled beers were naturally conditioned, which meant a yeast deposit, and the chance of cloudy beer if the customer did not take care. In 1897 the brewing scientist Horace Brown was reporting to the Institute of Brewing that brewers in the United States had solved the problems involved in chilling and filtering beers so that they would remain 'bright' in the bottle. It did not take long for the technology to cross the Atlantic. By 1899 the Notting Hill Brewery Company in West London was advertising its 'Sparkling Dinner Ale' as 'a revolution in English bottled beers, produced entirely on a new system . . . no deposit, no sediment, brilliant to the last drop, no waste whatever'. To compete, other brewers had to buy in the same

An enduring tradition: top, part of a banquet scene from a lapis lazuli cylinder seal found in the Royal Cemetery at Ur in Sumer, today southern Iraq, dated around 2600 BC, showing drinkers sipping beer from a pot through reeds and, below, twenty-first-century AD school teachers in Moroto, Uganda, drinking sorghum beer in exactly the same way

A baker and an alewife are carried to hell on the shoulders of demons. The alewife, condemned for defrauding her customers, carries the false-measure ale jug on her head, while the cheating baker's inaccurate scales and the oven peel, are also in flames. From the *Holkham Picture Bible, c* 1320–30

A scene from the story of the 'sinful hermit' in the *Smithfield Decretals*, about 1340. The hermit has stopped outside the alehouse, indicated by the pole with the bush at the end, and is drinking his ale from a mazer, a flat, handle-less bowl which demands a particular grip to avoid spilling

The hop market in the Borough, on the south side of the Thames from London, pictured in 1729 where pockets of hops are stacked up for sale in the shelter of the market house, and being carried away on wagons

Brewery workers cheer as Sir John Parsons, owner of the Red Lion brewhouse in Lower East Smithfield (now St Katharine's Way), Wapping, the Lord Mayor elect of the City of London, leaves by barge to go to his swearing-in on 29 October 1703

RED LION BREWHOUSE

Barclay Perkins's brewery in 1840, when it was already one of the 'must-see' places in London for visitors

The grubby reality, as opposed to the smoothness of the architect's impression: Watkins & Son's brewery, Eign Street, Hereford, in the 1880s

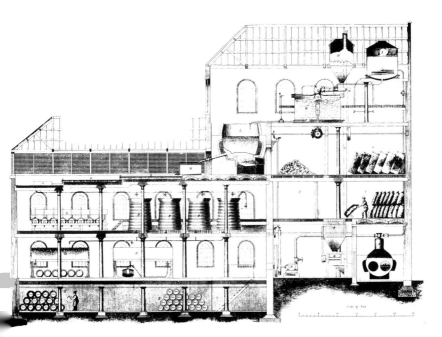

A typical steam-powered tower brewery, 1886, showing how gravity was used to help the brewing process move on, from the mash tun at the top to the copper, coolers, fermenting vessels, racking and cellaring

Employees at Glover & Sons' brewery, Harpenden, Hertfordshire, around 1899. Some of the men's occupations are clear: the malt man at the back carries his wooden malt shovel, a cooper next to him has a large hammer, and there are two more hammer-wielding coopers sitting down. The men on the barrels are most likely draymen

The union room at Younger's Holyrood brewery in Edinburgh in 1890, where India Pale Ales were made by the methods used at Burton-upon-Trent

Marchers on the Embankment, London, in the great demonstration of September 1908 against the Licensing Bill introduced in 1907, which would have banned the barmaid and allowed any district to vote itself 'dry' after 14 years

The brewery at Queen's College, Oxford, pictured in 1927. The brewer, J.F. Hunt, who was about to retire after 56 years, is seen by the mash tun holding the mashing rake or mash fork

Next he is seen by the copper, holding the handle of the sixteenth-century lead-and-wood pump that lifts the wort from the underback

nally he is down in the llar topping up still-rmenting casks from a opered filling can

Douglas Fairbanks jnr, the Hollywood film star, and Gertrude Lawrence, a British stage actress famous in her time, bring glamour to an advertisement from the mid-1930s meant to show that Whitbread Pale Ale could be drunk with a meal by the most sophisticated people at the smartest London restaurants

Bare boards, smoky oil lamp, faded paintwork, what this pub needs is leaving alone.

The ad Whitbread declined to run: it was turned down because it promised conservatism when the directors were keen to promote change

equipment themselves, and many – like the Notting Hill Brewery – gave their beers names that reflected the perceived advantages of filtered beers. The Chester Northgate Brewery, for example, sold 'All Clear' light dinner ale; in Scotland, Maclays of Alloa sold 'Sparkling Table Beer' (table beer was the standard Scots name for dinner ale).

Friary's 'Anglo Lager Dinner Ale', meanwhile, was a reflection of British awareness of what had been going on in mainland Europe for the past fifty or so years. A young German brewer called Gabriel Sedlmayr II, whose family ran the long-established Spaten brewery in Munich, spent several years in the 1820s and early 1830s making a tour of other European brewing nations, including England and Scotland. He came home to Munich fired with ideas to improve the local product. Bavarian brewers stored their beer in cool cellars and caves to mature it. A special strain of yeast had developed over the centuries for use in this cold-matured 'store-beer' (*Lager-bier* in German, *Lager* meaning storeplace): one that thrived in cool conditions and then settled to the bottom when it had used up all the sugars in the wort, rather than rising to the top as English ale yeast did. Using the knowledge he had gathered abroad, Sedlmayr developed *Lager-bier* so that it offered a more consistent, stable product at lower alcohol levels.

The reputation of the improved *Lager-bier* spread rapidly, and brewers across northern Europe began to adopt the new Bavarian style of beer-making, using its mashing techniques, cool fermentations and what were styled 'bottom-fermenting' yeasts (although 'bottom-settling' is a more accurate term: all types of yeast are in the middle of the wort when actually fermenting). Brewers in other countries took up the Bavarian method of lager brewing: in neighbouring Austria, Sedlmayr's good friend Anton Dreher adopted it alongside Viennese malting methods to make a style of rich, reddish beer. By 1843 the Bavarian influence had reached up into Sweden, where the style became known as *Bayerskt* – Bavarian. Everywhere lager beer began to dominate. In the Netherlands, Gerard Heineken, who had started in the brewing industry in Amsterdam in 1863 brewing top-fermenting beers, was having to brew bottom-fermenting *Beijersch Bier* by the late 1860s to cater for changing Dutch tastes.

All the beers in the Bavarian style were dark, the colour of an English brown ale at the lightest. However, in 1842 in the Bohemian town of Plzen (Pilsen in German), a newly built brewery began making beer brewed with bottom-fermenting Bavarian yeast, but pale English-style malt. With the local soft water extracting little colour from the grain, this resulted in a new style of beer – golden lager. Nobody knows why Josef Groll, the 29-year-old Bavarian brewer hired by the citizens of Plzen to run their new brewery, made a pale beer rather than a regular dark one. But the beer, which became known as Pilsner, was a big success locally, and over the decades the Pilsner style spread to overtake and almost displace the original dark Bavarian lagers.

British brewers remained aloof from the lager revolution. The first sighting appears only in October 1868, when the *Bradford Daily Telegraph* recorded that 'during the last hot weather the sale of Vienna beer was attempted on a small scale in the City [of London], and it was found to take so with all classes that there are now five establishments where this beverage may be procured in London, viz, three in the City and two in the Strand'. The *Telegraph* went on to say that 'when first imported into England, it was though that the Germans resident among us would patronise the favourite drink of the fatherland, they do so but Englishmen seem to like it quite as much as they do, and the quantity consumed is every day increasing'. The Bradford newspaper did not welcome this change, and wailed: 'Have our tastes changed or has our beer degenerated in its quality? It is feared that the brewers will have but themselves to thank if there is a material falling off in the quality of malt liquor consumed in England.'

Despite the *Telegraph*'s pessimism, it seems to have been another decade before anyone in Britain took up the challenge of lager brewing. A concern called the Anglo-Bavarian Brewery Company bought a brewery in Shepton Mallet in 1871, but there is no firm evidence it ever brewed lager beer. By coincidence, the country's first known lager brewer appears to have been from Bradford: Joseph Spink & Sons of the Brownroyd Brewery, Rose Street, Bradford, was brewing English lager in 1877. The *Brewers' Journal* commented that it compared 'most favourably with foreign productions'. The experiment did not last, however, for nothing more seems to be heard of Spink's lager.

The earliest lager brewer in Scotland was William Younger of Edinburgh, which mashed and fermented its first lager beer in 1879 at the Holyrood brewery, using yeast imported from the Carlsberg brewery in Copenhagen (which had originally come from Sedlmayr's brewery in Munich). The innovation was probably a reaction to the loss of overseas markets for Younger's top-fermented ales to German and other continental lagers. The strategy was: if they're beating you, brew what they brew. Younger's stopped brewing lager after a few years, its own bottom-fermented beer presumably not good enough, or cheap enough, to steal back world markets from the continentals.

The title of Britain's first lager-only brewery probably goes to the Austro-Bavarian Lager Beer and Crystal Ice Company in Tottenham High Road, north London (note the twin tribute to Sedlmayr and Dreher in the name), which was formed in March 1881 and brewing by 1882. It was run by an entirely German staff, backed with German capital. A year later it was reported that 'large quantities of genuine lager beer are sent out for consumption' from the Tottenham brewery. The same year, 1883, after more than eighteen months of building work, the new Wrexham Lager Brewery in north Wales was brewing dark Bavarian-style lagers.

Like Younger's foray into lager brewing, the Wrexham venture was largely a reaction to the success of continental brewers, and particularly, in the late nineteenth century, their triumphs in winning markets in places that had previously bought only British ales, from Burton IPA to Guinness stout. Increasingly, lager beer was now winning the war for overseas sales. Outside Europe, the locals were also producing their own lager beers: lager brewing was nearly a quarter of total beer production in the United States by 1860, and the first Australian lager brewery opened in Melbourne in 1885.

Although Professor Charles Graham of University College, London, noted in 1881 that lager beer 'has established a footing in our large cities', chauvinistic Britons saw nothing to fear at home. The journalist John Bickerdyke wrote in 1889: 'Neither German nor Anglo-German beers appear to make much headway over here, nor is this very surprising when we remember how far superior our own ales and beers are to any brewed in Germany.' Bickerdyke had spent some time studying in the German city of Baden-Baden, and presumably thought he knew what he was talking about.

Some were not so narrowly nationalistic, however. The young Hugh Tennent, a member of the family that owned the Wellpark brewery in Glasgow, one of Scotland's biggest beer exporters, had been sent to Germany and Switzerland in the early 1880s to convalesce after a serious illness. He came back with enthusiasm for the lager beers he had tried, and doubtless, like the Youngers in Scotland a few years earlier, his family too saw lager brewing in Glasgow as the way to counter the threat at home and overseas from lager brewers abroad. In 1884 Hugh, then only twenty-one, took control of Tennent's brewery by buying his elder brother's stake. Two continental brewers, a Dane and a German, were hired, new plant based on that found in a German lager brewery was installed in the Wellpark buildings, and lager brewing for export began in Glasgow in 1885.

By 1888 Tennent's was declaring that its lager would 'defy the most delicate palate to detect any difference between it and the best foreign article' – and it was cheaper, too. The following year a complete and separate lager brewery was built on the Wellpark site alongside the ale brewery. It opened in 1891 and ran until 1906, when it was reported that another new brewery 'complete in all details' had been built in the north-east part of the Wellpark site, 'devoted to the manufacture of lager, Munich and Pilsener beers', that is, both dark and light lagers.

Foreign sales were not the only reason some British brewers began producing lager. Commentators in the British brewing press continued to complain about the growing imports into Britain of German beers:

despite Barnard's sneers, between 1880 and 1895 the sale of German light beers, mainly Pilsner-type, in the UK increased fivefold. Baedeker's *Guide to London* in 1894 revealed that while bitter beer, ale or stout was 1½d or 2d a glass (that is, half-pint) in a 'Public House', 'good German Lager Bier' at 3d to 6d a glass 'is now very generally obtained at the larger restaurants, in some of which it has almost entirely supplanted the heavier English ales'.

However, early British lager brewers had technical problems their ale-brewing rivals did not suffer – for example, with the ice machines necessary to chill the brewery cellars where the beer was left to condition. Nor were the problems just technical: even when the product was right, the customers could not be tempted in sufficient quantities. The ale brewers had reacted to the demand for lighter, less alcoholic beers by producing mild and bitter ales of lower gravities, put on sale much sooner than in the past (and thus sweeter and less acid). Alfred Barnard wrote in 1889 that:

The cry of sedentary workers . . . has been of late years for a lighter and less heady beer. The gaseous German Lager has had a fair trial to supply this want, but except for about three weeks in the year, that beer seems ill-adapted to our climate. The English brewers have endeavoured to supply this want by brewing a light sparkling bitter ale, and from the encouragement they have received it is likely the importation of German beer will not increase.

Lager continued to be a minority product in Britain, more expensive than ale, and the specialist lager brewers faltered. Some survived by going for the export trade; others closed down. Several established English brewers tried making lager alongside their ales and stouts, including Henry Bentley's brewery at Woodlesford, near Leeds. In 1890 Alfred Barnard tried Bentley's 'English Lager Beer' in the brewery's cellars and wrote that it was 'quite equal to the Continental Lager, and equally sparkling'. In 1897 Allsopp's erected a 60,000 barrel lager plant at Burton upon Trent. But sales of lager in the UK remained at less than 1 per cent of total beer sales, and the vast majority of that continued to be imported from abroad. Allsopp's lager brewery equipment was eventually, in 1921, transferred from Burton to Arrol's of Alloa, in Scotland. That country was becoming the centre for what little lager brewing there was in the UK: John Jeffrey & Co. of the Heriot brewery in Edinburgh started lager brewing in 1902.

The interest in brewing lager by Allsopp's had as its background the increasing struggle for market share among Britain's brewers. In 1817 a House of Commons select committee found that about 30 per cent of the country's alehouses were tied to brewers through owner-ship or loans, a figure that rose to 50 per cent in London. The forces that had begun work in the eighteenth century meant that by the end of the nineteenth century the vast majority of pubs were tied to one brewer or another. This was particularly true in South-East England: a survey of Hertfordshire in 1903 found just 5 per cent of the county's pubs, eighty out of 1,566, were 'free' houses; seventy-three brewers, half of them from neighbouring counties, controlled the rest. (In Cheshire, by contrast, in 1897 43 per cent of the county's 1,589 pubs and beershops were free houses.) In many towns, one brewer had an effective monopoly: in Hoddesdon the local brewery, Christie & Co., controlled fifteen of the sixteen fully licensed pubs.

Several attempts had been made in the late 1810s and 1820s to bring in legislation to curb what was seen as the excessive power of the brewers who owned tied houses and introduce 'free trade' into the licensing system. Most of these Bills were defeated by the brewers' considerable parliamentary lobby, which included at least fifteen brewer-MPs such as Charles Barclay of Barclay Perkins, Sir Thomas Fowell Buxton of Truman's, Samuel Charles Whitbread and William Wigram of Meux Reid. One law change that did get through was the introduction of an 'intermediate' grade of beer in 1823, brewed at a strength between strong and table beer, to be sold by brewers not brewing any other type of beer. The advantage was meant to be that they paid just one guinea for a brewer's licence. If the idea was to give alehouse keepers an alternative source of supply to the big common brewers, the plan was a complete failure: only 137 intermediate beer brewing licences were ever taken out, and just seventeen intermediate beer brewers were still in business in 1830, against more than 1,500 'standard' brewers.

The next attempt by the government to tackle the perceived problems of the tied house came in 1830, with an Act 'to permit the general Sale of Beer and Cyder by retail in England', better known by its shorter name, the Beerhouse Act. The proclaimed motive of the Tory government of the time, led by the Duke of Wellington, was to promote free trade and encourage the drinking of beer rather than spirits; the Act allowed any householder who was eligible to pay the poor rate to sell beer, ale or porter by retail by purchasing a one-year excise licence for two guineas (£2 2s). The brewer's licence was fixed at 10s for the smallest operators, and only £2 for anyone producing 100–1,000 barrels a year.

The beerhouse system sidestepped the issuing of licences by magistrates, which was still necessary for anyone who wished to sell wine or spirits. Free traders wanted at least part of the licensing system removed from the magistrates' court because they suspected the magistrates of being too close to the big brewers, who now frequently mixed in the same social circles. They probably also hoped, optimistically, that the tied house system would be undermined by a flood of 'free' beerhouses. The Beerhouse Act further scrapped the duty on beer (though keeping it on malt), to encourage the new beerhouses to brew their own beer, while the duty on spirits was increased, again to encourage beer drinking.

The Beerhouse Act was one of the last pieces of legislation bought in by the Duke of Wellington's government before it had to face the electorate after the death of the king, George IV, and was at least in part an attempt to put a popular measure on the statute books to help ensure its re-election. It did not pass without a great deal of opposition from the growing teetotal movement, existing publicans and the magistracy, who objected strongly to the arrival of a new class of licensed premises over which they had no control. Many brewers also felt the new beerhouses would take business from brewers' tied full-licence houses.

There was an immediate rush to open beerhouses after 24 October 1830, when the Act came into force. Liverpool saw fifty new beerhouses open every day for weeks. Within six months there were more than 24,000 newly opened beerhouses, and by January 1832 there were just under 32,000 new 'persons licensed to sell beer' in England and Wales (the Act never applied to Scotland), of whom almost 13,500, or two out of five, brewed their own beer, representing 11 per cent of total beer production.

Many of these new beerhouses named themselves, in gratitude, after the new king whose signature passed the Act that gave them life, so that William IV is still the commonest king's name on English pubs, despite his comparatively short reign (the city of York had three King William IVs in 1872).

However, there is no hard evidence the Act either delivered a surge in drunkenness, as its teetotal opponents had feared, or damaged the business of the established brewers, as they had feared. In the area covered by one long-standing common brewer, Pryor's of Baldock – north Hertfordshire, mid-Bedfordshire and south Cambridgeshire – the three out of five new beerhouses not brewing their own beer were a terrific new market. Pryor's beer production leapt more than 50 per cent in 1831, the first year after the Beerhouse Act, and remained an average 66 per cent higher than it was in 1830 throughout the rest of the decade.

Over the nine years to 1841, in response to the large number of new outlets the Beerhouse Act had brought into being, the number of common brewers in England and Wales grew by a third, to 2,258, a leap of more than twice the rate of increase of the population. This upsurge in common brewers came despite a rise of some 3,000 each in the number of licensed victuallers (that is, full-licence inns and pubs) brewing their own beer, and in the number of brewing beerhouses. There were now almost 27,000 inns and pubs with breweries attached, 46 per cent of the total in England and Wales, and 16,600 beerhouses brewing their own beer, 39 per cent of all beerhouses. Together they represented 43 per cent of all licensed premises and 95 per cent of the 45,500 commercial breweries, and they made 40 per cent of the beer brewed commercially in England and Wales.

That year, 1841, was the zenith for home brew pub numbers. Thereafter inns, pubs and beerhouses brewing their own beer began to decline, in absolute and relative terms. By 1870, although there were 20,000 more inns and pubs in total than in 1832, and 15,600 more beerhouses, the numbers brewing their own beer had dropped to fewer than one in three pubs with full on-licences, and just one in five beerhouses. The common brewers, whose numbers had risen by 50 per cent in forty years to a peak of 2,512, now brewed three out of every four pints.

By the 1870s, particularly in the south of England, brewery openings were slowing as the market became saturated and the number of free houses available to sell to dropped. A boom in brewery openings was taking place in the industrialized and fast-expanding north-west of England, however: Lancashire and Cheshire saw a third of all new brewery openings in Great Britain in the 1860s, and the two counties made up a quarter of all new brewery openings in the 1870s.

The new breweries were frequently built in the 'tower brewery' style common from the 1870s, where gravity did as much work as possible. In a typical Victorian tower brewery, crushed grain would be carried to a hopper at the top of the tower by 'Jacob's ladder', a continuous steam-engine-driven belt. It would then be fed into the mash tun on the next floor down and mixed with hot liquor, often using a device called the Steel's Masher, invented by the Glaswegian brewer and brewers' engineer James Steel in the 1850s. By the second half of the century the bigger English brewers had largely stopped mashing their grain two or three times, and adopted the 'sparger', a mechanical device for spraying more hot water over the mash tun in use by Scottish brewers in the 1830s. When the grain had been mashed sufficiently, the resultant sweet wort flowed by gravity into the copper on the next floor, where it was boiled with hops.

From the copper the hot, now hop-flavoured wort ran down into a vessel called a hop-back or jack-back (back, or buck, being the old word for a water container, of which bucket is the diminutive). Here the hops still in the wort settled out, and the wort was then run into the coolers, shallow vessels no more than six or eight inches deep. The coolers were contained in a long room surrounded by louvred windows, which were opened to let the steam escape as the wort cooled; sometimes large air propellers, turned mechanically, were suspended above the coolers. It was a potentially unhygienic and dangerous cooling method: in relatively warm weather a brew could take hours to cool down sufficiently for fermentation to begin, and the wort was open to infection from wild yeasts and other bugs in the air around the brewery. Infected worts threw up a yeast head with a reddish tinge, which gave them the description 'foxed'.

'Artificial' cooling began to be introduced in the early decades of the nineteenth century – Brakspear's brewery in Henley, Oxfordshire, for example, had an 'attemperator' or 'refrigerator' supplied by Pontifex, the brewery engineers, installed in the 1830s, about the same time Guinness in Dublin installed wort refrigerators. By 1838 Samuel Morewood, author of a book on brewing, could declare that wort refrigeration was in general use. However, brewers continued to use open coolers along with paraflow coolers (which ran hot wort one way and cold water through a copper pipe the other), right into the twentieth century: the Hook Norton brewery was still using open coolers in the 1970s.

The coolers were generally in a long wing above the fermentation floor, from where the cooled wort ran next into whatever fermentation vessels the brewer preferred: squares, rounds or unions. Once fermentation and 'cleansing' (removing excess yeast) were complete, after about seven days, the new beer ran down one more floor to the ground, into racking tanks, where it could be racked into casks. Finally, if it was 'stock' beer, to be held back for maturing, the casks were transferred to the brewery cellars.

The bigger London breweries ran tours for middle- and upper-class sightseers. At Barclay Perkins, for a fee of one shilling to the brewery guide, you could sign your name in a visitors' book that included the signatures of Napoleon III, the future Edward VII, the Emperor of Russia and Garibaldi, liberator of Italy.

The Barclay Perkins brewery trip had its dangers. The guides liked to encourage first-time visitors to lean over the fermenting vessels and take a deep breath. The 'carbonic acid gas' – carbon dioxide – coming up from the strong beer as it fermented gave the unwary visitor a sharp and unpleasant punch in the back of the nose, as anyone who has ever done the same thing in a whisky distillery will know.

In 1851, the year of the Great Exhibition in Hyde Park, more than 50,000 visitors passed through the gates of Barclay Perkins's Anchor brewery in just five months. At the time it was certainly the largest brewery in Britain, and probably the largest in the world. Among the sights to be marvelled at were the 200 or so drayhorses which moved the beer about the streets of London – 'wonders in size and appearance' – and the almost equally magnificent draymen, fifty in number. One 'gigantic' red-faced drayman, with a 'dreamy, muddled look', admitted to William Rendle, the doctor treating him for erysipelas (a skin inflammation) that he drank 3 gallons of beer a day while out on his rounds, 24 pints – and he had one of the shortest delivery runs.

The horses in Barclay Perkins' stables were just a few of the estimated 3,000 owned by the larger London brewers in 1893, each one worth at least £90. The horses generally worked in threes, in what was known as 'unicorn fashion' – two at the pole and one in front – and they pulled a full dray weighing, including drayman, eight tons. Each team generally worked fourteen or sixteen hours a day, six days a week: out at 5 a.m. after an early breakfast of clover, hay and oats, and back in the stables at 7 p.m. (though Hoare's brewery in Wapping was famous for allowing its 160 horses to work only five days a week, and ten hours a day). The horses were trained to help lower the full butts, hogsheads and barrels of beer from the road down into the pub cellar, and a witness in 1868 said the greatest wonder he ever saw was a horse raising and lowering butts of beer outside a pub without any signal or word of command from the drayman, before moving back to the dray to be hooked on, and walk away to the next stop.

A horse, generally a Shire (considered the strongest of the native heavy breeds), was bought when six years old and sold when twelve. Its fate then was to end up, like another 26,000 horses in London each year, at one of Harrison Barber's seven slaughterhouses, such as the one in Garrett Lane, Wandsworth. There the horse carcasses would be transformed into everything from candlewax to catfood – or exported to Hamburg and made into sausage meat.

Like other breweries, even the biggest, Barclay Perkins was a family-run business. Even in 1889 the partners were all descendants of the Barclay, Perkins, Bevan and Gurney families who were the original investors in the concern in 1781. Each firm was run on the implicit understanding that it would be passed on to the heirs. If fathers passed away before sons were old enough to take over, then widows held the reins, as Sarah Eldridge did from 1846, when her husband Charles of the Dragon brewery, Dorchester died of apoplexy. If there were no sons available, only daughters, then sons-in-law were brought in, as happened to Eldridge's brewery when Sarah's son died in an accident and her daughter's husband, John Tizard, joined the business. If there were no direct heirs, the baton would be handed to more distant relatives. Edmund Fearnley was a 'beast salesman' at Smithfield Market in London, aged thirty-five, when his cousin at several removes George Whittingstall willed him a stake in a brewery in Watford in 1822. Edmund moved into the brewer's house, and in 1825, when George's sister Elizabeth died and left him the rest of the brewery property, changed his name by royal licence to Fearnley-Whittingstall.

There were 35,000 acres of hops under cultivation in Britain by 1800, and 50,000 by 1850. Hop growers were beginning to discover ways to combat the many ills that hops were heir to: around 1848, in an early form of biological pest control, ladybirds were introduced to the hop fields to eat the hop flies. Dusting with sulphur to control mould began around 1850, and simple insecticides such as tobacco juice and, later, quassia, were used from 1865 onwards. By 1884 spraying hops was all but universal.

Hop acreage hit a peak of 71,789 acres in 1878, with hops grown in forty English counties; however, the tiny Scottish hop industry, which operated in just five counties, disappeared in 1871, and Welsh hop growing ended in 1874.

New varieties of hop were still appearing: Bramling, an 'early' variety of Goldings, named after the Kentish village where it was discovered, was introduced in the 1860s. Richard Fuggle of Brenchley, Kent, unveiled the variety that still bears his name, the second great English hop, in 1875. Supposedly the first plant originated from a seed thrown out with the crumbs of a hop-picker's lunch at George Stace's farm in Horsmonden, Kent in 1861. By the 1930s 80 per cent of English hop production was Fuggles; unfortunately it is very prone to verticillium wilt, which first appeared in Kent in 1924, and acreage is now down to 10 per cent or so of the total.

After 1886 Britain's breweries rushed to turn themselves into partnerships, inspired by the extraordinary enthusiasm with which the share-buying public had greeted the flotation of Guinness's brewery for £6 million that October. This was the first big brewing partnership to turn itself into a limited company and offer shares to the public; the share offer was eighteen times over-subscribed, suggesting there was more than £100 million of investors' money looking for a brewery home: Barings, the bank handling the flotation, attracted much criticism by keeping a large part of the issue for itself and its friends, and most of the 6,000 members of the public who were actually allowed to buy Guinness shares ended up with just two or three £10 shares each.

Over the next fifteen years all the big brewing partnerships became limited companies: in 1889 alone, Whitbread, Ansells, Courage, Truman's and Watney's. The number of breweries with Ltd after their names rose from just seventeen 'pre-Guinness' to 111 in 1890 and 143 in 1895. Quite a few of the new limited companies were amalgamations of several small local brewers: Bristol United Breweries Ltd, floated in 1889, consisted of four breweries in Bristol and Bedminster;

Edinburgh United Breweries, formed the same year, was made up from four of the Scottish capital's brewers. The biggest amalgamation came in 1898, when three of the big old London porter breweries, Watney, Combe and Reid, came together to make the biggest brewing company in London, with its headquarters at Watney's brewery in Pimlico.

The rush to sell brewery shares to the public was not to enable the brewery owners to amass fortunes: the leading brewers in the counties were already wealthy from their partnerships. Rather, the need was generally to raise capital to join in the rush for tied houses. In 1869, a new Beerhouse Act began to bring beerhouse licensing under the control of magistrates for the first time, which meant that it became much harder to open new licensed premises. Licensing benches around the country were made up of men whose instinct was to restrict opportunities for drinking by members of classes 'lower' than their own. The temperance movement was growing in power, and many magistrates were sympathizers, at the least, with organizations such as the prohibition-favouring United Kingdom Alliance. Pub and beerhouse numbers remained virtually static between 1870 and 1880, though the population rose by more than 12 per cent, and outlets could no longer open virtually at will. Those pubs and beerhouses already in existence suddenly became more valuable. Brewers were realizing that tied houses, at one time perhaps a nuisance, because they often represented a client who had failed to pay off a beer debt, were now a necessity. Every free house snapped up by and tied to your rival was one fewer outlet to which you could sell your own beer.

To begin with, the increasing dearth of free houses was hardest on the smallest brewers. They were also hit, paradoxically, by Gladstone's Licensing Act of 1880, which removed all tax on malt. Instead, for the first time in fifty years, tax was imposed on beer, at a rate of 6s 3d per 'standard' barrel of 1057 OG, with the tax rate varying up and down pro rata to the strength of the actual beer brewed. Gladstone boasted that he was doing the brewers a good turn, by making the mash tun 'free' and allowing them to use what materials they wanted, so that they could replace malt with (cheaper) rice or maize if they liked. However, the beer tax represented a hidden increase of almost a shilling a barrel on the old malt tax. In addition, the excise was allowed to calculate the tax to be paid either on the strength of the wort or on the amount of malt and sugar used, whichever gave the greater amount of money to the revenue. This penalized the less efficient small brewer, who used more malt per barrel than the large brewers and thus found himself paying more tax per pint.

Gladstone's changes also hit the huge number of private brewers, who ranged from owners of stately homes where beer was brewed for servants and household guests, through farms that provided free beer brewed on the premises for the farm workers, to private households that brewed solely for the family. Now, if the house they lived in was worth more than £15 a year, they had to pay full duty on all the beer they brewed, which meant keeping records of all the raw materials used. In 1870 there were more than a hundred thousand householders, large and small, paying the then 4s private brewing licence. After the 1880 Act the number of licensed private brewers plunged precipitously, dropping more than 80 per cent to just over 17,000 by 1895.

The strength of the 'standard' barrel was reduced to 1055 OG in 1889, partly to try to compensate the smaller brewers, but they were still under increasing pressure. From 1880 the number of common breweries in England and Wales began to go into reverse: but it was only those producing fewer than 10,000 barrels a year which were closing. Larger breweries were becoming more numerous: the number of common breweries producing more than 20,000 barrels a year rose from 166 in the whole United Kingdom in 1871, 6 per cent of the total, to 296 in 1891, 13 per cent of the total. In 1891 the biggest two brewers were producing more than a million barrels a year each, five times the amount the biggest brewers managed in 1834.

Brewery openings plunged to little more than a handful in the 1890s, as one after another saw itself being taken over by a rival that wanted to increase its numbers of tied houses. While in the past breweries were bought for the continuing businesses they represented, now the breweries themselves were less valuable than their pubs. The proprietor of the Kingsbury brewery in St Albans retired in 1889, and the business was auctioned in two parts. The brewery and thirty-two tied houses went for £24,100; a week later, to the surprise of all observers, the twenty-six remaining tied houses went for £25,000 in total, twice the expected amount, as seven local brewers fought for the pubs.

Many big brewers, such as Worthington, tried to remain outside the tied house system, but by 1895 found they were having to play an expensive game of catch-up or lose considerable amounts of sales. Even in 1892 a Home Office survey of England and Wales identified seventy-six breweries which owned more than 100 pubs or beerhouses each. This was actually an under-estimation of the extent of large tied-house brewery estates, since the survey ignored pubs tied by lease to brewers: Georges in Bristol leased another 120 houses on top of the 350 it owned. Ownership of pubs by brewers was still mostly a regional phenomenon: only ten of the big pub owners were based in London, and only two of the biggest twelve were London brewers. However, the London brewers had always tied publicans to them by loans, rather than buying the pub: this worked well for the pub landlord, who would often have one loan from his porter supplier, one from his ale brewer and one from his spirits distiller.

At the same time, in some parts of the country, notably the West Country, the West and North Midlands, the Welsh borders and areas of Lancashire and Yorkshire, drinkers were still supplied by many pubs and beerhouses brewing their own beer. Back in 1823 two-thirds of the commercially sold beer in Yorkshire was made by publican brewers. Even in 1880, in Leeds 42 per cent of all beer produced locally was made by the city's 130-plus own-brew licensees. That figure had fallen by only a fifth in twenty years, though nationally the percentage of beer produced by pub and beerhouse brewers had halved over the same period. Other places where large numbers of home-brew pubs continued to survive in the 1890s included Derby (which had around fifty), Kidderminster (again around fifty), Worcester (more than sixty) and Preston and Nottingham (more than a hundred each).

The biggest centre of own-brew pubs was the Black Country, with more than 400 around 1898. Dudley had more than seventy pubs and beerhouses brewing their own beer in and around the centre of town, and the same number in settlements outside; Halesowen, Oldbury, Wednesbury, Wolverhampton and West Bromwich each had a dozen or more home-brew pubs; Tipton had forty; Walsall topped fifty; Stourbridge had more than sixty. However, all the home-brew pubs were under increasing pressure: their numbers across England and Wales more than halved between 1890 and 1900, from around 9,600 to fewer than 4,500. The only thing that went up was their average output, as the larger own-brew pubs survived while the smaller ones gave in. However, while average own-brew pub and beerhouse output doubled or trebled between 1832 and 1900, the average common brewer's output went up four times.

The situation in Scotland was rather different as the Beerhouse Act never applied there. The number of 'brewing victuallers' in Scotland was less than 2 per cent of all licensed outlets (less than 1 per cent after 1880), and the tied house system that developed was based almost entirely on loans to publicans, not ownership of pubs. This was in large part because the licensing system licensed the individual rather than, as in England and Wales, the premises. In Scotland, therefore, little extra value was attached to a building through its being used as a pub or bar, unlike in England. Even by 1914 only an estimated 60 per cent of Scottish licensed drink outlets were tied to brewers, mostly through loans.

Scotland also had a very different pattern of brewery openings from England and Wales, with a boom in the first twenty years of the century, a comparative slump from the 1820s to the 1870s (except for a slight rise in the 1850s) and a positive explosion from the 1880s. Much of this expansion was down to a significant leap in beer exports, both 'internal' (to England, particularly the North-East, Merseyside and London) and external, especially India (for the troops), Australia and the Far East. Allowing for the fact that Scots beer must also have left from English ports, the country's share of total UK beer exports may have been as high as 50 per cent by 1890. As it had only 5 per cent of the UK's total number of common breweries, this is a truly remarkable performance.

While Scotland had 8 per cent more breweries in 1900 than it had in 1890, south of the border brewery numbers dropped by more than 20 per cent in the same decade, with hundreds of sometimes long-established breweries disappearing. The pace was occasionally frenetic: to take just one example, in ten months from October 1897 to August 1898 one medium-sized brewery, Benskin's Watford Brewery Co. Ltd, took over five rivals across a thirty-mile arc of Hertfordshire and Bedfordshire, more than quadrupling its pubs and beerhouses estate, which had previously numbered just sixty. The directors of Benskin's planned for their expansion by commissioning a big new 150-quarter tower brewery from the brewery architect George Adlam. It was a busy time for Adlam, who was involved in four other projects, as it was for other brewery designers: openings may have dried up, breweries may have been closing at a rate of almost one a week, but between 1890 and 1900 more than 140 major extensions and rebuildings to breweries around Great Britain were carried out. Fewer but bigger: the theme of the 1890s was to dominate the coming century.

CHAPTER EIGHT

GONE FOR A BURTON

the twentieth century, part one

Good beer is the basis of true temperance.

Daily Express,
25 January 1919

The twentieth century started off badly for brewers. The tax on beer went up 24 per cent in 1900, to 7s 9d a barrel, supposedly to fund the Boer War. However, when the war was over, the tax stayed in place. An outbreak of arsenical poisoning in November 1900 in Lancashire and Staffordshire in which more than 3,000 people fell ill and seventy died was traced to contaminated glucose used in beer brewing. Beer consumption declined by around 7 per cent nationally between 1900 and 1910, and by around 14 per cent in England. The working classes had other distractions to spend their money on: football, the music hall and seaside excursions, according to Sir Austen Chamberlain, the Chancellor of the Exchequer, in his Budget speech of 1905. At the same time the temperance movement, growing in strength, was determined to close pubs and restrict drink sales.

Sunday closing had already been imposed in Scotland (in 1853), Wales (1881) and Ireland (1878), and was only narrowly defeated in England the year it was imposed on Wales. Licensing magistrates had begun to refuse licences to public houses on the grounds of 'super-fluity' – that there were too many pubs in the area. This policy the House of Lords declared perfectly legal in a landmark case in 1891 known as *Sharpe* v. *Wakefield*, after the Westmorland landlady whose pub had its licence taken away and the chairman of the local licensing board that removed it.

There was no compensation for the brewer if one of its properties was refused a licence, and after 1901 magistrates were starting to throw themselves into the cause of closing pubs: in 1903 240 pub and beerhouse licences were refused in England and Wales. After pressure from the brewers was exerted on the Conservative Party, the Licensing Act of 1904 was passed. This finally provided for a payment to the brewer or landlord if magistrates closed a pub as 'superfluous'. The money was to come out of a fund levied on the trade. The brewers and beer retailers, naturally, nicknamed this the 'mutual burial fund'. Up to the end of 1914, 3,736 fully licensed pubs and 5,881 beerhouses were closed under the Act, around 10 per cent of the country's total stock. Manchester alone had lost more than 300 pubs and beerhouses by May 1907.

However, over the years brewers worked out that not only did the compensation scheme increase the value of their surviving pubs, in many cases they actually made money out of the closures. Edward Lake of Greene King told the company's shareholders in 1911 that while the Bury St Edmunds brewer had paid a levy of £9,299 it had been given compensation of £11,071 for the pubs and beerhouses it owned that had been closed by magistrates, and had then made another £5,963 selling the de-licensed properties as homes – a net profit of £7,735.

Meanwhile the Liberals, who had become firmly linked to the temperance cause, as the Conservatives were to the brewers', felt the 1904 Act went nowhere near far enough in restricting the licensed trade. In 1907, when the Liberals were next back in power, they brought out a Bill which would have placed a fourteen-year time limit on all public house licences. At the end of that period, licences would be renewed only on payment to the Treasury of the 'monopoly value', the extra worth given to a house by virtue of its being a licensed pub, while the people in the area could vote on whether the pub should stay open. The Bill also gave licensing magistrates the right to refuse a licence to a 'tied' house, and banned the employment of women in pubs and beerhouses, thus killing off the barmaid.

This measure attracted huge public opposition, with a massive meeting in Hyde Park, London attended by half a million people who had arrived from around the country by special trains. There were also big demonstrations in Kent and East London organized by the hop growers (most of Kent's seasonal hop pickers came from the East End). Though the Bill passed the Commons, it was thrown out by the Lords in November 1908; and, since the Liberals had managed to lose eight by-elections while the Bill was being debated, no attempt was made to bring it back.

In 1909 the Liberals, with David Lloyd George as Chancellor of the Exchequer, tried to revenge themselves on the bigger brewers with a Budget that massively increased the cost of a brewing licence, from just £1 to 12s per fifty barrels over the first hundred. The Budget also put up the cost of a public house licence, from a maximum of £60 a year to – in a lot of cases in London – several hundred pounds. The additional burden would cost brewers £4 million a year. The London brewers reacted by lifting the price of beer from 4d a quart to 5d, the first increase for generations, which caused a furore: many members of the government interpreted the price rise as an attempt by the brewers to discredit the Liberals.

The Budget was voted down by the House of Lords, and the price of beer dropped to 4d again. However, the crisis caused by the Lords rejecting Lloyd George's Budget led to the introduction of the Parliament Act of 1911, restricting the right of the upper house to block legislation passed up from the lower house. The Budget, with its big increase in licence fees, was finally rammed through. The price of a quart, however, stayed at 4d: the brewers had found that a big increase in pub licence fees meant a much lower assessment for council rates, because the extra expense of the higher licence lowered the values of their pubs.

Breweries were still closing at an average of one a week. The United States had just, in 1904, pushed itself into second place in the league of beer-producing nations behind Germany, leaving the UK third. But there were still 1,503 common brewers left in England and Wales (ninety of them in London), 102 in Scotland and thirty in Ireland in 1907. In addition there were 2,066 fully licensed pubs and inns licensed to brew their own beer (all but one in England and Wales; only one in London) and 1,103 English and Welsh beerhouses still brewing their own (none in London). There were also eighty-eight brewing off-licences (a third of them around Worcester and Wolverhampton). However, two-thirds of common brewers each made less than 10,000 barrels a year, with the average for the 1,000 smallest commercial 'non-pub' brewers probably still below 1,200 barrels. At the same time, private brewers had more than halved in number from twelve years earlier, to just 8,605 'persons licensed as brewers not for sale' in England and Wales, forty-seven in Scotland and none in the whole of Ireland.

Business was not helped by the growing public demand for bottled beers, which had smaller profit margins than beer in cask, in part because it required expensive filtering and filling equipment. Many breweries that had spent unwisely in the rush to acquire tied houses at the end of the nineteenth century struggled to make decent profits in the first decade of the twentieth. They were hampered, often, by management which could not respond to falling sales and changing consumers. A business consultant called in to report on the management of Morgan's of Norwich in 1906 found that only one out of the company's five directors had any real managerial competency, and he turned up just twice a week for four hours a time. Several big-name brewers found themselves so financially embarrassed they were forced at least temporarily into voluntary liquidation or receivership, including the Burton brewer Thomas Salt & Co. in 1906 and Ind Coope of Romford in 1909.

Tastes were still altering, and brewers were inventing novel beer styles to cope. In 1902 Thomas Wells Thorpe, the long-serving head brewer and newly appointed managing director of Mann, Crossman & Paulin in Whitechapel, introduced what the firm later claimed was the first of a new kind of beer, bottled brown ale. Mann's Brown Ale was a version of dark mild in a bottle, and was said to be 'the sweetest beer in London'.

Another new style of sweet dark beer appeared in 1910, after the Kentish brewer Mackeson of Hythe acquired the patents to a method of brewing made with an addition of unfermentable lactose sugar, derived from milk. This was put into the wort at a rate of nine pounds to the barrel, half an ounce per pint. The new beer was called 'milk stout' ('stout' now meant simply 'black beer' rather than strong beer; Mackeson stout as brewed today is only 3 per cent alcohol, less than most surviving mild beers). Mackeson soon licensed the production of milk stout to other brewers: Massey's Burnley Brewery was advertising its 'new Milk Stout' by January 1911, for example, and thirteen other brewers were also making milk stout by 1912.

New technology had to be grasped, too. Steam drays had been replacing horses since the beginning of the century – Hanson's brewery at Kimberley, near Nottingham, bought its first steam dray from Thorneycroft's of Basingstoke in 1902 for £652, for example. Around the end of the decade brewers began buying lorries, with Phipps' brewery in Northampton, to name one, acquiring two 'petrol wagons' in 1910 and three more soon after.

If brewers thought life was tough, it soon become much tougher. Three days after the outbreak of war with Germany and Austria on 5 August 1914, Asquith's Liberal government passed the Defence of the Realm Act, better known as DORA, which included powers for the Home Secretary to make Orders dealing with the production and sale of all alcoholic drinks. At the end of August the Intoxicating Liquor (Temporary Restrictions) Act gave licensing magistrates the power to limit opening hours in any area, on the recommendation of the local chief constable. In London, where opening hours had been 5 a.m. to 12.30 a.m., pubs were ordered to shut at 11 p.m.

A month later, a universal closing time of 10 p.m. was imposed. By the end of January 1915 more than 420 of the country's 1,000 licensing districts had imposed even stricter hours. Meanwhile, in November 1914 beer duty was increased almost threefold, from 7s 9d to £1 3s a 'standard' (1055 OG) barrel, sending the price of a pint up 20 per cent from 2½d to 3d.

Even then, there were those who said alcohol was still hampering the war effort: Lloyd George did not pass up the opportunity to attack his old enemies the brewers, declaring in a speech at Bangor in February 1915 that drink was 'doing us more damage in the war than all the German submarines put together'. A few weeks later, when he had become Minister of Munitions, he met a deputation of shipbuilders complaining about production being affected because of heavy drinking by their workforce. In response to their call for complete prohibition for the duration of the war (as happened in Russia), Lloyd George said: 'The feeling is that if we are to settle German militarism, we must first of all settle with the drink. We are fighting Germany, Austria and drink; and as far as I can see, the greatest of these three deadly foes is drink.' The words were quickly quoted in the press and, understandably, infuriated both the drinks trade and the shipbuilding unions.

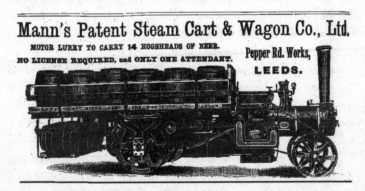

New technology, Edwardian-style: a motor "lurry" (sic) of the sort that began to replace horse-drawn drays from about 1903.

The government backed away from any thought of a full ban on alcohol, despite a petition signed by two million people in 1916 calling for prohibition 'during the war and for six months after'. It did consider nationalizing the entire drinks industry, but passed over the idea because of the cost of compensation, estimated at £225 million. Instead it brought in the Defence of the Realm No. 3 Act, which established the Central Control Board (Liquor Traffic) in June 1915. Permitted opening hours in many parts of the country, especially in Scotland and the north of England, were slashed from the pre-war sixteen or seventeen hours a day (nineteen and a half in London) to five and a half hours on weekdays and five hours on Sundays. An 'afternoon break' in serving was imposed, and evening closing had to be at 9 p.m. or 9.30 p.m. 'Treating' – buying a drink for someone else – was banned, thus outlawing the great social institution of the 'round'. The new regulations covered half of Great Britain by the end of 1915, and 94 per cent of the population by the end of the war.

Much scandal was caused by reports of munitions workers drinking away their wages when they should have been making shells for the guns on the front line. To show the government was in charge of the situation, it was decided to put pubs and breweries under state direction in areas where this was supposed to be happening. In what became known later as the State Management Scheme, the Control Board took direct control of pubs in three areas: Enfield Lock in north London (where there was a huge, if secret, munitions factory); Invergordon/Cromarty in Scotland, where a naval dockyard for the Home Fleet had been built; and Carlisle/Gretna Green, where another big munitions factory at Gretna had brought in thousands of workers from outside. The Carlisle nationalization eventually included state purchase of five local breweries (all but one of which were ultimately closed), and all the pubs on both sides of the Solway Firth, an area of 500 square miles.

Brewery workers had been encouraged to join the army or navy, with many breweries promising to give half pay to their dependants while they were away. Many bigger breweries lost four out of ten men to the forces. The subsequent labour shortage led brewers to what one, Sydney Nevile of Brandon's brewery in Putney, called the 'desperate expedient' of employing women for labouring tasks such as rolling barrels and cask-washing, and, in some breweries, malting. Nevile discovered only one problem with hiring some 'surprisingly efficient' females: the cellarmen complained about the ladies' foul language. Brewers also found their lorries, and even their drayhorses, requisitioned by the War Department.

Beer duty rose only slightly, to £1 5s a barrel by April 1917, but increasingly stringent restrictions on output were brought in from April 1916. The restrictions were expressed in terms of 'standard' barrels of 1055 OG, and effectively meant that brewers could brew less of their regular-strength beers, or more of weaker brews. The first restriction was a comparatively benign limit of 85 per cent of the previous twelve months' production, April 1915 to March 1916. In 1917, however, with Lloyd George now Prime Minister, and German U-boats squeezing food imports from America, the policy was to save grain for food production rather than use it in alcoholic drink: in February all malting of barley was ordered to stop, and in April brewers were ordered to produce no more than a third of 1915/16's 'standard' barrelage. Committees were drawn up to look at the cost of nationalizing the brewing industry and closing down much of the existing production, concentrating it in a few large centres.

Beer was suddenly in short supply, with production falling from thirty million bulk barrels in 1916 to nineteen million barrels. Many pubs could get only one barrel a week, and were having to keep their doors shut. Worse, when you got any beer, it was dreadfully weak, as breweries tried to make the grain they were allowed go as far as possible: the average strength of beer in 1917 was a fifth lower than in 1916, and three-quarters of the pre-war level. It also cost twice as much as pre-war beer, at fourpence a pint. Industrial unrest in the summer of 1917, at least in part caused by the beer situation, made the government think again, and the restrictions were eased for the second half of the year. One music-hall artist, Ernie Mayne, performed

a song called 'Lloyd George's Beer', about the 'Government Ale', as
the weak brew was nicknamed:

> *Lloyd George's beer, Lloyd George's beer,*
> *At the brewery there's nothing doing –*
> *All the waterworks are brewing*
> *Lloyd George's beer.*
> *Oh they say it's a terrible war*
> *And there never was a war like this before*
> *But the worst thing that ever happened in this*
> *   war*
> *Was Lloyd George's beer.*

It was probably no consolation to soldiers home on leave and faced
with far weaker beer than they remembered from before the war that
German brewers were having to brew at no more than 25 per cent
of pre-war production. The Central Control Board quickly banned
brewers from using the term 'Government Ale' for beers under 1036
OG on price lists. A strange note went out from the Ministry of Food
in November 1917 to all hoteliers asking them to put up prominent
notices urging guests 'to refrain from drinking beer, in order that there
may be more beer for the working classes'. Instead, the ministry said,
hotel guests should drink light wine, on which all import restrictions
had just been lifted.

In August 1917 Lloyd George declared himself against brewing
industry nationalization, not least because the estimated cost had risen
to £1 billion. But the next year, April 1918, the restrictions on the
industry were tightened again, with duty doubled to £2 10s per standard barrel, production limited still further, and a maximum average
gravity of 1030 for 50 per cent of all production imposed. (Ireland,
however, was allowed an average gravity of 1045; partly because the
big stout producers such as Guinness simply could not brew to an
average of 1030 OG and still make a recognizable stout, partly so as
not to add weak beer to the many grievances the Irish already had in

1918.) Beer production in 1918/19 actually increased by around 22 per cent, though average beer strength dropped by a similar amount, to 1030.5 OG.

The end of the war did not bring much respite. Beer duty was raised to £3 10s a standard barrel in April 1919 and £5 in 1920, almost thirteen times its pre-war level. Even taking inflation into account, the tax on a pint was more than five times higher than in 1913. Output control ceased in 1919 but a maximum average OG remained in place: 1044 in Great Britain, 1051 in Ireland. Price control, imposed in October 1917, was not removed until August 1921, a month before OG restrictions were lifted, and almost three years after the war ended.

By now there were far fewer brewers around to celebrate: between 1910 and 1920 the number of brewing companies in the UK (including Ireland) dropped by more than a quarter, from 1,284 to 941, while the total number of brewers-for-sale, including pubs and beerhouses brewing their own, fell 35 per cent from 4,512 to 2,914. Ironically, the war years had been good for brewery profits, particularly after 1917, and particularly for the larger brewers such as Whitbread in London and Mitchells & Butlers in Birmingham, and national concerns such as Bass and Guinness. It has been estimated that average profits for brewers who were limited companies were around 75 per cent higher in 1917–20 than they were in 1910–13.

Although production rose to thirty-five million bulk barrels in 1919, a similar level to that of the Edwardian era, this was beer at a much lower strength than Edwardian drinkers would have accepted. The problem was that taking beers back up to their pre-war gravities would have meant, because of the higher tax on stronger beers and increased raw material costs, a price increase of a penny or penny-halfpenny a pint. This represented a 20 per cent rise when the average cost of a pint in the public bar was just 5d. The permanent effect of the Great War on British beer was thus to push down the strength of each style by around 20 or 25 per cent. Porter, for example, dropped from a pre-war 1055 OG to 1036 post-war, IPA on average from 1065 to 1048 over the same period, mild from 1048 to 1032. The government also brought in an extra incentive to produce more but weaker beer in 1923: duty regulations were changed so that brewers were taxed on the number of 'standard' barrels they produced, but given a 20 per cent rebate per bulk barrel. The more bulk barrels per standard barrel, that is, the weaker the actual output, the less tax was paid.

Even Guinness, in the newly independent Irish Free State, was not immune: the Dublin government was not going to give up tax revenues by reducing beer duty from Westminster's levels. Guinness Extra Stout, 1074 OG before the war, had hit 1049 in 1918 and recovered only to 1054 a year after the war ended. It stayed at that strength, four degrees below the gravity of pre-war Guinness porter, until the Second World War brought further restrictions. Guinness porter, at the same time, dropped from 1058 OG to 1036 during the war, before rising slightly to 1041 in 1923.

The war brought human tragedies to many breweries. At Watney Combe Reid, 1,051 directors, staff (the salaried) and employees (the waged majority) joined His Majesty's forces and 110 were killed, roughly one in ten. Casualties among officers were proportionally more than double those among the rank and file; since the sons of brewery directors and partners, thanks to their social backgrounds and education, were recruited straight into the officer classes, the young men who were meant to be the next generation of brewery managers were prominently represented among those doubly decimated in the slaughter of battles such as the Somme and Ypres. Statistically, probably one company in five had someone killed who was a director or partner, or in line to become a director or partner. Alfred Pope of Eldridge Pope, the Dorchester brewers, had ten sons; four never returned from the battlefield.

In Hertfordshire three of the five biggest brewing concerns in the county were affected. At Simpson's of Baldock, Lieutenant Arthur Shaw Hellier, the only son of the brewery's owner, Evelyn Shaw Hellier, was killed in action in the Dardanelles in August 1915, aged twenty-nine, leaving his spinster sister as the heir to the company. A few months earlier, in May 1915, Lieutenant Geoffrey Reid, only son of

Percy Reid of Pryor Reid in Hatfield, was killed near Ypres, aged twenty-seven, a short time after he had joined the Pryor Reid board. His father decided that, with no heir to carry it on, the company should be wound up once the war was over. In 1919–20 its 150 pubs were split between two rising regional concerns, Green's of Luton and Benskin's of Watford.

At the Hoddesdon brewery of Christie & Co., Captain John Christie came back from the war with the Military Cross, and debilitating headaches from wounds received in the trenches. He was apprenticed to a brewer in Kent (it was normal practice for young men destined for the family brewery to spend their pupillage with another company) and came back to Hoddesdon, where he rose to be under-brewer and a board member. He never had the chance to succeed his father as chairman, however: in 1927, still suffering pain from his war wounds after twelve years, he shot himself in the head. A month after his death the company and its 150 or so pubs were sold to the Cannon Brewery of St John Street, Clerkenwell, for just over £500,000.

The takeover of Christie's brewery was one among many: between 1920 and 1930 the number of brewery companies in the UK fell by around 40 per cent, to 559, as their rivals bought them for their pub holdings. The list of acquisitions of Mann, Crossman & Paulin was typical of the trail large companies were cutting through their smaller brethren: Michell, Goodman Young & Co Ltd at the Stamford Hill brewery, Stoke Newington, bought for £80,000 in 1919; Brandon's brewery, Putney, with seventy-six pubs, acquired in 1920; Best's brewery, Camberwell, and six pubs, taken over in 1924 for £44,000; the Hornchurch Brewery Co. Ltd in 1925, for £171,000; Henry Luker & Co. Ltd at the Middleton brewery, Southend-on-Sea, for £285,000 in 1929, with forty-three pubs.

The City of London – the actual Square Mile – lost its last brewery in 1922, when the former Calvert's brewery in Upper Thames Street, known since 1860 as the City of London Brewery Co. Ltd, closed and transferred production to Stansfeld & Co.'s Swan brewery in Fulham, which it had taken over in 1919. Another of the great nineteenth-century porter breweries, Meux, closed its brewery at the bottom of Tottenham Court Road in 1921 and moved production to Thorne Brothers' brewery in Nine Elms Lane, Vauxhall, which Meux had acquired in 1914. (The Meux site eventually became the Dominion theatre.)

Own-brew pubs and beerhouses, meanwhile, were stopping brewing and taking common brewers' beers instead at a rate of two a week in the 1920s, as their numbers more than halved to below 900. Some own-brew pubs, like the Old Star in Stourbridge, Worcestershire, kept by William Hughes, had malted their own grain as well, and sold malt to local grocers, who would retail it by the peck (a quarter of a bushel; very roughly, 10½ pounds in weight) to housewives who still brewed in their own homes. The Old Star also supplied beer to pubs in the surrounding Black Country villages such as Lye, Brierley Hill and Netherend. When the First World War ended, Hughes still had plenty of local competition: there were more than twenty other own-brew pubs and beerhouses in Stourbridge itself, and another forty-two in the five nearest villages. The numbers fell away rapidly. Ten were gone by 1921, another sixteen by 1923, fifteen more by 1930, including Hughes: two-thirds of the local own-brew pubs ceased brewing in ten years. The same was happening elsewhere.

The problem was that beer-drinking was declining: consumption per head, which had already dropped from 242 pints a year in 1900–4 to 215 pints a year by 1910–14, was just 132 pints a year during the First World War, and stayed close to that level, 45 per cent below consumption when Queen Victoria died, throughout the 1920s. Even rising real incomes in the late 1920s failed to lift beer sales: there were now too many other things to spend money on, and besides, pub opening hours were not much better than they had been during the war: the Licensing Act of 1921 was a long way from a return to the sixteen- or nineteen-hour drinking day available in August 1914. It effectively set in concrete for the next sixty years many of the First World War's restrictions. In London, permitted drinking time was now any nine hours between 11 a.m. and 11 p.m., with a compulsory two-hour break in the afternoon; elsewhere, pubs could open for only eight hours and had to shut by 10 p.m., again with a two-hour afternoon break. On Sundays pubs could open for just five hours, which generally meant a five-hour dry gap between 2 p.m. and 7 p.m.

One set of drinking establishments was free from many of the restrictions placed on pubs and beerhouses, particularly Sunday closing (in Wales) and afternoon closing. Clubs as an upper-middle-class phenomenon had grown up in the eighteenth century; the working men's clubs movement had begun in the 1860s in an attempt to offer the working classes a teetotal alternative to the pub. Its promoters rapidly realized that establishments which banned drinking would attract very few members, and the sale of alcohol was soon allowed. In 1887 there were just under 2,000 registered clubs in England and Wales, 328 of them members of the Working Men's Club and Institute Union. By the start of the First World War there were more than 8,700 registered clubs, 1,600 of them CIU members, and CIU clubs had almost half a million members. During the war the CIU felt strongly that its clubs were being discriminated against by the brewers: the clubs complained loudly that they were being conned into paying too much for their beer by brewers who applied wartime taxes as if the beer the clubs received were full strength instead of watered-down 'Government Ale'. In addition, when beer was short, the clubs found they were at the end of the queue, with brewers giving their pubs preferential treatment.

The resentments boiled over in calls towards the end of the war among CIU members for the establishment of 'clubs' breweries', to be owned by the clubs themselves. Three clubs' cooperative breweries had actually been started before the war, though with limited success. The Burnley Clubs Brewery Ltd dated back to 1901, and ran for almost fifty years. The North of England Clubs brewery leased the Rainton brewery in East Rainton, County Durham, in 1905 but collapsed in 1909. A brewery was started in Leeds in 1911 by the local Liberal clubs, 'in practical protest against brewers' profiteering', and had collapsed within a couple of years, but was reformed in 1914, and was still thriving in 1919.

That year it became possible to obtain new brewers' licences again, and the number of commercial breweries going out of business meant clubs had a wide choice of premises in which to start their own breweries. The clubs were booming: there were 2,000 CIU-affiliated clubs in 1920, with just under a million members, out of 9,000 registered clubs in total. The Coventry Clubs' brewery was running by June 1919. One month later the lengthily-named South Wales and Monmouthshire United Clubs brewery began brewing at the former D. & T. Jenkins' Crown brewery near Pontyclun, Glamorgan. The Medway Federation of Clubs Brewery Ltd acquired Thomas Danes & Son's Anchor brewery in Aylesford, Kent in 1920. The Northants & Leicestershire Clubs' Co-operative Brewery opened in Leicester in 1921. In 1924 (by which time there were 2,500 CIU clubs) the Yorkshire Clubs Brewery Ltd was founded in Robert Cattle's former brewery in Pocklington in the East Riding, moving to York in 1933.

The Northern Clubs Federation Brewery, which was to become the largest and longest-lived of the clubs breweries, and the only one still open in the twenty-first century, got off to a poor start. It put down a £2,300 deposit on the disused Smart's brewery in Alnwick, Northumberland, in 1919, but found the equipment, which had not been used for almost twenty years, covered in rust and verdigris and useless for brewing. In 1921 it bought John Harper Graham's Hedley Street brewery in Newcastle upon Tyne, which had been used during the war to produce beer for the troops. By 1927 the Federation brewery was successful enough to move to larger premises, leasing John Buchanan's Hanover Square brewery, and then buying it outright two years later.

The same themes that characterized the post-1918 years would continue throughout the century: massive overcapacity in the brewing industry, so that overheads were too high and profits too low; the need to maintain production volumes, made manifest in regular takeovers of and mergers with other pub-owning brewers, to acquire their outlets and customers; the fall in beer turnover in the pub, coupled with the drop in strength of beer, causing quality problems in the glass that would challenge the brewers.

The next great hurdle, however, was the effect of the Great Depression, and in particular the Budget introduced by the Labour Chancellor of the Exchequer, Philip Snowden, in 1931. It was intended as a response to the crisis being caused by unemployment, but the more than 40 per cent rise in beer duty it introduced, to £5 4s a barrel, equivalent to an extra penny a pint, brought a new crisis for Britain's brewers. Output fell nationally by around eight million barrels between 1931 and 1933; consumption per head dropped to just 104 pints a year, 20 per cent down on the 1920s.

The Brewers' Society, formed in 1904 from three bodies representing the country, London and Burton brewers, lobbied furiously. The Chancellor in 1933, Neville Chamberlain, agreed to rebase beer duty in a way that effectively meant a 35 per cent cut in the tax on a beer of 1040 OG, to below the level of 1930. However, he got the brewers to agree that for their part they would drop the price of beer by a penny a pint; lift the average gravity by two degrees; make more beer available; and use more home-grown barley.

The brewers agreed, but secretly they were a little worried about promising to produce more beer: there was a feeling about that only middle-aged and elderly men drank beer, and that consumption was falling because the people who drank it were dying out. Certainly this was what was happening to porter: like London's old porters, who had given the beer its name, it was fading away. There were only fifty former Fellowship porters still alive in 1924, and just sixteen left in 1932. Truman's, once one of the three great porter brewers, stopped making the beer in 1930. In Ireland Guinness was still brewing it, mostly for the Dublin and Belfast markets, but as early as 1921 the chairman of Murphy's brewery in Cork had declared that 'porter is now practically dead in the South of Ireland'.

To try to ensure that all beer did not go the same way as porter, the Brewers' Society under Sydney Nevile, now of Whitbread, decided to commission an advertising campaign, paid for by a levy on the membership, under the slogan 'Beer is Best'. It was launched in the first week of December 1933, by coincidence the same week that prohibition ended in the United States. The campaign was condemned as a 'sinister attempt to enslave youth to the Drink Habit' by temperance activists, who defaced the posters saying 'Beer is Best' by adding the words 'Left Alone'. They failed to halt the advertising: dozens of different advertisements appeared over the following years, with several new slogans, including 'Stick to Beer' and 'The Best Long Drink in the World'. No real research exists to show if the campaign made any difference, but beer consumption did rise 37 per cent from the record low of just under 18 million bulk barrels in 1932/3 to 24.7 million barrels in 1938/9.

Whitbread launched its own effort to raise the image of beer, with a series of magazine ads showing beautiful people drinking Whitbread pale ale from stylish goblets in glamorous surroundings. The first one used Gertrude Lawrence, a 1930s stage actress considered the acme of sophistication at the time; other famous figures who appeared in the ads included Douglas Fairbanks Jr and the 1920s matinée idol Owen Nares.

The brewers were also trying to make pubs more attractive, under the general banner of 'public house improvement'. Whitbread actually had a subsidiary called the Improved Public House Co., formed in 1920, which ran large managed pubs with an emphasis on good architecture, on food, and on drinking at tables rather than 'vertical drinking'. In many places, however, when brewers tried to replace cramped old boozers they had problems with temperance-inclined licensing magistrates who could not believe that larger, more attractive pubs would not mean more drunkenness. This prejudice on the licensing bench against pubs meant that generally if a pub was being built on, say, a new council housing estate or by the side of a new road the brewers had to surrender the licence of another, older pub elsewhere in the district before they could get a licence from the magistrates for the new one. Many large new architect-designed pubs were built during the 1920s and 1930s by brewers in places such as

London, the West Midlands and Liverpool, and thousands of other pubs were rebuilt and refurbished. Eventually, however, there was a reaction against the big 'palace' pub, partly because, as the *Brewers' Journal* admitted in 1943, customers preferred their pubs 'to be homely, individual and personal' and partly because brewers discovered larger pubs had higher overheads per barrel sold.

Brewery mergers, takeovers and closures were still reducing numbers, with brewery companies going out of business at a rate of just over one a month. By 1940 there were 428 companies, and 840 breweries in all, including perhaps two or three hundred surviving own-brew pubs. Brewery companies were now getting much bigger:

It's a cracker . . . an advertisement from Christmas 1933, one of the first in a long-running series from the Brewers' Society designed to promote beer generically.

Bass and its great next-door rival Worthington had merged in January 1927, swallowing a third big Burton brewer, Thomas Salt & Co., a few months later for £1.28 million. In 1934 Samuel Allsopp & Sons in Burton merged with Ind Coope of Burton and Romford to form Britain's biggest brewery company, with 3,400 tied houses. By 1940 the top ten brewery companies were producing 40 per cent of all the beer sold in Britain, against 25 per cent in 1914.

The Second World War brought brewers the same problems of dramatically increased taxation and sharply reduced supplies of raw materials to brew with as the First. This time, however, official hostility towards the whole drinks trade was missing: the forces of temperance were nowhere near as strong, largely because Britain could be seen to be a much more sober nation. Whether it was down to changed social conditions or simply weaker beer, the number of annual convictions for drunkenness in England and Wales fell by three-quarters between 1913 and 1935, from 196,000, a rate of 52.6 per 10,000 people, to 48,000, or 11.9 per 10,000 people.

When war broke out in 1939 the National Temperance Federation urged the government to reintroduce all the restrictions of the First World War, including the 'no treating' rule, plus extras, such as banning clubs in Wales from opening on Sundays, and stopping pilots from drinking for a set number of hours before they went on duty. The temperance movement tried to argue, as it had in the past, that brewing 'destroyed' grain that should be used for food production. However, the government recognized that on the 'home front' the pub had a vital role. Lord Woolton, the Minister for Food, declared in May 1940 that while the strength of beer would have to fall to make raw materials go as far as possible, there would be no halt to brewing, nor any cutback in barrelage. He said: 'It is the business of the government not only to maintain the life but the morale of the country. If we are to keep up anything like approaching normal life, beer should continue to be in supply, even though it may be beer of a rather weaker variety than the connoisseurs would like.'

It was also beer of a rather dearer price. Basic beer duty was doubled immediately the war broke out to £2 8s a barrel, and rose twice more in 1940 to end the year at £4 1s a barrel. The price of a pint of mild, the standard working man's drink, rose from 5d before the war to 8d. In April 1942 duty was lifted more than 45 per cent, to £5 18s 1½d, pushing mild up to 10d a pint, twice its pre-war level. Average strength, meanwhile, had fallen from 1040 OG in 1939 to 1034 in 1942. But while even the government had expected a decline in beer consumption as a result of higher prices, production actually increased, from 24.7 million bulk barrels in 1939 to 29.3 million barrels in 1942. Emboldened, the Chancellor of the Exchequer increased beer duty twice more in 1943 and 1944, so that mild now cost a shilling a pint. Production, meanwhile, rose to 31.3 million barrels in 1945, the highest level since 1920.

Consumption increased despite brewers being asked to use flaked maize, flaked oats and even, in 1943, flaked potato to make up for a lack of malt. In June 1941 brewers were ordered to reduce hopping rates by 20 per cent. The call-up, which saw a company such as

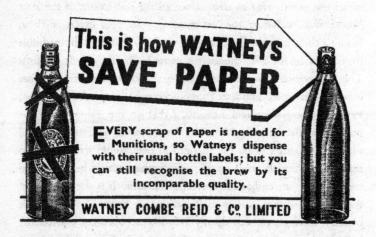

This is how WATNEYS SAVE PAPER

EVERY scrap of Paper is needed for Munitions, so Watneys dispense with their usual bottle labels; but you can still recognise the brew by its incomparable quality.

WATNEY COMBE REID & Cº. LIMITED

A Second World War advertisement showing how brewers tried to help by doing away with bottle labels.

Watney's lose more than 600 staff and workers to the forces, once again meant women were employed in the brewery, shifting casks and loading hops into coppers. Lorries were again commandeered by the forces, with Charrington's in London, for example, losing half its fleet to the army. From 1943 the country was 'zoned', and brewers restricted to delivering only in the area local to their breweries. Pubs were reduced to closing one day a week or more to try to conserve supplies. Stronger beers, such as Burton, disappeared completely. There was even a shortage of glasses: at least one pub, the Bell Inn, Keresley, near Coventry, was selling beer in jam-jars in the autumn of 1941. However, the government resisted urgings by teetotal MPs to ration beer in the same way as food.

German bombs hit thousands of pubs; by August 1943, 1,300 were so damaged they were forced to shut. Many port cities, such as Swansea and Plymouth, lost a quarter of their pubs to bombs. More than a dozen breweries in ports and industrial cities were also put out of action by bombing, though in every case they either kept production going through a subsidiary or found former rivals were happy to help out. Devenish's brewery in Weymouth, near the naval base at Portland, was unable to brew for two years after a bomber attack on the town in August 1940, relying on its next-door neighbour John Groves & Co., and Eldridge Pope up the road in Dorchester, to supply its pubs.

In October 1940 a bomb landed on the brewhouse at Barclay Perkins in Southwark, wrecking three of the brewery's five coppers and mash tuns. Whitbread's brewery survived a massive incendiary attack on London in December 1940 only thanks to the brewery fire brigade, while the surrounding area was flattened. The buildings lost included Brewers' Hall, which had already been destroyed once before, in the Great Fire of 1666. Boddington's brewery in Manchester lost everything but the bottling stores in a raid in the same month. The Cornbrook Brewery, Manchester, was damaged badly enough to put it out of commission for two years, and two breweries in Sheffield were razed. The Tamar brewery in Devonport, Plymouth, a subsidiary of Simonds of Reading, was partly wrecked in 1941, and Bent's brewery in Liverpool was badly damaged the same year, as was Taylor Walker's brewery in Limehouse, hard by the London docks.

Few London brewers escaped: Watney's in Pimlico, Guinness's brewery in Park Royal, built only in 1936, Charrington's and Mann's in the East End, Young & Co. in Wandsworth and Fuller, Smith & Turner in Chiswick were all hit several times during the war. Ind Coope in Romford suffered in at least six attacks, including a raid in 1944 which partly destroyed the roof of the fermenting room, but kept brewing throughout. Elsewhere, the fermenting room at William Cooper & Co.'s East Street brewery, Southampton, was completely destroyed in Luftwaffe raids on the port. In June 1942, in what were known as the 'Baedeker raids' by the Luftwaffe on historic towns and cities, Morgan's brewery in Norwich was blown up. Once again it was probably no consolation that the enemy drinker was suffering even more: beer brewing in Germany had stopped entirely by March 1943.

While output on the home front kept up, even if the only beer available was weak and pricey, drink for the forces overseas was a problem. In the Far East complaints came back that were almost identical to those made by Henry VIII's commanders in Picardy exactly 400 years earlier. The troops in India and South-East Asia were rationed to three bottles a month each, but in December 1944 the Earl of Munster reported that supplies were so short there was not enough beer even to maintain this. One attempted solution was the same as Henry VIII's – mobile breweries. Soldiers fighting in Burma were supplied in 1944 with beer made on the back of fifteen hundredweight trucks. These were equipped with miniature boilers, mash tuns, coppers, coolers and fermenting vessels. The beer only kept for twelve hours after its three-day fermentation was complete, but with temperatures of 95° Fahrenheit in the shade it is doubtful much of it remained undrunk when that time was up.

Plans were also made to put breweries into ships. Two former liners were acquired by the Admiralty and sent to Vancouver in Canada to be fitted out with breweries built by Adlams of Bristol. In the middle of work the war in the Far East ended after the dropping of atomic bombs on Japan. It was decided to continue fitting out one of the ships, the *Menestheus*, which made its first brew on 21 December 1945, using malt extract and hop concentrate, and brewing liquor purified from sea water. Only one beer, a darkish mild, was made in the 'Davy Jones Brewery', as it was called. The ship, which also had its own bars to dispense the beer, and a theatre and cinema on board as well, sailed for the Far East, arriving in Tokyo Bay in March 1946. The beer sold at 9d a pint, and appeared to be popular with those who tried it, but with the war over the Admiralty had lost interest, and when the *Menestheus* arrived back home the brewery was removed from the ship, just six months after its first beer was made.

With hostilities over, the country continued to face problems that resulted in even greater restrictions than during the war. A worldwide food crisis in 1946 saw the new Labour government order every brewer to reduce its standard barrelage to 85 per cent of the previous year's. Soon after, the maximum permitted average gravity was lowered by 10 per cent, with the minimum average reduced to 1030 OG. Pubs were still having to put signs on their doors saying 'Sorry – No Beer'. The brewers blamed the lack of beer on everything from shortages of coal to 'the fact that many more young girls are drinking beer to-day', apparently because they could not afford cocktails any more and mineral waters were unavailable.

The gravity restriction was withdrawn the following year, but by now the country was in economic crisis. More cuts in standard output were ordered, to 78 per cent by January 1949, while beer duty was raised twice in 1947 and 1948 to push the cost of a pint up by 2d: 'The price of beer today seems fantastic' the writer Maurice Gorham said in 1949, when bitter was on average around 1s 4d. Beer output dropped by 10 per cent in 1946 to 29.3 million bulk barrels at an average OG of 1032.6. It rose slightly in 1947, and then fell away almost continuously for the next six years, dropping below 25 million bulk barrels in 1950, though average gravity rose to 1037.

Mild was still 'the staple drink in public bars, much drunk by darts players', and if you ordered 'a pint' without qualification in the public bar of a pub, mild is what you would be served. In the more middle-class saloon bar, the normal drink was bitter. Porter had disappeared from Great Britain: Whitbread 'brewed its last gyle of porter in 1941', according to the beer writer Andrew Campbell, exactly 199 years after Samuel Whitbread started in business. Whitbread, which had been the world's biggest porter brewer in the eighteenth century, published a book on beer in 1948 which said, rather sadly: 'Once the pride of the great London breweries, porter is today an almost obsolete term.' Burton was still common: in the same book Whitbread asserted that 'In this country there are four chief types of beer: pale ale, mild ale, stout and Burton', and a year later Maurice Gorham was agreeing that 'the drinks kept on draught in the ordinary London pub are bitter, Burton and mild ale'. Lager, however, was rare. Gorham wrote in 1949: 'Lager is not a very popular drink in pubs, except in fairly high-class saloon bars during very hot weather. One can usually get bottled lager but it is not always iced. A few houses keep it on draught.' Even in 1956 lager could be dismissed by Andrew Campbell with the sentence: 'The very light mild flavour is popular with the ladies.'

Between 1940 and 1950 the number of breweries in the UK had dropped by a third, from 840 to 567. Though many brewery companies, particularly in the West Country, still marketed a bottled brown ale under the name 'Home Brew' for those who preferred the own-brew pubs' beers, most own-brew pubs had ceased operation. Those that had survived the 1920s and 1930s had been borne down during and after the Second World War by a lack of raw materials and the quality problems associated with brewing at enforced lower gravities. But the local brewery was still a familiar site (and smell): there were nineteen breweries in total operating in London in 1952, eighteen in Edinburgh, fourteen in Manchester, nine in Sheffield, eight in Birmingham, Newcastle and Preston (though in Preston six were own-brew houses), six in Burton, and five each in Alloa, Bolton, Cardiff, Halifax, Leeds, Sunderland and Warrington.

With beer on average about 10 per cent weaker than before the Second World War (and about 30 per cent weaker than before the

First World War), drinkers had spotted that, as Maurice Gorham wrote in 1949, 'the keeping and serving of the beer make almost more difference now than the brewing, and the quality in any bar can change with a new landlord or even a new girl behind the bar'. Draught beer had become much more unreliable, and the 'quality question' would be a dominant theme for the rest of the century. Drinkers' initial reaction was to order more bottled beer, where the quality was at least consistent, if not as good as the very best draught beer. Bottled beer was more expensive, and many drinkers, to save money, would mix draught and bottled together, creating the 'brown and mild' (bottled brown ale, draught dark mild), the 'light and bitter' (bottled light ale, draught bitter) and other drinks that helped disguise cheaper but poor, flat, stale draught beer with the livelier, carbonated bottled variety.

The swing to bottled beer after the Second World War was so rapid that by 1952 the *Statist* magazine was declaring: 'It is probable that within a decade draught milds and bitters will no longer make up the major part of brewery production.' The *Statist* was guilty of the common economist's sin of extrapolating trends without considering that they might slow down: even so, by 1959 'packaged' beer, which meant almost entirely bottled beer, was 36 per cent by volume of the UK beer market. For some brewers the proportion was even higher: Mann's brewery in London, famous for brown ale, estimated in 1958 that bottled beer made up nearly 70 per cent of its production. At Whitbread, nearly half the trade in 1959 was in bottled Mackeson milk stout, which the company had acquired after a series of takeovers in the 1920s. Mackeson was one of the heavily advertised beers, with the veteran actor Bernard Miles appearing on television to tell viewers: 'Looks good, tastes good – and by golly, it does you good!' It is not a message that would be allowed today.

One solution to the problem of pubs that could no longer be trusted to keep draught beer well was 'bottled beer in a cask'. Equipment to pasteurize bulk beer had been in use on the continent since the 1920s. Guinness in Dublin was experimenting with metal containers made by Krupps of Germany for its draught stout in 1928. In 1930 Watney's bought a container beer pasteurizing machine from a German manufacturer and set it up at the Mortlake brewery. Originally Watney's intended the beer for sale on board ship. However, one of the brewers at Mortlake, Bert Hussey, was convinced that 'container beer' had a future on land as well, particularly in the free trade, and arranged to supply the new form of beer to the East Sheen Lawn Tennis Club, near the Mortlake brewery.

These pre-Second World War experiments with pressurized beer came to nothing, partly because the equipment was too expensive to make it economic, partly because of technical problems such as valves becoming sticky with beer. The economic crisis that followed the war meant that brewers were slow to spend money on further experiments with container beer. In 1955, however, the Luton brewery J. W. Green (now known as Flower's, after a reverse takeover of the Stratford upon Avon brewery in 1954) started producing a pasteurized container beer, pressurized with carbon dioxide, called Flower's Keg. This, too, was originally meant for small, low-turnover, free-trade outlets that had particular problems keeping draught beer in good condition; but within a few years, as technical developments made keg beer even less vulnerable to mishandling, and less likely to pick up a taint from the metal of the cask, it was being supplied to Flower's tied pubs, which were eager to take it.

The Flower's success with pressurized container beer (which quickly became known generically as 'keg', to Flower's annoyance) encouraged the bigger brewers to bring out their own versions. Flower's had based Keg on a draught beer, Flower's Original. Bass decided its beer for kegging would be Worthington E, like Original an existing premium draught bitter. Whitbread went for an entirely new brew when it introduced its own keg beer, Tankard, in 1955. Other big brewers decided that as 'keg' beer was 'bottled beer in a cask', they would use their best-selling premium bottled pale ales as the basis for their own keg brews. The advantage was that these bottled beers already had well-known, heavily advertised brand names, so that drinkers would know what they were getting. Thus Watney's introduced keg Red Barrel, Ind Coope put its Double Diamond pale ale into kegs, and Courage kegged Tavern, the bottled pale ale made by Simonds of Reading, which Courage took over in 1960.

All the first keg beers were 'premium' strength and cost more than standard draught beers. But through the 1960s their popularity grew: while keg bitter brands took just 1 per cent of total beer sales by volume in 1959, they were taking 8 per cent by 1966 and 17 per cent by 1971. At the same time many brewers were deciding that their 'non-keg' beers were best dispensed under a pressurized blanket of carbon dioxide as well, a style of serving known as 'top pressure'. Hand-pumps, which had been used to serve draught beers since the start of the nineteenth century, were disappearing. By the start of the 1970s, in many areas up to 90 per cent of pubs were serving only pressurized draught beers, keg or top-pressure, from taps on the bar behind brightly-lit boxes.

The roll-out of keg ended the mass popularity of bottled beer. Sales drifted slowly down from 34 per cent of all beer sold in 1960 to 27 per cent in 1969, and then dropped rapidly: 20 per cent in 1974, 12 per cent in 1979, 9 per cent in 1984. Only the increased popularity of bottled premium lager pushed sales of all bottled beer back up, to around 13 per cent in 1998.

Meanwhile, canned beers were taking off. They had been pioneered in the United States in 1933, shortly after prohibition ended, and reached Europe the same year, when a French brewery called Moreau and Co. of Vezelise, Lorraine, in 1933 advertised its *bières en boites* as *Le Gout du Jour* – 'The Taste of Today'. The first canned beer in Britain was made in 1935 by the little Welsh brewery of Felinfoel, near Llanelli, which was owned by the John family, who also had a financial interest in a tinplate works which supplied the metal for the cans. The next brewer in Britain to can beer, and the first to can lager, appears to be Jeffreys of Edinburgh. The main interest was among brewers of beers for export: Barclay Perkins, Simonds of Reading, McEwan's of Edinburgh and Tennent's of Glasgow, all big beer exporters, were all early canners. By the end of 1937, twenty-three British breweries were making canned beer. But even after the Second World War, canned beer remained at less than 2 per cent of all British beer sales. It was not until the ring-pull can crossed the Atlantic in 1964 that canned beer began to replace bottled beer for home drinking. Sales of canned beer were 3 per cent of all UK beer consumption in 1971, 8 per cent in 1976, 15 per cent in 1986 and 24 per cent in 1996.

Other changes were happening to the beer styles on offer. Burton ale, which had still been a popular winter drink in the early 1950s, especially in London, was disappearing as brewer after brewer stopped production. By the start of the 1970s in London only Young & Co. of Wandsworth was still brewing a beer called Burton Ale, and in 1971 the decision was taken to change the name of the beer to Winter Warmer. Nobody at Young's can remember why the name Burton was dropped, but probably drinkers were already expecting that anything called Burton would be a pale ale: one story is that the brewery felt the Trade Descriptions Act now outlawed anything called Burton that was not actually brewed in Burton.

Mild ale, the great staple of the early twentieth century, was also declining rapidly, hit by an ageing customer base and its association with the working classes. A study published by *The Times* in 1958 summed up mild's problem: 'Traditionally bitter is looked on as the bosses' drink. Any man reckons today he's as good as his boss. So he chooses bitter.' In 1959 draught mild was still 42 per cent of all beer sales by volume, twice as great as draught bitter. By 1964 draught mild was down to 33 per cent of beer sales by volume. Around 1969 sales of draught bitter overtook those of draught mild for the first time. Six years later, in 1975, as draught mild plunged to barely one pint in eight of total beer sales, it was passed in popularity by a beer that had hardly existed in Britain in 1959 – draught lager.

CHAPTER NINE

THE COUNTER-REVOLUTION

the twentieth century, part two

For many years Watney's spent enormous sums associating their name with the colour red: the pubs were all painted red, the beer was called Watney's Red and so on. Early in 1975 many of their pubs in London were painted in any colour other than red. The company appeared to be trying to camouflage its pubs, to conceal the fact that they were Watney's houses. I can think of no parallel for such behaviour in any industry.

Richard Boston, *Beer and Skittles*
(1976)

The first assault on British indifference to lager beer had come from Canada, rather than Europe. A Canadian industrialist, E. P. (Edward Plunket) Taylor, had started building up a brewing empire in Canada and the United States in 1930. One of his earliest acquisitions was Carling Breweries Ltd of London, Ontario, which had been founded in 1843 by an immigrant from Yorkshire, Thomas Carling. In the 1920s it was brewing a beer called Black

Label Rice Beer, which was changed in 1927 to Black Label. Taylor closed the Carling brewery in 1936 and transferred production of Black Label to another of his acquisitions, the Kuntz brewery in Waterloo, Ontario. By the start of the 1950s, Taylor's Canadian Breweries had a dominant position in its home country, while it was also building a reputation in the United States through a subsidiary, Carling Brewing Company Inc., in Cleveland, Ohio.

In 1951 Taylor was visited by the managing director of the Hope & Anchor brewery in Sheffield, Thomas Carter. Hope & Anchor, a specialist bottled beer brewer, had been very successful with a milk stout called Jubilee, first produced in 1935, the year of George V's Silver Jubilee. Carter was sure there was a market for Jubilee Stout among Canadians. Taylor agreed to brew and bottle Jubilee Stout in Canada if, in return, Hope & Anchor would brew and bottle Carling's Black Label lager in Britain.

Jubilee Stout was a flop in Canada, to the chagrin of Hope & Anchor – but Taylor's team found it was pushing at an open door in its efforts to sell lager to the British, helped by its access to Hope & Anchor's 200 tied houses. Sales of lager, though still tiny, were increasing. Much of this increase, according to *The Times* in 1958, was down to 'one of the most successful mixed drinks in recent years, lager and lime-juice, of obscure origin and drunk mostly by the young'. The same year Thomas Carter had a row with Taylor over the comparative efforts being put into selling Jubilee in Canada and Black Label in Britain. It was resolved by an adjusted agreement that saw Taylor's Canadian Breweries take over the now considerable liabilities of the Canadian Jubilee Stout operation, while Taylor and Carter signed a joint declaration of intent to promote the creation of a national brewery group in Great Britain. Taylor's intention was to become at least as dominant in the UK as he was in Canada.

In October 1959 Taylor set up a company called Northern Breweries Ltd, through which he made his first acquisition, John Jeffrey & Co., a little Edinburgh brewery that specialized in lager. Four months later, in February 1960, Hammonds United Breweries of Bradford and

Hope & Anchor came into Northern Breweries, turning it into an £18 million group with H. L. Bradfer-Lawrence of Hammonds (who had entered the brewing business fifty years earlier) as chairman and Taylor as vice-chairman.

Taylor took the lead in the speedy acquisitions of the next few months. As soon as Northern had been set up, Taylor had got his stockbroker to buy £25 of shares in every quoted brewery company in the UK, so that he would be able to get hold of the financial information available to shareholders, but not normally made free to outsiders. This, according to Philip Bradfer-Lawrence, son of Northern's chairman, 'created an absolute uproar in the Brewers' Society. It just wasn't done'. Neither was what Taylor did next: in ten months, by the end of 1960, he acquired stakes in over twenty British brewers and took over, on behalf of Northern Breweries, six of them. Three more Scottish breweries were acquired by May 1960, and in July the small Welsh brewery Webbs of Aberbeeg, in Monmouthshire, became the first acquisition south of the Trent. A month later draught Black Label went on sale for the first time. In October a fifth Scots takeover was followed by the acquisition of the Ulster Brewery in Belfast. That month Northern changed its name to United Breweries, as its ambitions spread out across the UK.

Northern/United was the biggest mover in a storm of brewery takeovers in 1960, but it was far from the only predator. Over the previous decade, medium-sized regional brewing concerns had been growing at the expense of their smaller brothers, with an average of ten to a dozen takeovers a year around the industry. Occasionally these included bigger deals, particularly among London brewers: Courage and its Southwark neighbour Barclay Perkins came together in 1955, Watney Combe Reid and Mann, Crossman & Paulin merged in 1958 and Ind Coope of Romford and Burton acquired Taylor Walker of Limehouse the following year. Then in 1959 an outsider tried to burst in: not Taylor but the property developer Charles Clore.

Watney's was in the middle of selling its Stag brewery site, close to Victoria station in London, an asset worth £6 million. Its net book assets, including by now almost four thousand pubs, stood at almost £38 million, but its market capitalization was only £27 million. Clore clearly felt this was a crime, and Watney's assets would be better with someone who understood property. On 25 May his Sears Holdings put in a bid worth 60s a share, when Watney's shares were 51s 3d. It was the first ever approach by an outsider for a big brewery company, and it absolutely stunned the 'beerage', as the family-dominated big brewers were known: later, each board member of a big brewery would have his own 'Kennedy moment', remembering for ever where he was when he first heard of Clore's bid. One Watney's director, George Mann, was described as 'visibly shocked' when the news was told to him. Clore's bid was rejected by Watney's chairman, Simon Combe, as 'preposterous'. The market, expecting Clore to come back with a bigger bid, drove Watney's share price up to above 70s. Clore refused to bite, and eventually walked away with a good profit on the 500,000 Watney shares he had bought before the bid was made.

It would be an exaggeration to say, as some have, that Clore was responsible for the blizzard of takeovers and mergers that characterized the late 1950s and early 1960s. But he had helped make brewers more aware of their true returns on capital, which looked good on paper but only because pub values were entered into company books at unrealistically low prices. Some breweries had not revalued their properties for more than twenty years. At least one revalued its property upwards by 50 per cent in the wake of Clore's bid, 'and that was conservative because we didn't want to frighten the board'.

As family brewers decided they would rather realize the capital tied up in their firms and invest it somewhere more lucrative, brewery takeovers doubled from eleven in 1958 to twenty-two in 1959 and then rose again to thirty in 1960. Total brewery numbers fell to 336 in 1961, a 38 per cent drop in ten years, leaving just 210 brewery companies still in existence (many now had more than one site, after the takeovers of the previous ten years). Beer production dropped in 1958 to 23.8 million bulk barrels, the lowest output for twenty-one years. Since the eighteenth century the industry had been polarized between a small number of very large brewers and a large number of very small brewers, but now the large brewers were producing the majority of the nation's beer. It was reckoned in 1961 that the eight largest brewery companies supplied 60 per cent of British beer, the next fifty largest supplied 30 per cent and the remaining 150 supplied just 10 per cent.

One of the most important drivers of this increasing concentration was the wish by owners of big beer brands, the so-called 'national' beers such as Whitbread's Mackeson, Ind Coope's Double Diamond and Bass's bottled pale ale, to secure national tied house coverage. That way they could derive economies of scale from national advertising campaigns, which had grown after the arrival of commercial television in September 1955 (Watney's was one of the advertisers to appear on screen on Day One of ITV). Among larger companies after 1959 there was also a desire to stay out of the hands of Taylor and his United Breweries, and make deals on their own terms.

Indeed, Taylor was starting to have more effect on the British brewing industry simply by making offers to companies than he was by actually taking them over. In 1960 he approached Walker Cain of Warrington, a considerable power in the Merseyside/Manchester area, which immediately took fright and merged with Tetley of Leeds to form Tetley Walker. Early the next year Taylor tried to acquire Bristol Brewery Georges, whereupon the Bristolians threw themselves at the newly formed Courage Barclay Simonds of London and Reading. Taylor's United made a higher offer, but Courage, supported by the Bristol directors, had already received enough acceptances to give it control.

Shortly afterwards the biggest merger yet took place, to create the UK's first truly national brewer. Ind Coope, strong in the south and with a presence in Scotland, joined forces with Ansells, one of the two big brewers in the Midlands, and Tetley Walker, the new dominant force in the north. The combined ICTA group (it changed its name to Allied Breweries in 1962) had almost 8,000 pubs. It was in part, like Walker's merger with Tetley, a defensive coming together against

Taylor, and in part a move to nurture and grow national brands such as Ind Coope's Double Diamond keg beer and its own offering in the nascent lager market, Skol.

While lager was still only a tiny fraction of total British beer sales, companies such as Ind Coope knew demand was growing: production at its Wrexham lager plant (acquired in 1949) increased ninefold between 1955 and 1961. Ind Coope deliberately aimed Skol at young people, featuring pictures of young drinkers in its advertising for the brand, and telling the *Morning Advertiser* (the trade paper for pubs) that the 'boy and girl' (its own words) in the Skol adverts, 'the biggest advertising campaign Britain has ever seen for any lager', were 'changing the taste of Britain'.

One company convinced that Britain would eventually take to lager was Guinness, the stout giant. Early in 1958 Guinness decided that cheap summer holidays abroad were bringing more and more Britons into contact with lager, and suntanned holidaymakers would be taking a desire for the pale, cold continental beer back home to Britain. Guinness found itself an expert German lager brewer, Dr Hermann Münder of the Dom brewery in Cologne and started to construct a lager brewery at the Great Northern brewery in Dundalk, founded in 1897, which it had bought for the purpose. (An Irish launch was felt necessary to solve any problems before hitting the much larger British market.) Dr Münder confessed later he was not very impressed with the Dundalk site as a potential lager brewery, describing the existing set-up as 'like an alchemist's kitchen'.

Several names for the new beer were considered, including Atlas, Cresta and Dolphin, before Harp was picked as the perfect label: a harp was, of course, the Guinness trademark. Test brews using water from the Mourne mountains were carried out at the brewing research centre in Weihenstephan, Bavaria, and a cask of yeast from Weihenstephan was used to start the first brew of Harp in June 1960.

Harp was launched in Dublin and Belfast, using a different recipe for each market. It was successful enough to plan for a British launch within a year: the first tank of Harp arrived on a rain-swept quay at

Salthouse Dock, Liverpool, in April 1961. Guinness, already accustomed to selling its stout in other people's pubs, set up a consortium of brewers to sell Harp that consisted of itself, Scottish & Newcastle in the North, Mitchells & Butlers in the Midlands and Courage in the South. This way it guaranteed shelf space for the beer from the start in the consortium's tied houses. After six months of selling only in north-west England, Harp went on national sale in November 1961.

By the summer of 1963 Harp had become the best-known lager on the market, after considerable spending on marketing: even in 1960 lager took 19 per cent of all UK beer advertising, despite having only 1 per cent of the market. But sales had flattened out, and while the lager market had doubled in size in three years it still represented only 2 per cent of British beer sales. Almost all of this was in bottles: but the first kegs of draught lager were beginning to be seen. Harp was not the first keg draught lager, but the Harp consortium solved the technical problems of serving up a glass of beer rather than a pint of froth more quickly than their rivals, and the first draught Harp hit the pubs of Britain in 1965.

It was enormously successful, particularly in Scotland, where in three years draught lager captured 20 per cent of the beer market, and in Northern Ireland, where a huge increase in lager-drinking occurred. Few drinkers knew, or cared, that at an OG of 1033 it was weaker than most continental lagers, and weaker than many draught British beers. This new, light (in several senses), 'modern' beer had arrived at a time when the motivation for beer-drinking was changing, and its success was helped by everything from the decline in heavy manual work, which lessened the demand for a filling, energy-giving drink, to the rise in central heating, which meant a cold drink was more welcome than even a cellar-cool one. The semi-conscious reason for drinking beer had moved from 'restoration' to 'refreshment'. Lager, served cold, with more carbon dioxide 'bite', was more 'refreshing', and for lager drinkers strength (or flavour) was irrelevant to the appeal.

During the 1960s each big brewer was anxious to get the smaller brewers to stock his national lager brand rather than a rival's. Small firms found themselves wooed like eighteenth-century heiresses. Bill Kington, managing director of the Border brewery in Wrexham (and father of the humorist Miles Kington) was visited on successive days one week in 1961 by E. P. Taylor, pushing the virtues of Carling Black Label; Edward Guinness, trying to interest him in Harp; and Mr Le Fanu of Ind Coope, courting him with Skol. 'It is all going to my head,' he told Edward Guinness.

United Breweries, meanwhile, managed five acquisitions in 1961, giving it a total at the year's end of 2,800 pubs. However, it still lacked a partner in the south-east; so at the end of the year it began talks with the Charrington family, which still controlled the company. When the deal was completed in April 1962, the new company, Charrington United, controlled 5,250 pubs. Only Watney Mann, which had taken over three big regional brewers in 1960 to grow to more than 6,400 houses, and the new Allied Breweries at 7,846 pubs, were bigger.

A rather different route was being taken by Whitbread to ensure it kept a place among the big boys. The company's main aim was to ensure it still had a national market for its bottled beers larger than its own 1,300 tied houses. Every regional brewery that was acquired by a rival such as United meant one opportunity fewer for Whitbread to sell Mackeson or Forest Brown (named for the old Forest Hill brewery Whitbread took over in 1924) through that regional's tied pubs. The company could not make the usual sort of share-exchange takeover, as that would have diluted the power of the Whitbread family, which still held around half the stock. Whitbread therefore set up a scheme to try to bolster regional brewers who wished to remain independent, buying a big block of their shares to decrease the chance of their being taken over by another company.

The first such stake was bought in 1955, when Whitbread acquired a £100,000 slice of Morland's of Abingdon, in Oxfordshire, which used the money to modernize its brewery. Other holdings quickly followed, and the 'Whitbread Umbrella', as it became known, extended its shadow over more and more companies, so that by the end of the

1950s the company had stakes in some twenty regional breweries owning 15,000 pubs, all selling at least some Whitbread beers.

To Whitbread's alarm, as the 1960s arrived, the umbrella proved an inadequate defence against a determined predator. In 1961 it lost two of the companies it had stakes in: Hewitt Brothers of Grimsby, to United, and Wells & Winch of Biggleswade, to Greene King of Suffolk. Alarmed, the Whitbread board changed its policy. From that year the umbrella turned into a crocodile, swallowing the little fishes that had swum into its open jaws for protection from the sharks. When Charrington, Whitbread's rival London brewer, tried to move in on one of the oldest and largest of Whitbread's umbrella associates, Tennant's, Whitbread swiftly made a counter-offer for the Sheffield brewer that was accepted by the Tennant's board.

Between 1961 and 1968 Whitbread bought twenty-two different regional and local brewers from Devon to Scotland, acquiring along the way more than 9,000 pubs. It did not buy all the brewers it had formerly sheltered: Marston's of Burton, Buckley's of Llanelli, Devenish of Weymouth and Morland's of Abingdon, for example, stayed family-owned despite Whitbread having a stake in each, and when Allied Breweries tried to buy Boddington's of Manchester in 1969 Whitbread used its holding to keep Boddington's independent.

Bass had been in a similar position to Whitbread in the 1950s, with 70 per cent of its beer sold through other brewers' pubs or in the free trade. The Bass board had thought, much as Burton brewers had initially believed during the rush for tied houses of the 1890s, that the quality of its beers and public demand for its products meant its market share was safe. By 1959, however, as bottled beer sales finally started to fall, the company realized a merger was inevitable if it wanted to survive, and talks were held with Watney Mann. They collapsed because neither side would give way over who was to be chairman of the combined concern, and also because in the middle of negotiations, Watney's had bought Wilson's of Manchester, which had sold a great deal of Bass and Worthington beer through its pubs, without bothering to tell Bass what it was doing.

The next year Bass was approached by Alan Walker, chairman of Mitchells & Butlers of Birmingham. Bass's 71-year-old chairman, whose ego had got in the way of the Watney Mann merger, had now died, and the new chairman, Sir James Grigg, had no objection to Walker being chief executive of the combined concern. In 1961 Bass, Mitchells & Butlers was formed. Although presented as a merger, it was really a takeover of an old-fashioned, rather dozy member of the beerage by a newcomer with drive: within a year half the former Bass management had resigned or been fired.

Walker, who had already shaken up the cosy family-dominated board of Mitchells & Butlers when he arrived as an outsider in 1955, knew that even Bass, Mitchells & Butlers was not a big enough concern to survive in an era of national companies. After stop-start negotiations with Charrington United over some years, Bass Charrington was born in August 1967. It was the biggest brewing company in the country, with more than 11,000 outlets.

Bass Charrington apart, even at the end of the 1960s almost all the other big brewers were still family-run. Whitbread's chairman was a seventh-generation direct descendent of its founder. Watney Mann's chairman, Peter Crossman, was descended from one of the partners who formed Mann, Crossman & Paulin in 1846. The family of Truman's chairman, Maurice Pryor, had joined that company in 1816. Scottish & Newcastle's chairman, Sir William McEwan Younger, was a great-nephew of the founder of the McEwan side of S&N. At Courage, Barclay and Simonds there were two Courages and one Simonds on the board of directors, with the chairman, Richard Courage, again descended from the founder. Six Guinnesses sat on the board of the stout giant. Even at Allied Breweries the chairman, Sir Derek Pritchard, was descended from a family that had run a wine and spirits firm in Manchester taken over by Ind Coope in 1949.

In all, almost 200 breweries were taken over in the fifteen years between 1955 and 1969. The pace of takeovers slowed after 1968 simply because there were so few family brewers left. A handful of acquisitions early in the 1970s helped fill in some holes, and by 1972 the 'Big Six' brewers – Bass Charrington, Allied, Whitbread, Watney (Grand Met), Courage and Scottish & Newcastle (the result of the merger between Newcastle Breweries and the Younger/McEwan combine Scottish Brewers in Edinburgh that had taken place in 1960) – controlled 56 per cent of all pubs, against 24 per cent in 1960, and just 16 per cent of pubs for the six largest brewers of 1952.

The Big Six now brewed 82 per cent of beer made in the UK, from 57 breweries. The number of independent brewers was now down to just 88, including the Channel Isles and the Isle of Man. They brewed just 9 per cent of the nation's beer, against around 70 per cent for the 380 small to medium independents of 1952 (the other 9 per cent in 1972 went to Guinness). The independents owned only 13,800 tied houses between them, an average of fewer than 160 each. Shareholders in the remaining independents were probably not encouraged by a survey in 1970 that confirmed brewers were lagging behind in providing a decent return on capital: 11.1 per cent, against 14.5 per cent for 'all industrials', 16.1 per cent for 'leisure' and 16.7 per cent for food retailing.

Own-brew pubs had now almost vanished completely as brewing publicans retired or died, or their equipment developed faults that were too costly to repair. Three closed in 1971: the Druid's Head, Coseley, near Wolverhampton; the Friary Hotel, Derby; and the Nag's Head, Belper; and another, the Britannia, Loughborough, stopped brewing when the landlord died in 1972. At the end of 1972 there were just four own-brew pubs still operating in Great Britain: the All Nations near Telford, Shropshire; the Three Tuns at Bishops Castle, also in Shropshire; the Old Swan in Dudley in the West Midlands; and the Blue Anchor in Helston, Cornwall. One hundred years earlier there had been almost 30,000 pubs and beerhouses brewing their own, and they had made almost a quarter of total commercially brewed beer.

The demise of so many breweries, and the rise of a handful of nationally promoted keg beers, was beginning to cause considerable consumer resentment. While many drinkers had rushed to the new keg beers in the early 1960s, when they seemed to offer a respite from poorly kept draught beer served by unskilled landlords, by the end of the decade the feeling was growing that keg beers and their cousins top-pressure beers were too gassy, too sweet and nowhere near as satisfying as properly kept traditional cask ale. In 1968 the marketing department at Whitbread, having picked up on this growing hostility, asked the London advertising agency CDP to come up with a corporate campaign to reassure drinkers that all was well, and that their beloved pubs and local beers were safe with Whitbread.

Two advertisements were designed, one showing an old-fashioned pub with bare boards, an oil lamp hanging from the ceiling and three elderly drinkers, with copy that indicated Whitbread wanted to leave this pub exactly as it was. The other showed a pint of beer and a loaf of mass-produced, polystyrene-like sliced white bread, with the strapline: 'The British pint – must it go the way of the British loaf?' The copy listed fourteen different breweries taken over by Whitbread, all still at that time making beer under their own names as well as selling keg Whitbread Tankard, with the promise that Whitbread wanted to keep those breweries and their beers 'alive and kicking'.

The marketing people approved, and the ad agency, delighted, made a presentation to the Whitbread board, expecting to be told how well they had done. Instead, there was a furore: the board made it clear that their interest was in modernization. The ads never ran. Instead, over the next two decades Whitbread shut a dozen of the breweries it owned at the start of the 1970s – including its Chiswell Street home, which closed in 1975 after 225 years.

The brewing industry had never been very good at being told its policies were wrong: it was generally product-oriented rather than customer-oriented, producing what it felt the customer ought to be drinking. If keg beer avoided all the problems of short shelf life and careful handling requirements associated with traditional cask beer, then keg would be what was sold. Unfortunately, there were many customers who thought keg, to quote one group of four young men in March 1971, 'too fizzy, no character, tastes sickly'. They also loathed the tone of much of the advertising for keg beers, and the corporate branding that spread the same colours and typefaces over thousands of pubs. One particularly disliked campaign came that same year from Watney Mann, which relaunched its Red Barrel keg beer as Watney's Red, with the slogan 'Join the Red Revolution!' and posters that featured unconvincing lookalikes of Communist icons such as Khrushchev, Mao and Castro.

The quartet of young English beer-drinkers quoted above soon decided they had had enough fizzy, sickly beer, and formed an initially semi-serious group called the Campaign for the Revitalization of Ale. The four were on holiday in Ireland at the time, where the only ale generally available was keg Smithwicks from Kilkenny, a beer even sweeter and fizzier than most British keg bitters. The choice they saw in nearly every Irish bar – just two beers, Smithwicks or Guinness – was a warning of what might happen in Britain if the mergers of the 1960s continued unabated.

The Campaign for the Revitalization of Ale, Camra for short, was a comparatively tiny affair until a year later. In the autumn of 1972 a much older organization of anti-keg-beer enthusiasts, the Society for the Preservation of Beer from the Wood, founded in 1963, tried to take a stall at a brewers' beer exhibition in Alexandra Palace, north London. Brewers who were promoting keg beer at the exhibition refused to let the SPBW through the door, whereupon it and Camra immediately organized a picket. Since three of the four founding members of Camra were journalists, they knew how to turn a protest into a national newspaper photo-opportunity, and the anti-keg-beer message received far wider publicity than it would have done had the brewers not shut the door on it.

Although the SPBW had provoked the Alexandra Palace boycott, it was Camra that seemed to benefit from the resulting exposure. By early 1973, when the organization's name was changed to the Campaign for Real Ale, membership had reached 1,000; by February 1974 the campaign had 9,000 members. The first *Good Beer Guide*, published that year, sold 30,000 copies. The first national 'real ale' festival, in Covent Garden, London in May 1975, attracted 40,000 visitors. The national brewers began to realize that there were beer-drinkers – often young beer-drinkers, with lots of money to spend – they were failing to capture with their supposedly modern keg beers and lagers. These 'real ale' enthusiasts were drinking hand-pumped, unpressurized beers from those local brewers the nationals had not either succeeded in taking over or scared into ripping out the hand-pumps themselves.

Watney's, which had become the most vilified of the Big Six for its removal of unpressurized beer from 90 per cent of the 7,000 outlets it controlled ('Grotneys' was its Camra nickname) introduced a new real ale in 150 of its London pubs in 1975. Allied Breweries was hailed in 1976 when it launched a premium cask ale, Ind Coope Burton Ale, the first ever widely distributed new cask beer from a national brewer. (There were two ironies here: Burton Ale took the name of a long-vanished darkish, sweet beer, even though it was a pale bitter ale, and it was based on Double Diamond, which in keg form was one of the beers Camra hated.) It was the first breakthrough in a series of policy reversals in Britain's brewery boardrooms that led Camra to be described as Europe's most successful campaigning consumer organization. A few years later there was an even more satisfying victory for the real ale campaigners: in 1979 Grand Metropolitan, now owner of Watney's, axed Watney's Red after a dramatic decline in sales. The one-time king of the kegs was dead.

While the national brewers were changing their minds about unpressurized beer, and rushing to reinstall hand-pumps in their pubs, a remarkable revival was taking place down at the tiniest end of the brewing scale. At just the point when it looked as if little one-man-and-a-dog breweries were all going to vanish, they started opening up, inspired by the success of Camra in boosting the sales of cask beer. There are several contenders for the title of Britain's first 'new wave' brewery, notably the Selby brewery in north Yorkshire, which began brewing again in 1972 after an eighteen-year gap (ironically, it used equipment salvaged from two just-closed pub breweries in the

Midlands, the Druid's Head at Coseley and the Britannia at Loughborough); the Miners Arms in Priddy, Somerset, a restaurant that started making its own beer in 1973; and the Litchborough Brewery in Northamptonshire, founded in 1974 by Bill Urquart, a brewer at the Watney-owned Northampton brewery, who was made redundant aged fifty-eight when the new Carlsberg lager brewery in Northampton was built.

When the 1976 *Good Beer Guide* came out, it listed five 'new' or 'micro' breweries that had started since Camra was formed. The pace picked up: six more new breweries opened in 1977, seven in 1978, sixteen in 1979, eighteen in 1980, thirty-six in 1981. By the end of that year, 104 new breweries, either own-brew pubs or stand-alone brewing operations, had opened, and only nine had closed, leaving ninety-five new breweries selling their beers to the free-house sector. Already, in nine years, the number of new breweries in operation had passed the number of surviving regionals. All the new breweries were producing cask ale: many had been started by brewers made redundant, like Bill Urquart, from national brewery companies. Some had even been opened by the nationals, anxious that here was another trend they might miss out on – eventually Grand Met/Watney opened seven own-brew pubs, Whitbread eleven, and Allied twelve – though most of these were later to close. The success of this new sector was helped by a leap in beer consumption, with total production rising to 41.7 million barrels in 1980, the highest level ever, and 75 per cent up on the post-war low of 23.8 million barrels reached in 1959.

Of those ninety-five small breweries open in 1981, only eighteen were still in business in 2001. However, a survival rate of one in five over twenty years compares very well with most small business sectors, where the average age of a new company when it dies is said to be just four years. In total since 1973, around 850 or so new breweries have opened in Great Britain, a rate of one every twelve days. Of those, more than half are still open. There are more breweries in operation today than at any time since 1952, though the big brewers have continued to shut plants. The top five 'micro' brewers, including Black Sheep of Masham in North Yorkshire, Ringwood of Hampshire and Hopback of Wiltshire, all brew more than the bottom eight 'regionals'. All the same, the total amount of beer produced by all the hundreds of 'micros' in a year would take just one of today's national brewers only a few weeks to brew.

The rise of Camra, with its emphasis on traditional ales, encouraged beer enthusiasts to investigate vanished elements of the country's brewing heritage, such as porter. Michael Jackson's seminal book the *World Guide to Beer*, published in 1977, had a section given over to porter, which Jackson called 'a lost, though not forgotten, beer'. The next year, apparently inspired by Jackson, two English brewers brought out the first draught porters to be seen in English pubs for around forty years. One was a small Yorkshire family brewer, Timothy Taylor and Co. of Keighley, West Yorkshire, whose porter was a 1920s-style 1042 OG; the other was one of the first wave of new breweries started since Camra was founded, Penrhos, based near Kington in Herefordshire. Its Penrhos Porter had a more authentically nineteenth-century OG of 1050.

Porters were picked up briefly by three national brewers who had once been famous for the style: Watney, Whitbread and Guinness. However, none of them lasted very long. The country's growing number of micro-brewers were more enthusiastic: more than sixty different porters were being brewed in Britain and Ireland in 1999, with around one in five of Britain's 'new' breweries making a beer supposedly in the porter style.

While Camra was fulminating against keg and top-pressure bitter and mild, another type of non-traditional beer was capturing more and more drinkers. By 1971 lager, both keg and bottled, was taking just under 10 per cent of total sales. Britons' belief that lager was a drink only fit for women, homosexuals and foreigners was crumbling. Indeed, a European heritage of some kind was now regarded as essential for a new lager to succeed in Britain. Whitbread, after unsuccessful talks with the Belgian brewer Artois, had begun brewing a lower-gravity version of Heineken in 1968 under licence from the Dutch giant, moving production to its new Luton brewery in 1969.

The Dutch took a little convincing that the British beer should be weaker, at an OG of 1033 (the same as Harp), than the version of Heineken sold around the world, which was at 1048 OG. Within two years of the move to Luton, however, Heineken had 20 per cent of the lager market in England and Wales. Watney had gone into business with Tuborg's Danish brother, Carlsberg, to brew another weaker version of a continental lager, once more at an OG of 1030. By 1973 lager sales in Britain had increased 50 per cent in two years – despite, or perhaps because of, the premium prices being charged for draught lager: Tuborg, brewed by Truman's in London, sold for 22p a pint in the early 1970s and Carlsberg for 18p, while even the heavily promoted Watney's Red keg bitter was only 14p a pint, despite having an OG of 1037.

The next three or four years saw a series of unusually hot summers, perfect for the lager marketers, and sales continued to climb like a rocket. By 1976 keg lager had passed sales of keg bitter, and total lager sales nationally were equal to almost one in four pints, a tremendous achievement for the lager marketers against the one in fifty pints of fifteen years earlier. At the same time, lager was still getting a disproportionate amount of advertising money: one-third of all beer advertising in the twelve months to June 1976 went on lager brands. In Scotland lager had risen to 40 per cent of sales in 1977, the year after Scottish & Newcastle started brewing McEwan's lager at the New Fountain Brewery.

In 1986 lager sales reached 43.5 per cent of total beer sales. Lager advertising was now firmly targeted at 'lads': researchers found that eight out of ten pints of lager were drunk by men, two-thirds of whom were under thirty-five. In the late 1980s newspapers were writing of 'lager louts', meaning young men who consistently drank lager to excess and were aggressive and rowdy. The 'lager lout' tag failed to stop the drink's rise, however. By 1989 lager in all its forms, draught, bottled and canned, had finally captured the majority of the

UK beer market, with sales of 50.3 per cent by value. Mild, meanwhile, was down to about 5 per cent of beer sales.

While lager was increasing in popularity, there were still new styles of British beer being developed. The invention of 'summer ale' is generally credited to John Gilbert of the Hop Back brewery in Salisbury. Gilbert, who had previously worked at Watney's brewery in Mortlake, started Hop Back in 1987. In 1989 he decided to try to brew an ale that would be as refreshing during the warm months as a lager. The resulting pale, dry, hoppy beer he called, after a novel by P. G. Wodehouse published sixty years earlier, Summer Lightning. It won numerous awards at beer festivals, and inspired equally numerous imitators: by 1999 there were at least sixty similar premium-strength, pale, thirst-quenching cask ales being made by other British brewers, many with 'summer' or 'sun' in their names.

The next innovation came about because the Scottish brewer Belhaven found itself struggling to sell cask ales in a local beer market where lager ruled, and most of that came from two giants, Tennent's and Scottish & Newcastle. Belhaven took its inspiration in part from Guinness, which had been serving its draught stout using a mixture of nitrogen and carbon dioxide for more than thirty years. In 1989 Guinness had perfected a method of serving a draught-like glass of stout, with the authentically creamy head, from a can. The new drink, which used a pressurized plastic 'widget' in the can to create the head, was hugely successful in the take-home market. In 1991 Belhaven decided to try serving draught bitter under mixed nitrogen/carbon dioxide pressure, reasoning that a beer served this way would have less 'bite' than normal keg beers.

Belhaven Best Draught, 3.2 per cent ABV, and delivered under pressure by a mixture of 70 per cent nitrogen and 30 per cent carbon dioxide, was based on the recipe for Belhaven Heavy, which itself was based on the now-vanished Campbell, Hope & King's 70/- ale. It went slowly at first after its launch in 1991, but when the first advertising appeared in 1992 sales began to speed up as drinkers decided here was a new substitute for the blandness of many lagers and the inconsistency of too much cask ale.

Imitation was again the sincerest sign that competitors were impressed. The big national brewers brought out their own versions of the new beer style that was known as 'smoothflow' by its friends and 'nitrokeg' by those such as Camra who feared another threat to cask ale. The most successful of the first 'nitrokeg' beers was one that Bass spent several years perfecting before launching it in 1994 under the name Caffrey's. Thomas Caffrey was the man who built the Ulster Brewery in Belfast, and Bass probably felt that this 'bitter served up like a stout' needed an Irish heritage.

Brewers had made technological changes in brewing, as well as serving beer. The conical fermenter, which had been pioneered by the Swiss in the 1920s, took off only with the increase in lager drinking of the 1970s. Contrary to popular belief, many warm-fermenting ale yeasts also settle out to the bottom of the fermenting vessel, like cold-fermenting lager yeasts. Brewers found brewing ales with bottom-settling yeasts in conical fermenters at last solved the problem of how best to remove excess yeast from finished beer. However, most of the country's best beers were made with yeast that insisted on floating to the top when its job was done, and traditional-minded brewers had to keep their older style of fermenting vessel or lose the characteristics their top-fermenting yeasts gave the beer.

The same problem of taste eventually halted expansion of another technological shift, into continuous fermentation. By 1970 continuous fermentation plant was being used by Bass, Mitchells & Butlers in Birmingham and by Watney in London, Edinburgh and Cork. It was reported that Watney's could now produce its Stingo strong ale in two days, rather than the nine months of the old system. However, while Stingo apparently did not suffer, there was one problem with many of the beers brewed under the continuous fermentation system: the flavour did not appeal. When one was test-marketed in the pubs owned by the Northampton Brewery Co., drinkers declared that it tasted 'like nail varnish'. Needless to say that one never made it to the wider market. This, together with problems getting the workforce to operate the new and more complex technology, meant continuous fermentation never advanced as its advocates once hoped it would.

By the 1980s the market dominance of the big brewers had been causing unease for more than twenty years in those circles of government charged with looking at industrial competition. Between 1966 and 1986 the brewing industry was the subject of fifteen official reports; and even in 1969 the Monopolies Commission had concluded that the tied house system, which at that time gave brewers ownership of 78 per cent of all pubs, was A Bad Thing.

Ministers put off tackling the perceived problems of the tied house. But the 1969 report on the brewing industry sparked the Errol Committee investigation into licensing law in England and Wales in 1972, and the parallel Clayson report on licensing in Scotland of 1973. The Erroll Report, which backed liberalized licensing hours and the lowering of the age limit for drinkers to seventeen, disappeared onto a top shelf somewhere in the Home Office. But the Clayson Report resulted in the Licensing (Scotland) Act of 1976, which effectively gave each licensing area the right to choose its own opening hours. Gingerly at first, and then more enthusiastically, the Scots extended evening and afternoon hours until they met in the middle, ending the mid-afternoon shutdown. Finally, in October 1977, Sunday drinking was permitted in Scotland for the first time in 124 years.

Despite the failure of Scottish society to collapse now the country's pubs were open all day, England and Wales had to wait twelve years for similar reforms to arrive. Only in September 1988 did a new Licensing Act allow pubs in the two countries to stay open from 11 a.m. to 11 p.m. without a break, six days of the week, for the first time since the Kaiser invaded Belgium. A House of Lords amendment extending Sunday lunchtime opening to 3 p.m. was slipped in (the government minister who failed to shout 'not content' and block the move admitted later he stayed silent because he thought someone else had been deputed to say the words). It was another seven years before in August 1995 pubs in England and Wales were finally to open all afternoon on Sundays.

Meanwhile, in 1989 the Monopolies and Mergers Commission had ended another investigation into the brewing industry with the conclusion that a 'complex monopoly' existed, based on high levels of vertical integration. Ironically, brewers' ownership of pubs had dropped in the previous twenty years to 58 per cent of the total, as the national brewers in particular sold off pubs: Watney's, for example, sold seven hundred in 1988. However, the 1980s had seen a series of takeovers in which a dozen old-established brewers disappeared into the arms of their peers. The rise of the 'new small brewers' sector, and the way the tied house system locked these new producers out of the chance to sell their beers in most of the country's pubs, undoubtedly influenced the MMC in its two main recommendations: that no brewer be allowed to own more than 2,000 pubs, and that every tenanted tied pub be allowed to have a 'guest' beer from an outside brewery.

The man whose job was to reject or accept the recommendations of the MMC was the Secretary of State for Trade and Industry in Margaret Thatcher's Conservative government, Lord Young of Graffham. Young, a strong believer in 'free enterprise' and as few restrictions on business as possible, was sympathetic; but Conservative MPs were 'uniformly hostile'. Young blamed this reaction on 'the brewers' support for constituency associations up and down the land' – brewers had been financial backers of the Conservative Party since at least the time of Gladstone and the Liberal Party's support of temperance campaigners in the nineteenth century.

Young stitched together a complicated compromise, the 'Beer Orders' of December 1989, that went part-way to applying the MMC's recommendations without actually satisfying anybody. From 1 May 1990 the 'big six' national brewers had two years to take the tie completely off half the pubs they owned over the first 2,000 each (a total of around 11,000 pubs): the rest (around 20,000) had to be allowed to take one 'guest beer', which had to be a cask beer (to ensure pubs did not bring in the nationally advertised keg bitters and draught lagers as their 'guests'). Even though it did not go as far as the MMC and Camra wanted, the ultimate result of the Beer Orders was by far the biggest shake-up the British brewing industry has ever seen in its history.

There were three main results of the Beer Orders. The first was a short boom in the number of new small breweries: the guest beer rule meant they had many thousands of potential new customers to serve, which encouraged hundreds of brewery start-ups in the first half of the 1990s. By 1996, the best year ever, when sixty-seven new small breweries opened, the number of micros operating in the UK had passed three hundred. Another, linked effect of the 'guest cask beer' rule was that in 1991 and 1992 ales increased their share of the market, and it looked as if the lager boom might be over. But this hiccup in the rise of lager did not last.

Meanwhile the big brewers quickly realized that there was no point in owning a pub if they could not supply it with beer. However, the new Secretary of State for Trade and Industry, Nicholas Ridley, had ruled in October 1989 that there was nothing to prevent them from selling their 'excess' pubs to an outsider, cheaply, but with a supply agreement that meant those pubs still took the national brewer's beer. They would also be allowed to 'tie' the same number of pubs as before the sale. The second result of the Beer Orders was thus an explosion in big retail pub operators such as Enterprise Inns and Century Inns, which grew from nowhere to owning a quarter of all pubs by 1994.

The third result, and ultimately the most revolutionary, was that, with the century-old link between brewing and pub owning now fractured by the rise of the non-brewing pub companies, brewers realized that they could stop brewing but continue owning pubs and retailing beer, buying the beer from stand-alone brewing specialists who owned no pubs themselves. As retailing was generally more profitable than brewing – it was claimed by one big brewer in the 1990s that pub retailers 'made six times more profit' than brewers – this seemed to make good economic sense. The biggest brewers in Britain began to jump one way or the other, becoming either brewers or retailers but, with the sole exception of Scottish & Newcastle, no longer both.

In 1991 Grand Metropolitan, the owner of Watney's, sold its brewing operations to Courage, owned since 1986 by Elders IXL of Australia, which also owned Foster's. In return, Courage with Grand Met set up a new concern, Inntrepreneur, which combined all Courage's former pubs with most of Grand Met's, to create a huge pubs-only concern owning 4,300 pubs. The same year Allied Breweries, now merely a subsidiary of the food and retailing group Allied-Lyons, announced it was selling all its breweries in the UK to a joint venture with Carlsberg of Denmark, to be called Carlsberg-Tetley, while the pubs would pass to a new Allied-Lyons subsidiary, Allied Retail. The sale was held up by a long MMC investigation, but finally passed in 1994.

As the 1990s progressed, the revolution triggered by the Beer Orders gradually worked its way through the industry. The pub companies – 'pubcos' – grew larger. More regional brewers gave up on brewing or sold up to someone else. Eldridge Pope, the Dorset brewer, also sold its brewery to a management buy-out, in 1997, to become another pure pub company. Gibbs Mew of Salisbury, with 300 pubs was bought by Enterprise Inns in 1998 and its brewery site sold, the first instance of a pure pubco buying a brewer. A row split the board of another family brewer, Morrell's of Oxford, in 1998, over whether to continue producing beer, with the chief executive, Ken Hodgson, declaring: 'Nobody but a bloody fool would make a commitment to stay in brewing.' Within a few months the company had been sold for £48 million and the brewery closed.

The 'national' brewers underwent an even more dramatic shake-up between 1991 and 2001. In 1995 Scottish & Newcastle bought Courage from its renamed owner, Foster's Group, to become the UK's biggest brewer, with a market share of more than 30 per cent. The takeover was passed by the government, though in 1989, before the Beer Orders, the MMC had blocked the bid by Foster's/Courage to buy S&N. In 1996 Bass bought Allied's share of the Carlsberg-Tetley set-up, only to have the MMC force it to let go, so that Carlsberg of Denmark ended up owning all of C-T. Allied (since 1994 called Allied Domecq, and one of the world's biggest drinks companies) which was on its way out of the British pub/brewing scene: in 1999 it sold the last of its pubs, with more than 1,800 going to a company called Punch Taverns, formed two years earlier to acquire 1,450 leased pubs from Bass.

Observers had expected both Bass and Whitbread to leave brewing eventually and concentrate on hotels, into which both had expanded, and retailing. It was no particular surprise when, early in 2000, it was revealed that Whitbread had sold its brewing operations to Interbrew, the Belgian brewing giant, for £400 million. What was a surprise, however, was the announcement several months later of the identity of the company that was purchasing all Bass's brewing operations for £2.3 billion – Interbrew, again. Since Interbrew owning both Whitbread's and Bass's brewing operations gave it somewhere between 32 per cent and 36 per cent of the entire UK beer market, and two of the country's biggest beer brands, Stella and Carling ('Black Label' had been dropped in 1997), the government's competition regulators had a fit. Early in 2001, after an investigation by the Competition Commission (the new name for the MMC), the Department of Trade and Industry ruled that Interbrew would have to sell all of Bass Brewers on competition grounds. However, Interbrew immediately went to the High Court, which threw out the DTI's decision on the grounds that Interbrew had not been given a chance to state its case for keeping at least part of the Bass brewing set-up.

The government dithered, and after a new investigation it decided in September 2000 that Interbrew could keep the 'Celtic Fringe' parts of Bass Brewers: the Tennent's brewery and its lagers in Scotland, and the Ulster Brewery in Belfast. The rest, including Carling, it would have to sell. On Christmas Eve 2001 Interbrew announced it had agreed to sell the Carling operation to Coors, the third-biggest brewer in the United States, for £1.2 billion. Many were surprised: Heineken or South African Breweries had been seen as the most likely purchaser, with a venture capital consortium as the next most likely. Coors, although it had been one of the under-bidders when Interbrew bought Bass's brewing arm, had barely registered on the radar as a possibility this time. Acquiring the Carling set-up practically doubled the size of the Colorado-based company.

The Carling deal, which went through in February 2002, let Interbrew keep the Bass brand, while Coors owned Worthington, as well as Carling and Caffreys. It put the Americans at number two in the UK beer market, still some way behind Scottish & Newcastle. It also put 75 per cent of the British beer market in the hands of four companies, and left more than 50 per cent of British brewing in foreign hands.

Seventeen years earlier, six brewers had owned 77 per cent of the market: if the Beer Orders had been intended to increase competition, they had completely the opposite effect. In addition, the beer market has become increasingly dominated by big brands. In 1989 the top five best-selling beers had just under 21 per cent of the total market, the top ten 31.6 per cent. Over the next ten years the independent pub companies increasingly bought the beers they perceived to be the most popular, that is, the existing best sellers, and sales of the big brands rose accordingly. In 1999 the top five beer brands in the UK had 34 per cent of all beer sales, the top ten just under 50 per cent.

Of the original Big Six, only Scottish & Newcastle remained in brewing from 1989, and it came under increasing pressure from investors to divest itself of its pubs. Grand Met had merged with Guinness in 1997 to form a world-wide drinks firm, Diageo. Bass – by now renamed Six Continents – announced in 2002 it was floating off its hotels arm and its retail operation as separate companies, with the retail side, which would take the revived name Mitchells & Butlers, controlling some 2,000 mostly branded pubs. Whitbread had sold 90 per cent of its pubs, and was down to around 600 or so pub-restaurants to sit alongside its hotel, health-club and coffee-bar operations. The Inntrepreneur estate formed by Courage and Grand Met had been taken over by the Japanese bank Nomura in 1997, and eventually sold in 2002 under the name Unique to a consortium that included Enterprise Inns, which had grown in ten years to be the biggest of the pubcos. Enterprise had the right to buy Unique in 2004, which would make the combined operation as big a pub-owner as any of the big brewers had ever been. Nomura had also bought Greenall's 1,240 franchised and tenanted pubs in 1999, selling them to Pubmaster in 2002. The result was that ten companies, seven of them pure retailers, owned 41 per cent of all the 66,000 or so pubs in the UK. How much better that is than 1989, when the Big Six brewers owned 33,400 pubs out of 76,000, or 44 per cent, is a subject for the moot.

If all this – the beer business still dominated by a handful of brewers, the pubs business dominated by a double-handful of pub owners – was a surprise to the people who drew up the Beer Orders, in the expectation they would increase competition, it should not have been. The situation had been predicted half a century earlier, by a right-wing economist called Arthur Seldon, writing in *The Economist* back in 1950.

Seldon had foreseen that the growing national brewers with heavily advertised brands would destroy the local monopoly of the small brewer, and place him under intense competitive pressure. (Seldon thought this competition would come from bottled beers, then the only national brands available.) 'Such competition,' Seldon wrote perceptively,

> may lead some small brewers to sell out to the larger; others may attempt to make their houses profitable by turning themselves into . . . chains of 'free' houses and selling the beer in greatest demand. Beer would then be supplied by a smaller number of specialist brewers who had disposed of their houses. The industry would then tend to separate into its two parts as the economic conditions in which the licensing system led to their integration faded away. The controversial 'tied house' system might in time come to be recognised as a phase arising from the peculiar social and economic conditions of the nineteenth century.

Seldon, whose scenario must have seemed inconceivable in 1950, when there were still more than 400 pub-owning family brewers, thought the division of beer production and distribution would take 'several decades' to develop, as it would be hampered by the big brewers' investments in bricks and mortar. As it happened, the mindset of the family brewers (heroically conservative or rigidly traditionalist, depending on your viewpoint) meant they could not see becoming retailers of other peoples' beers as an alternative to being taken over and closed. The development of the specialist national brewer and the specialist independent pub owner was thus delayed for forty years as the national brewers added more and more pubs to their estates, instead of sloughing them off as Seldon had predicted. Once the Beer Orders forced the first independent pub companies and pub-free national brewers into being, however, the two sides of the industry, pub-owning and brewing, sprang apart within a decade, just as Seldon said they would.

As the British brewing industry grapples with the twenty-first century, it is very different from the industry of even two decades earlier. Eight out of ten pints now come from brewers who do not own any pubs. Conversely, five out of six pubs are now owned by non-brewers. The number of independent local brewers has almost halved in thirty years, from around ninety in 1971 (depending on your definitions) to fewer than fifty. Old-established regional brewers are under continuing pressure to quit brewing, as they find that unless they put in a great deal of effort the returns do not justify the investment: Brakspear of Henley on Thames, for example, announcing in 2002 the decision to contract another company to brew its beers and concentrate on retailing, revealed it was actually losing money on every pint it brewed. Beer-drinking is under threat from new alternatives such as 'flavoured alcoholic beverages' or FABs: bottled, generally fruit- or spirit-flavoured drinks, around 5 per cent alcohol by volume, which provide young drinkers with the easy route into alcohol that lager-and-lime did in the 1950s. Despite increasing liberalization of licensing hours, total beer sales have continued to fall, to fewer than 35 million barrels a year, though this is still higher than any year from 1913 to 1972.

However, the decision in the 2002 Budget to take the equivalent of 14p a pint off the tax burden of the smallest brewers gave an instant boost to the microbrewery sector, which may be tiny but is enormously enthusiastic: the country's 500 small and medium-sized brewers produce some 1,700 different beers. A survey in 2001 found that even after forty years of rising lager sales, most men still drink draught ale at least once a week, with two out of three men aged eighteen to thirty-four being ale drinkers. In addition, those brewers that survive today, from the tiniest to the largest, are brewing beer because they want to, not because their great-grandfather founded a brewery and they know no other way of making a living.

Britain's favourite drink has a long history ahead of it still.

THE LOCAL BREW

Until the last thirty years of the twentieth century, beer was essentially a local product. This chapter traces the history of brewing first through a regional company that just missed becoming a substantial national player, and second through the vicissitudes of the industry in a single Scottish city.

When John William Green started work in Luton, the Bedfordshire town was best known for hats rather than beer. However, the company to which he gave his name became the biggest brewery business in the region, and brought Luton-brewed beer to millions.

Green's father Joseph, a Quaker ironware merchant, came to Luton in 1840, and John William was born in the town seven years later. When he left school at sixteen, in 1863, he was apprenticed to one of Luton's many straw-hat companies. After two years, in 1865, he left to join the tiny Phoenix brewery in Park Street West, Luton. This, one of only two breweries in the town, was run by H. and F. Pearman. In 1869, the twenty-two-year-old John William Green bought the brewery from the Pearmans, leaving them to concentrate on their wine merchants' business.

A description written years later of his working day emphasizes how closely the young brewery owner had to be involved in all sides of the business – beginning at 6 a.m., when he would be up to help with mashing the malt, and continuing after breakfast with a round of visits by dogcart to call on the brewery's customers and check that everything was all right.

John William's father remained a Quaker all his life (he was buried in Luton's Quaker burial ground in 1886, aged seventy-eight). But John William had become a Freemason as early as 1868, something he would not have done if he had remained a practising Quaker. There was nothing to prevent Quakers being brewers, however – in nearby Hitchin, across the border in Hertfordshire, the Lucas family, Quakers for 200 years, still ran the town's biggest brewery in the nineteenth century.

The Phoenix brewery's first takeover came in 1875, when Green acquired another small Luton brewer, Wadsworth and Thaire of Market Hill. The boost to business this brought meant that the brewery soon needed to expand. In April 1876 the *Brewers' Guardian* announced: 'Mr J. W. Green of the Phoenix Brewery, Luton has entrusted Mr Kinder with the enlargement of his brewery from seven to 15 quarters' – that is, from around thirty-five barrels of beer from each brew to a capacity of seventy-five barrels at a time. Arthur Kinder was a well-known Victorian brewery architect, and his services would not have been cheap.

By 1884 the only rival in the town to Green's growing business was the much older brewery in the New Bedford Road. This was properly known as the Luton Brewery Co. Ltd, which had been established when the brewery's owner, Thomas Sworder, retired in February 1874. However, the concern seems to have continued trading under the name Sworder's. It had ninety tied houses, and its first manager, C. R. Rigg, was appointed at the substantial salary, by 1874 levels, of £500 a year.

Brewing had been started in the New Bedford Road by the Gray family, who built the Crown and Anchor pub and a brewhouse alongside in 1831 (until it was demolished at the end of 1974, the back of the house still bore the inscription 'Gray's Celebrated XX Ales'). Sworder, a Hertfordshire lawyer, bought the Grays' brewery in 1849. Eight years later, in 1857, he acquired Burr's brewery in Park Street, with thirty-three pubs and beerhouses, for £41,250. He then erected a new brewery in the Bedford Road, and built up his stock of pubs so that eventually he owned thirty-five in Luton and another thirteen in nearby Dunstable, as well as others further away.

In any fight for dominance in Luton, Sworder's firm must have looked the favourite. But Green lured Sworder's master brewer from Bedford Road to join him at Park Street West, and concentrated on establishing the Phoenix brewery's reputation for the quality of its beers. By 1897, according to knowledgeable Lutonians, Sworder's brewery was almost bankrupt. That May, the 16 quarter Bedford Road brewery, together with fifty-eight hotels, pubs and beerhouses, was put up for sale in London.

The auction attracted tremendous interest (the scramble by brewers to acquire tied houses was at a peak) and the bidding started at £50,000, leaping up by as much as £10,000 a time and finally stopping at £139,000. Only at the end of the auction was the buyer's name revealed. The man with the winning bid was an agent acting for John William Green. The *Brewers' Journal* reported after the auction: 'We understand Mr Green has subsequently received several tempting offers for his purchase, but to no avail.' In his fiftieth year, Green had achieved domination of Luton's brewing business, and he was not going to let it go.

Green did not actually have the money to pay for the purchase: his own brewery, with forty or so pubs, was valued at only £85,000, not even two-thirds of the price he had just agreed for Sworder's. But he had until September, when the Luton Brewery Co. Ltd would be officially wound up, to work out a scheme. In an early version of the 'leveraged buyout', Green decided to use the assets of the company he was acquiring to pay for the acquisition. In August 1898 the *Brewers' Journal* announced that Green would be merging the two breweries, his own and Sworder's, as one company, J. W. Green Ltd, with a share issue of £300,000. By selling some of the shares in the new concern, the funds were found for the absorption of Sworder's.

By 1900 the Phoenix brewery had been rebuilt (by Adlams of

Bristol, another well-known firm of brewery architects) to cope with the increased business the takeover of Sworder's had brought. The brewery now had forty horses to pull the drays, and the men, who started work at 6.30 a.m., were allowed six free pints of beer a day. They were expected to wear the red stocking cap traditional to brewers, though in most other breweries this was already a dying fashion.

John William Green, meanwhile, had not restricted his interests to brewing. He had become active in politics, first as a Liberal, later as a Liberal Unionist and Conservative. He was elected to the first Luton town council, and then the first Bedfordshire County Council, on which he served for almost thirty years. He was also on the board of the Luton gas company, president of the Luton Conservative Association, a Justice of the Peace and, in 1906, High Sheriff of Bedfordshire.

A price list for private customers from around 1910 shows the company producing a range of eight different draught beers, typical of the time:

Beer	Price per 9 gallon firkin
Pale ale 'Standard Ale'	9s
Pale ale No. 1, Fine Tonic Ale	10s 6d
India Pale Ale	13s 6d
XXX Strong Ale	12s
XX Mild Ale	9s
AK Light Ale	7s 6d
Double stout	12s
Porter	9s

The brewery also sold three of its beers in stoppered bottles – Lutonian pale ale at 2s 6d per dozen large, and Lutonian XXX Strong Ale and Double Stout at 3s 6d per dozen – as well as Bass and Guinness in bottle.

While Green's survived the First World War without much trouble, others were less lucky. Over in Hertfordshire Percy Charles Reid of the Hatfield and Harpenden Breweries, the county's second largest brewer, lost his son, a young lieutenant, in action near Ypres. Reid decided that, with his son dead, he would break up the company, an amalgamation of Pryor Reid of Hatfield (which had roots going back at least as far as 1635) and Glover's of Harpenden. In 1919 J. W. Green bought the Harpenden brewery and some twenty-five pubs and beerhouses, including ten in and around Luton. (The rest of the pubs, including eleven more once owned by Glover's, were acquired by Benskin's of Watford the following year.)

The next year Green's acquired the small north Hertfordshire brewery of W. and S. Lucas Ltd, Sun Street, Hitchin, and its fifty-two tied houses. For not quite three years the Lucas brewery carried on making its own beers for its own pubs, but in 1923 Green's closed the Hitchin brewery, and incorporated the Lucas tied houses into the Green's estate. The Lucas family had been brewing in Sun Street since at least 1709, and maintained a tradition of giving the eldest son the name William, so that there were eight William Lucases from the seventeenth century to the twentieth. They were early members of the Quakers, and when the brewery became a limited company in 1896 its first chairman, William Lucas VII, was a professed teetotaller.

The Lucases had family and business connections with another old-established Quaker brewery, Morris's of Ampthill, in Bedfordshire, which was bought by Green's in 1926, its seventy-two pubs and beer-houses taking the Luton brewery's tally of tied houses up to the 250 mark. Morris's could follow its roots back to 1738, when William Morris of Ampthill left his smith's shop and brewhouse to his son John. The 'Mr Morris of Ampthill' who bought Buckley & Garnish's brewery in Bury St Edmunds for his nephew John Clark in 1792 was almost certainly a member of this family. Buckley & Garnish was the brewery where Benjamin Greene started in Bury St Edmunds before he acquired the Westgate brewery to brew on his own account, thus founding what is now Greene King.

John William Green retired from the chairmanship of the company he had founded, and its board, in 1930, aged eighty-three. He was followed in the chair by his sons Sidney Green, until 1932, and Colonel Harold Green, who reigned from 1932 until 1937, and again from 1942 to 1944. John died, aged eighty-five, in 1932, and the flags flew at half-mast on every public building in Luton, for he was a local hero. Every one of his company's 300 or so tied houses declared on the signboard that they sold 'noted LUTON ales'. Every bottle of beer that left the brewery bore the legend 'Lutonian brand'. Every cask that left the company cooperage, painted in the company colour, malachite green, was stamped 'J. W. Green LUTON'. Even the brewery dray-horses had names such as 'Lutonian Sensation'. Green was proud to be a Lutonian, and Lutonians were proud of him.

But his death in 1932 brought the family financial problems, and in 1935 the company had to be reorganized, with a triumvirate of managing directors. They were W. W. Merchant, Green's brewery manager, who had become a director in 1917; Colonel J. B. S. Tabor, John William's grandson, who had joined the board in 1932; and Percival Lovell, the company secretary, who had also joined the board in 1932. Another new member of the board was Richard Ottley, a director of the merchant bank Erlangers; the relationship with Erlangers was a key element in Green's subsequent expansion.

The following year, 1936, Green's bought another Hertfordshire brewery, Adey & White of St Albans. Its fifty-six pubs made 'an ideal purchase', the Luton firm's directors said, pushing Green's trading area down towards Watford. The St Albans brewery was another eighteenth-century foundation, whose first owners, the Kinder family, had bought up pubs in the 1730s. It became Adey & White in 1868, and took over two other small breweries in the city in 1878 and 1918. By the time the brewery was sold to Green's its equipment was old and out-of-date, the pubs needed money spending on them, and neither of the two directors had male heirs to whom they could pass the business on. It was closed within two months of Green's taking over, with the last brew poured down the drains.

Green's head brewer since 1932 had been Bernard Dixon, previously the head brewer at Greene King's Panton Brewery in Cambridge when in 1931 it won the champion challenge cup at that year's Brewers' Exhibition. In 1940 Dixon became one of Green's managing directors. Brewers everywhere were struggling to cope with the problems of wartime, including shortages of everything: malt, paper for bottle labels, fuel for lorries (even in November 1945, 20 per cent of Green's deliveries were being made by horse-drawn dray). But there were plenty of customers, and for Green's one important group of eager beer-drinkers was the United States Army Air Force. The flat Bedfordshire plains were ideal for bomber airfields, and from 1943 onwards there were many American airmen stationed in the area. However, they could not get on with traditional English ale: it was much too warm and flat for their lager-conditioned palates. What they did like were the sharper bottled beers. But bottles were rationed, even for Americans.

The commanders of the US forces turned to their nearest big brewer, 'JW's', and promised to supply the company with all the necessary malt and hops if it could come up with an answer. The solution was not entirely new: Watney's, the Pimlico brewer, had been experimenting with something similar in the 1930s. What Dixon did with the Americans' ingredients was to brew a beer that was then chilled, filtered and put into special casks under pressure – 'bottled beer from barrels', as a contemporary newspaper reporter on the *Luton News* described it in a report from December 1944.

It was a long way from traditional English beer, but the GIs for whom it was brewed loved it. Lorries from far-off bases made long journeys to Luton to pick up supplies. No delay was allowed before the beer got to the lips of gallant US airmen returning from action, the *Luton News* reported: 'The special serving apparatus which is needed for the beer, including an icebox for the cask, is fitted onto jeeps, and when the great bombers touch down after smashing at the Hun, out dash the jeeps with a drink for the crews.' Dixon must have been impressed at the news that his beer could be served up straight after a hurried journey across a bumpy airfield. Any drink that could stand that kind of handling was clearly immune to the most careless pub landlord.

The *Luton News* ended its report with the wish that 'perhaps when the war is over the Luton people will themselves be able to try this special beer so much liked by the boys from over there'. But the experience with pressurized beer was put on the back burner after the war, and Green's concentrated on expanding its operations in a spectacular fashion. Bernard Dixon had decided that in twenty years' time there would only be a dozen or so brewers left in the UK, and he wanted the Luton brewery to be one of them.

In the five years from 1948 to the end of 1952 the Luton brewery took over seven other breweries from Sunderland to Sussex and tripled in size to just over 1,000 pubs. First to be acquired, in 1948, was E. & H. Kelsey of Tunbridge Wells, in Kent; with eighty-four tied houses, it had had a trading agreement with Green's since before the war. (Indeed, it was American and Canadian servicemen drinking in Kelsey's pubs who had given Green's No. 1 bottled pale ale the nickname Dragon's Blood, which the brewery later adopted officially.) Beer production carried on at Kelsey's Culverden brewery, not finally stopping until 1956.

Early in 1949 Green's looked at a brewery on the Isle of Wight, but decided against a purchase. The board agreed, though, that they wanted it to be known they would look at companies 'however remotely situated they might appear from the home premises at Luton'. The next purchase, in fact, was just twenty-five miles down the road: at the end of 1949 Green's acquired J. & J. E. Phillips of Royston, in north Hertfordshire, and another 149 pubs. The Phillips family, which had owned the brewery since its foundation in the 1720s, had been trying to sell up since at least 1926. They made at least three approaches to Greene King, the Bury St Edmunds brewers, and talks had been held with two more local breweries, Wells & Winch of Biggleswade and Simpson's of Baldock.

Even though the family was delighted to sell, it was Green's who had approached Phillips suggesting a sale, the Phillips board told its workers. Two members of the Phillips family, Harold and his cousin Eric, would join the Green's board. The Royston brewery closed in January 1950, the workers being paid off with £7 a man for every year they had worked at Phillips, the equivalent of several months' wages for many. Within ten years Green's had conducted a ruthless purge of the weaker Phillips pubs, closing down one-third of the total. The necessity to renovate the rest, however, was a drag on Green's finances for some years.

In July 1950, operating through E. & H. Kelsey, the J. W. Green Group acquired George Ware & Sons of Frant, Sussex, and sixteen tied houses. The next year, in September 1951, Green's took over Soulby Sons & Winch Ltd of Alford, Lincolnshire, which brought in another 143 pubs. The Alford brewery remained open for a short while, but in February 1952 the Luton men made a successful bid for another Lincolnshire brewery, Mowbray & Co. of Grantham, with 204 pubs. The Alford brewery closed, and Mowbray's stayed open for another twelve years. The Lincolnshire takeovers brought Green's a bottled beer brand that it would eventually sell throughout its estate, Poacher Brown.

Seven months after buying Mowbray's, Green's turned its acquisitive eye back nearer to home, with the purchase of E. K. & H. Fordham of Ashwell in north Hertfordshire. The company had lost its heir apparent, Anthony Hill, grandson of one of the brewery's founders, when his Spitfire was shot down in 1942 while on a photographic reconnaissance mission. After the war the remaining shareholders were mostly elderly, and several were keen to realize their assets. The offer by Green's (which had first expressed an interest in buying the Ashwell brewery in 1942) was announced in the local newspaper on 4 September 1952. By 13 September, shareholders representing 76 per cent of the total holding in Fordham's had accepted the offer. Within another fortnight any resistance that remained was over, and Fordham's ninety-one surviving pubs were finally in Green's hands. The brewery, by far the largest employer in the village, stayed open as a reserve brewery and subsidiary bottling plant, bottling Guinness, Worthington and Bass for Green's. It finally closed in 1965.

Just before Christmas 1952 the J. W. Green Group bought R. Fenwick and Co. of Sunderland from its owner, George Younger & Sons of the Candleriggs Brewery, Alloa, in Scotland. George Younger had acquired Fenwick's in 1898, when it was already around 130 years old, and carried on brewing there even after the brewery was badly damaged by bombing in 1941. But George Younger decided it needed cash to build a new bottling hall at its Alloa brewery and buy pubs in Scotland, and Green's was an eager buyer of brewing capacity (the Sunderland brewery only finally closed in 1964). The purchase meant that in January 1953 J. W. Green was the ninth largest brewer in Britain, with 1,010 pubs, just behind Courage and ahead of Ansells and Barclay Perkins.

While it was expanding, Green's was still trying to maintain some old traditions. The *Luton News* in 1947 was reporting that the brewers at the Luton brewery were sporting red tassel caps, which had been supplied by the company since the 1930s to encourage the wearing of the traditional brewer's red stocking cap. (The company's maltsters wore green ones.) The J. W. Green Group annual convention programme for 1953 recorded, under the heading 'Traditional Headgear', that

> an interesting tradition at the Luton Brewery is that of the men in the brewing department wearing red stockinette caps whilst at work. The Luton Brewery has always been noted for this particular form of cap, which, of course, is the traditional brewer's headgear. Long after its use had ceased elsewhere, this link with the past survived at Luton, and there is no intention of dropping the custom.

By now Green's had actually adopted as a trademark a figure of an eighteenth-century brewery worker in red cap, apron and breeches, holding a beer cask. He replaced several earlier marks, including the phoenix, John W. Green's signature, and a curious example (p. 248) from the 1930s showing a drayman sitting astride a cask of XB beer, a full glass in his hand, with the slogan: 'When you're on a good thing, stick to it!'

The company's beers around this time were a light mild called BB (the staple beer in most houses), a dark mild called AK and a bitter. Prices were 1s 1d for mild, and 1s 4d for bitter. Bernard Dixon had banned the old malachite green 'house' colour of John William's era, and pubs were now painted black and white. Refurbished pubs were given new bar tops in the wonder material of the day, Formica, and new pubs were fitted with copper bar tops. Display fittings had a backing of peach-coloured glass.

The year 1953 passed without any further additions to the J. W. Green empire, though there was much sizing-up of potential bid targets: at a board meeting on 27 August 1953, eleven different brew-eries were discussed. But if Bernard Dixon's ambitions to turn Green's into a leading national brewer were to be fulfilled, he needed some-thing he had not yet been able to find: a brand, an image that would put it alongside the likes of Bass and Watney. The chance came early in 1954 when Flower & Sons of Stratford upon Avon agreed to sell out to the Luton brewery.

The Stratford company had been founded in 1831 by Edward Fordham Flower, whose father Richard had been a partner between 1785 and 1802 in a brewery just off St Andrew's Street in Hertford with his brother-in-law John Fordham, uncle to the Ashwell Fordhams. Richard Flower was a member of a family of radical campaigners, and his brother Benjamin was gaoled for six months for libelling a bishop in a pamphlet he published. Richard Flower's own efforts included a pamphlet in 1802 entitled 'Observations on the Malt Tax', which urged the government in verse to 'tax not that liquor which cheers up the poor'. Sadly, successive governments have ignored this call.

In 1818 Richard left Hertfordshire for America, taking with him his youngest son, Edward Fordham Flower, who was then thirteen.

The Flowers settled in southern Illinois, near the Wabash river, on what later became the township of Albion (family legend says they turned down a site further north on the shore of Lake Michigan, believing it to be too marshy. Others were less fussy, and the city of Chicago was eventually founded there.) Richard and Edward returned to England in 1824, and Edward stayed behind when his father went back to America. He married Selina Greaves, a girl from Barford, near Stratford upon Avon, and eventually went into the timber business in Stratford.

The year after the Beer House Act was passed in 1830, dramatically increasing the number of places selling beer, Edward Fordham Flower, then twenty-six, built his first brewery in Stratford. He chose a site by the canal in what became known as Brewery Street, just off the Birmingham Road. The brewery was a relatively small operation, with only six men and a boy on the payroll, and at first it produced just three beers, strong ale XX, table ale X and stout porter. But the well water used by the brewery came from similar geographical strata to those of Burton on Trent, with beds of marl and gypsum, which helped brew sparkling, easily clearing ales. Sales figures in 1833 were £3,423; fourteen years later they had trebled to £10,220 a year. By 1866 the company was turning over £100,000 a year, probably more than any other brewery outside the big brewing centres, and Flower's had opened agencies in Manchester, Birmingham and London.

The brewery became a limited company, Flower & Sons Ltd, in 1887, with Charles Flower as chairman. Charles, who had no children, died in 1892 and was followed in the chair by his brother Edgar, who had secured the future of the dynasty by siring ten offspring. When Edgar died in 1903 he was succeeded as chairman by his son Archie, later Sir Archibald Flower.

Between 1896 and 1930 Flower's took over half a dozen other brewers, starting with William Turner of the Caudlewell Brewery, Shipston-on-Stour, and finishing with Rowland's of Evesham, and acquired a reputation for producing quality pale ales. At one time two train loads of Flower's beer left Stratford for London every week, on Tuesdays and Fridays. Five years after the end of the Second World War the brewery was employing around 110 brewers and labourers and making 2,500 barrels of beer a week, with 80 per cent sold on draught and the rest, around 30,000 dozen bottles a week, bottled on site. Three malthouses at the brewery produced all the malt needed. Flower's controlled 357 tied houses, forty-five managed and the rest of them tenanted.

But by the early 1950s the company was in some trouble after overspending on a new brewhouse. The old family management, led by Dennis and Fordham Flower, had been forced aside, but the new leadership soon hit problems of its own, particularly with the quality of the beer. Directors' meetings, held in meeting rooms at hotels such as the Savoy, Mayfair and Grosvenor House in London, far from the brewery in Stratford, were frequently acrimonious as different family factions fought.

The alliance with Green's brought in both technical expertise to help solve the problems at the Stratford brewery (drains, it was said later) and extra demand to fill its vats (the Flower family secured a guarantee that brewing would continue at Stratford for at least twenty years), while the Luton company acquired the well-known brand name it was seeking. Although Flower's had only brought 350 tied houses to the party, and had just three out of nine directors on the board of the new company, the name of the concern was now Flower's Breweries Ltd.

The next year, 1955, Bernard Dixon used his new brand name to launch a beer he had been perfecting since first brewing something like it for the American servicemen in 1943. Flower's Keg, an easy-to-handle, pressurized, filtered beer, was essentially the brew the GIs had loved so much. The beer in the kegs was Flower's Original bitter ('a very suitable beer for the kegging process', according to the company), brewed at Stratford and trundled by the tanker-load across the South Midlands to Luton for kegging.

The cost of installing the pressure taps and other apparatus for serving keg beer in pubs was high, the company admitted, a factor that delayed its introduction. But the consistency of the new product, 'bottled beer in a cask' as it had been called twelve years before, was a great success at a time when the often poor quality of cask beers meant many pubgoers drank only bottled beer, or spiked a half-pint of draught bitter or mild with a bottle of pale ale or brown ale. At first Flower's used keg bitter only to introduce its beers to small free-trade customers, such as working men's clubs and cricket club bars, which did not have sufficient turnover for cask-conditioned ales to be kept in good condition. The first dispense for Flower's Keg was

WHEN YOU'RE ON A GOOD THING STICK TO IT

The trade mark registered by JW Green in the early 1930s. It was later replaced by a brewery worker from an earlier time, the Brewmaster.

installed on the bar of the Napier Club at the Napier Aero Engines factory, Luton airfield (as Luton airport then was).

As the beer gained more free-trade outlets, drinkers began to demand it in their own Flower's pubs, and by 1960 Flower's Keg was widely available in the brewery's tied estate, after a new kegging hall was built in a converted maltings at Stratford. It was not the first container beer, but it was the first to be presented to drinkers wary of the dodgy standard of much draught ale as a new class of 'quality-controlled' beer. Other brewers, such as Watney Mann with Red Barrel and Ind Coope with Double Diamond, soon began to market more widely their own versions of 'container' beer. To Flower's annoyance the word 'keg' could not be registered as a trademark, and it became the generic term for pasteurized, pressurized beers.

Brands were important to Bernard Dixon, and he always looked for opportunities to advertise Flower's beers. For the Soho Fair of 1957 Flower's had a float carrying a giant Brewmaster figure, to publicize the company's strong pale ale of that name, while the low-loader lorry which pulled the float was mounted with a huge dragon from the Dragon's Blood bottle label which breathed flames from its nostrils, powered by a gas bottle hidden in the dragon's body (alas, this proved too dangerous to use except for publicity pictures in the brewery yard).

The same year, during redevelopment work at Park Street West, the company applied for planning permission to erect a 14 foot tall, revolving, floodlight Brewmaster figure on top of its new, 120 foot high lager conditioning tower (Dixon also believed in the coming importance of lager, though as yet it had only a tiny market). Fortunately for the Luton skyline, the borough planning committee threw the application out. One sarcastic councillor managed to ask if the scroll in the Brewmaster figure's hand contained the chemical formula for the beer, a remark which must have hurt Dixon, since he had designed the Brewmaster himself.

Flower's now had 1,500 employees and controlled 1,125 pubs from Cumberland to Kent, covering twenty-three counties, as well as the Thresher off-licence chain, taken over in 1957. But the company still wanted to grow. It was buying individual pubs in the London area and running them as managed houses under a separate subsidiary, whose identity as an arm of Flower's was kept quiet so as not to alarm the London brewers. In 1956 Bernard Dixon had turned up at Meux and Co.'s Nine Elms brewery in south London, which would have filled a large hole in the Flower's empire, and announced to the doorman: 'Tell your managing director Mr Dixon is here to see him.' Dixon's activities had not made him a universally popular figure in the brewing industry, and when the doorman announced to his boss the name of the visitor at the front door, he was told: 'Give my compliments to Mr Dixon and tell him to f*** off!'

What amounted to a fundamental disagreement over company strategy was approaching crisis point. It had become clear to the Flower family board members that their managing director wanted to concentrate brewing at Luton, despite an agreement at the time of the merger that production would continue at Stratford for at least twenty years. There were also fears about the size of the company's borrowing, and its future gearing. In 1958 the row over strategy boiled over: Dixon was forced into premature retirement, his place at the helm taken by Sir Fordham Flower.

But if the Flower family had had difficulties with their smaller brewery back in the early 1950s, there was little chance of their making a decent fist of events at the end of the decade with a company so much bigger. One senior employee said later that 'within a short time it became apparent the steam had gone out of Flower's management, the remaining directors being mostly charming country gentlemen totally lacking in BD's drive'.

Even to the charming country gentlemen it was clear Flower's had to take action to survive, and the board explored several different options: it bought shares in Usher's of Trowbridge in 1959 with a view to a takeover (though Usher's was bought by Watney Mann the following year) and merger talks were held with Tennant Brothers of Sheffield and Brickwood's of Portsmouth. There was also a proposal floated in 1959 for a loose merger of Flower's, Greene King of Bury

St Edmunds and Simonds of Reading, which went nowhere (Simonds merged with Courage and Barclay in 1960). Meanwhile, in July 1959, Flower's signed a 25-year trading agreement with the London brewer Whitbread (which had owned around 2 per cent of the company since 1954), and Colonel Bill Whitbread joined the Flower's board.

But the sharks were loose in the brewing pond, and in 1961 there were rumours that Eddie Taylor, the Canadian who was welding together an empire of regional British breweries to promote his Carling Black Label lager, was interested in Flower's and had built up a stake. By this time Whitbread had invested some £1 million in Flower's, giving it, at January 1962, around 11 per cent of the equity. Flower's directors owned only around 2 per cent of the company, and were starting to worry about their vulnerability to a hostile takeover. There was some support in the company for an amalgamation with Watney Mann. However, there was a 'friendlier' option available. Whitbread had acquired Tennant's of Sheffield, another company in which it had held a 'friendly' stake, in December 1961. The Flower's board asked the Chiswell Street brewers if they would like to acquire Flower's as well. The answer was 'yes', and by May 1962 Whitbread's takeover was complete.

In January 1963 Whitbread announced that a new bottling plant would be built for Flower's in Oakley Road, Luton, three miles from the Park Street West brewery. But the proximity of the new site to the M1 motorway, with all that implied for fast delivery by lorry to far-away areas, must have soon occurred to someone in the Whitbread hierarchy. In August 1965 the intended bottling plant had become an intended new brewery, and another announcement was made: Park Street West was to be closed down.

In Stratford, meanwhile, modernization work was being carried out up to the end of 1966. However, the year after Whitbread acquired Flower's it had also taken over West Country Breweries, which had a brewery in Cheltenham. In 1967 the Londoners announced that they would be closing the Stratford brewery and moving production to the Cheltenham brewery. Stratford brewed its last beers in February 1968, and the town's largest employer and largest ratepayer was gone. The name remained, however: the Cheltenham brewery now operated under the title Whitbread Flower's Ltd. Flower's still had a pull other brands lacked.

A few months later the Oakley Road brewery in Luton began brewing, becoming fully operational in 1969, when Park Street West was closed. Oakley Road cost £9 million to build; the first entirely new brewery in Britain for thirty years, it was designed to replace both Park Street West and Whitbread's own Chiswell Street brewery. It was largely automated, and brewed only keg beers and 'container' beers (bottles and cans).

Just before Park Street West closed, in April 1969, Flower's at Luton had officially become part of Whitbread (London) Ltd, and the Flower's name began disappearing from pub fronts and bar tops. A few old Green's brands survived for a while – Poacher brown ale, Brewmaster pale ale – but with the Whitbread name on the label. When, after years of debate over what to do with the site, the Park Street West brewery was finally demolished in January 1978 (it ended up as hardcore on the road up to a Hertfordshire pig farm), there was little to show it had existed apart from a few pub windows still etched with the slogan 'J. W. Green's noted Luton ales'.

Oakley Road was not a happy new home for Luton's brewers, however. At the local paper, the *Luton News*, the file on the Park Street brewery is filled only with reports of successful company horticultural shows and tenants' association dinners. However, the files on the Oakley Road brewery are thick with cuttings covering strike after industrial dispute after stoppage. There were two strikes by workers at Oakley Road in 1969, the first year of full production, and others in 1970, 1973, 1974, 1976, 1977 (three times) and 1978–80.

Although there was no more trouble between 1981 and the final catastrophe in 1984, it looks with hindsight as if Whitbread might have been waiting for something to happen to give it the excuse to close the brewery, since the eventual shut-down happened so quickly. Whitbread openly admitted it had too much brewing capacity in a declining market, though in 1983 it spent £1 million updating the Gold Label barley wine production line at Oakley Road.

In March 1984 pay talks began for the 305 Transport and General Workers Union members at Oakley Road. The TGWU might have been expecting only the usual ritual huffing and puffing from both sides before a mutually acceptable figure was found, but negotiations dragged on. A 'lightning' 24-hour strike took place on the eve of the bank holiday, 3 May. Whitbread declared the workers had broken their contracts, and reinstatement would 'depend on disciplinary hearings for each man'. True to their word, the management called in the first worker through the gate on the Monday after the strike, a security guard, and told him he was dismissed. Faced with this, the workers escalated the action into an all-out strike.

A warning that the brewery could close was made on 31 May, four weeks into the strike. Less than two weeks later, on 11 June 1984, the main Whitbread board declared that the brewery would not reopen. Each of the workers was offered an average of £6,200 in compensation. The company admitted that excess production capacity was 'a factor' in the closure: Oakley Road's 1.5 million barrels a year would not be missed.

Ironically, the Flower's name had made a return in 1981, when Whitbread, responding to the growing interest in cask-conditioned ales, had revived Flower's Original for the name of a new cask beer, brewed at Cheltenham. It later brought back Flower's IPA as well. However, in 1998 Whitbread announced the Cheltenham brewery would be closing, with the Flower's beers likely to go to the Boddington's brewery in Manchester.

As an epitaph for Cheltenham, and also for Stratford and Park Street West, one could do little better than to quote a speech made in 1955 when the Cheltenham brewery was under threat from a finance group that wanted to liquidate it and sell its assets:

A well-managed company like the Cheltenham and Hereford Brewery [the former name of West Country Breweries] has a local tradition and is a human activity with staff and employees who have worked with the company for many years, and their fathers and grandfathers, in some cases, before them; they may also hope that their sons will be employed in the organisation. It seems to me that a company such as this, with all its staff and employees, is of great human importance and it would not be in the best interests of the brewing industry or indeed of the country for such an entity to be liquidated for the benefit of a quick profit for purely financial interests . . . with complete disregard for those who work in the company . . . I am convinced that the continuance of old-established concerns, run on progressive lines, is in the public interest and consequently sound business.

The occasion was the Whitbread annual meeting of 1955; the speaker, Colonel Bill Whitbread.

The city of Edinburgh has every claim to be one of the great brewing centres of Europe. It was a leader in the production of the best-known local beer style, Scotch Ale, and Scotland's biggest brewing centre: even in 1958 the city had eighteen surviving brewery companies, as many as London had at that time.

Edinburgh brewers had several immediate advantages over brewers elsewhere in Scotland. Most importantly, fine brewing water was available from wells around the city, especially on a line west from Holyrood through Canongate, Cowgate and the Grassmarket to Fountainbridge. In addition, the farms of Lothian supplied good grain, while coal could be brought in from local mines to boil water (the city's nickname, 'Auld Reekie', is sometimes said to come from the clouds of smoke, 'reek' in Scots, that issued from all the brewery chimneys). Finally, a large and thirsty population was to be found just outside each brewery gate.

However, large-scale commercial brewing was slow to develop in Edinburgh. Entrepreneurial brewers found they were restricted by a meddlesome town council eager to impose its own excise tax of two pennies Scots on every Scots pint (a Scots pint being approximately three English pints).

The city's brewers were crammed in among their neighbours, not all of them savoury. The father of the Edinburgh lawyer George Combe ran a brewery in Livingston's Yards, 'close under the south-west bank and rock of the Castle', and in his memoirs Combe described the brewery's locality during his childhood in the 1790s:

> to the east a Scotch acre of ground was a filthy swamp in winter, and covered with dunghills in summer. All round, to the east and south, were tan-works and a magnesia-work, which poured their refuse into open ditches with small declivity. The public drain, charged with the soil of the Grassmarket and Westport, two humble localities of Edinburgh, ran past uncovered . . . a more unhealthy residence can scarcely be conceived.

One Edinburgh brewer, now forgotten, helped advance the cause of science in the 1750s by allowing a young doctor, Joseph Black, to collect the contents of the bubbles that rose off the fermenting wort in his brewery. Black had discovered that if you poured acid on to chalk, an invisible gas was produced which would stifle a candle flame; this gas he called 'fixed air'. In 1757 Black's experiments in the brewery proved that the bubbles given off by fermenting beer contained this same 'fixed air': shaken up in a glass with lime water, it would precipitate out chalk.

Black's experiments in Edinburgh were the first steps towards a truly scientific understanding of the chemistry of brewing, and strongly influenced another great British scientist, Joseph Priestley, who made his own experiments into the gas given off as beer ferments at the Meadow Lane brewery in Leeds around 1770. However, another twenty years would pass after Priestley's investigations before the French chemist Antoine Lavoisier showed Black's 'fixed air' to be made of carbon and oxygen, in the form of carbon dioxide, and a century before a proper understanding emerged of the role of yeast in producing carbon dioxide as it turned sugar into alcohol.

Edinburgh's breweries were still small even in 1795, with only two known to have fixed capital greater than £1,000. Two decades on, when Robert Stein & Co. of the Canongate brewery went bankrupt in 1819, it was a big concern in local terms, valued at over £5,000, but its inventory suggests its maximum output was only around 9,000 barrels a year.

Edinburgh's brewers were lucky enough to be able to tap into two very different sorts of water. One was soft, suitable for making the comparatively dark, sweetish, strong, malty type of beer known as Edinburgh Ale or (in its export version) Scotch Ale. The other was hard, and similar enough to the gypsum-laden wells of Burton upon Trent, the great centre of pale ale brewing, for Edinburgh brewers in the second half of the nineteenth century to be able to make a very acceptable version of Burton's most renowned beer, India Pale Ale. William Younger & Co., for example, brewed six draught beers in 1871: IPA and five versions of Edinburgh Ale, from X Mild (the youngest) to XXXX Stock (the most matured).

From the 1850s onwards, Edinburgh brewers found their feet in the export trade. The capital fielded two of the very biggest exporters, William Younger and William McEwan. By 1880 it is reckoned the bigger brewers in Edinburgh were selling half their output locally, a quarter in Scotland generally and the rest in England and abroad: outside Scotland, only the brewers of Dublin and Burton upon Trent had similar sales splits between local and distant trade.

The city's brewers were heavily concentrated in the historic centre of Edinburgh: there were at least six breweries along North Back Canongate (today's Calton Road) alone. In the 1890s, as sites grew too cramped for further expansion, the water table dropped because of increased extraction and wells became contaminated by other local industries, and several moved out to greenfield sites to the east and west. (It is claimed that pressure to move was also put upon the brewers of Edinburgh Old Town by Queen Victoria, who was aggrieved by what must have been the almost continual smell of malt and hops in the air whenever she stayed at Holyrood Palace.) The

Duddingston/Craigmillar area, where the water was similar to that found in the centre of the city and where new rail links made it easier to supply drinkers further away, saw seven new breweries employing an estimated total of 2,000 people opened in the sixteen years between 1886 and 1902.

The first new brewery in Craigmillar was opened by William Murray, who moved his operation there in 1886 from the village of Ednam in Roxboroughshire, some 40 miles to the south-east of Edinburgh. Six years later Andrew Drybrough & Co. was under pressure to move from its home, the Craigend brewery at the west end of North Back Canongate, because the North British Railway Company wanted to build a new tunnel through Calton Hill behind it to double the number of lines into Waverley Station. Seeing Murray thriving, Drybrough shifted to a greenfield site on the Duddingston Road in Craigmillar, which was handy for the recently built suburban railway line.

Shortly thereafter, in 1895, Pattison, Elder & Co. opened the New Brewery in Duddingston. This concern was built by the Pattison brothers, Walter and Edward. However, three years after the brewery opened the business collapsed, having never made a profit. Investigation showed that Pattisons Ltd had been trading insolvently almost since the beginning, and the affair ended with the brothers' trial and imprisonment in 1901 on charges of fraud.

In 1899 the New Brewery was bought by Robert Deuchar of the Sandyford brewery, Newcastle upon Tyne, which eventually concentrated all its output in Duddingston. Farquar Deuchar, Robert Deuchar's son and the main shareholder in the company, died in 1950 and soon afterwards his stake was put up for sale by the family trustees. The successful tender was made at the end of 1953 by Newcastle Breweries, which carried on brewing at Duddingston until 1961.

At the start of the new century, Edinburgh had thirty breweries operating within its borders. But business was becoming harder, and seven small to medium-sized concerns closed between 1902 and 1913. They included Alexander Melvin & Co. of the Boroughloch brewery, which closed in 1907, it was said, because Alexander Melvin junior, the then proprietor, was enamoured of a rich American lady who was fervently anti-drink and who told him she would agree to marriage only if he gave up the beer-brewing business.

The scandal of the Pattisons' collapse was nothing to the shame and disgrace surrounding the demise of Edinburgh United Breweries Ltd in 1934. Edinburgh United had been formed in December 1889 as an amalgamation of four concerns in the city, including Robert Disher & Co. of the Edinburgh & Leith brewery in Canongate, famous for the strong Disher's Ten Guinea Ale, and Ritchie & Son of Bell's brewery, Pleasance. The Bell's brewery premises, one of the oldest in the city, took its name from its owner in the mid-eighteenth century, Bartholomew Bell, who brewed a famous beer called Black Cork. Sadly, the recipe for Black Cork died with the owner of the brewery in 1837, Robert Keir.

Edinburgh United never thrived, and it appears that by the late 1920s someone had decided the only way to survive was to get out of paying some excise duty. Every brewery in the country had a resident excise man whose job was to be present at each brew and measure the strength of the wort and the amount brewed, so that the beer tax to be paid could be calculated. From at least October 1926, Edinburgh United began producing 'secret' brews, made late at night and over weekends and public holidays, about which the excise man was never told and on which the brewery paid no tax – though its drinkers were still charged the full amount.

In December 1934 Edinburgh United dismissed its head cellarman, supposedly, it was later said, after a row over whether he should get more money for not revealing the scam. The angry cellarman went straight to the local customs man to tell him about the fiddles at the brewery. On Christmas Day Customs and Excise raided the brewery premises. After examination of the books and documents that customs men had taken away, in February 1935 Edinburgh United was handed a demand for almost £52,000 in unpaid excise duty.

Unsurprisingly, the brewery could not pay. A liquidator was

appointed, and the managing director of Edinburgh United and three of the brewers went to court charged with offences to do with hiding brews from the excise. The two most junior were let off without sentence, but the MD, William Lawrie, and his head brewer, a one-armed First World War veteran called John Clark, were found guilty and sentenced to gaol.

In 1931 Edinburgh's two biggest brewers, William Younger & Co. and William McEwan & Co., had merged to form Scottish Brewers Ltd. Younger's always claimed the date of 1749 for its own foundation. However, this was merely the year William Younger, aged sixteen, moved from the family home in Linton, Peeblesshire, to Leith, Edinburgh's port. Traditionally, William's first job is said to have been in a brewery in Leith. Unfortunately, there seems to be no documentary evidence that William ever brewed commercially anywhere. In 1753, Younger, now twenty, was appointed an excise man. He won this potentially lucrative post (excise men received commissions on the sale of contraband goods they seized) through a typical eighteenth-century chain of nepotism: the father of Grizel Sime, his fiancée, worked as head gardener to the Earl of Dundonald, whose heir, Thomas Cochrane, was a Commissioner of Excise and a childhood playmate of Grizel's.

William was a reasonably prosperous property owner when he died, aged only thirty-seven, in 1770. Grizel, a widow at thirty-one with six children to support, the eldest only thirteen, remarried two years later; her new husband, Alexander Anderson, was another Leith brewer, who had been brewing since at least 1758. When Anderson died in 1781, Grizel ran the brewery herself before retiring in 1794, aged sixty-five. Grizel and William's eldest son, Archibald Campbell Younger, had been apprenticed to his stepfather's brewery at fifteen. When he reached twenty-one, in 1778, Archibald left Leith to start his own brewery in the precincts of the Abbey of Holyrood House in Edinburgh. The attractions of this location included more than the excellent local well-water: it was outside the jurisdiction of Edinburgh Town Council, and Archibald and the three other brewers in the Abbey precincts did not have to pay the council's 2d-a-pint impost.

Archibald's business expanded enough in eight years for him to buy a larger brewery in 1786, nearby in Croft-an-Righ ('Farm of the King' in Gaelic), a lane behind Holyrood Palace. His beers included Younger's Edinburgh Ale, which sold in the bothies of Edinburgh for 3d a bottle, 20 per cent more expensive than ordinary ale. After five years, Archibald moved again, to a new brewery in North Back Canongate with a capacity of some 15,000 barrels a year, where he was in business with his brother-in-law, John Sommervail.

Another brother, Richard Younger, was brewing in his own right at James Gentle's old brewery in Gentle's Close, off Canongate, from at least 1788, though by 1796 he had moved to London. That year the youngest Younger, William II, then twenty-nine, opened his own brewery in the Abbey precincts, having graduated from selling ale and porter in Leith. By 1802 William Younger's 'much admired' ale was being advertised for sale at the Edinburgh Ale Vaults in London, in cask and bottle.

In 1803, with sales growing, William II bought James Blair's Abbey brewery close by. When Archibald died in 1819, he left his brewery to William, who promptly sold it to another brewer, George Hastie. William II was now in partnership with Alexander Smith, the brewer and superintendent of the Abbey brewery. There was now only one Younger brewing in Edinburgh, for the first time in more than thirty years.

It was only in 1836, when William II was sixty-nine, that he finally made his son William Younger III, aged thirty-five, a partner in the business, along with Andrew Smith, son of Alexander Smith. William Younger III had no real interest in the business, but Andrew Smith had worked there since he was sixteen; and by the time the two senior partners, William II and Alexander Smith, both died in 1842, Andrew was twenty-nine and an experienced brewer. Under his direction the company began bottling for sale overseas in 1846, and exports started to grow. The reputation of its India Pale Ale and Edinburgh Ale helped it rise to be easily the biggest brewer in Edinburgh by 1850, mashing 10,292 quarters of malt. This was nearly a third as much again as its nearest rival, Alexander Berwick, who had bought Richard Younger's old premises off South Back Canongate (now Holyrood Road), 300 yards away.

Eight years later Younger's acquired Berwick's premises from Alexander's nephews for £1,600. It eventually concentrated production of India Pale Ale (brewed, like the Burton article, in unions) at the Holyrood brewery, while the Abbey brewery made the Edinburgh Ale. William Younger III had died in 1854, and by the early 1860s the brewery partners were his two sons, William IV and Henry Johnston Younger, and the energetic Andrew Smith. By now the firm was exporting its ales as far afield as Honolulu and New Zealand, but the bulk of trade was still at home: Scotland took more than half of all Younger's sales, Tyneside took around a quarter of total output, and a fifth went through London. In 1861 Younger's opened a branch office in London, which was important enough for Henry Younger to be put in charge.

After William Younger IV and Andrew Smith retired in 1869, the brewery was run by Henry Younger, his younger brother David, and Alexander Smith, son of Andrew. Under these three, joined in the mid-1870s by Alexander Low Bruce, son-in-law of the great African explorer David Livingstone, Younger's maintained its position as Scotland's leading brewer, with home sales alone of more than £400,000 a year by the 1880s. Bruce was made a director on the specific instructions of William IV in 1875 in an attempt to curb the excesses of Henry Younger, who had been running up the firm's overdraft to such a degree that Younger's bankers were threatening to pull the plug. Over the next five years the financial pressures eased, and between 1881 and 1886 the company was able to increase production from 90,000 barrels a year to 215,000 barrels, some one-sixth of all the beer brewed in Scotland.

In 1887 Younger's became the first big brewer in Scotland to register as a limited company. Alexander Bruce, without whom the company might not have made it that far, died of pneumonia in 1893, aged fifty-four. Responsibility for running the company eventually devolved to Harry George Younger, son of Henry, who was to become managing director. With his hand on the tiller, Younger's began increasing the number of tied houses it owned, both in Scotland, where it had the largest tied trade of any Scottish brewer by 1914, and England, where it bought up pubs both on Tyneside and in London. By 1905, it was reckoned Younger's produced a quarter of all Scotland's beer.

In 1921 the character Father William, with his slogan 'Get Younger each day' appeared for the first time in the company's advertising. Soon he was also on the labels of Holyrood Ale, a new light, artificially carbonated bottled beer, and in 1927 Father William was registered by Younger's as a trademark.

Then, in December 1930, came the announcement that Younger's was combining 'certain of their financial and technical resources' with those of McEwan's, though 'each company will continue to be carried out as a separate business with its present organisation'. From January 1931 the two companies were now under a new umbrella, Scottish Brewers Ltd, with Harry George Younger as first chairman; the relationship, however, remained as loose as these words suggested.

McEwan's was one of the youngest 'big' brewers in Britain, founded only in 1856 by William McEwan, the son of an Alloa ship owner. One of William's uncles was John Jeffrey, who owned the old-established Heriot brewery in the Grassmarket, Edinburgh, and in 1851, aged twenty-four, William entered into an apprenticeship at the brewery, carefully paying the required 'entrance money' to the brewery workers; 10s had to be given to those engaged on the actual brewing side, 8s to the maltsters and coopers. From early on it looks as if McEwan intended starting his own brewing business: in 1852 he went all over Bass's and Allsopp's breweries in Burton upon Trent, having crossed his fingers and told the Burtonites he was not connected with the trade. The next year he checked out more breweries in Burton and Liverpool, apparently looking for one to rent.

In the end McEwan decided to build his own brewery from scratch, on land in Fountainbridge, Edinburgh (where there had been breweries in the early eighteenth century) using as capital £1,000 borrowed from his family and another £1,000 from the bank. The first beer was brewed in December 1856 and delivered to customers in January 1857. By April that year he was accepting orders for pale ale to be exported to Australia.

Two years after Younger's became a limited company, in 1889 McEwan's followed suit. Like Younger's, it was capitalised at £1 million, with the founder retaining a stake of £430,000. His sister Janet's fourth son, William Younger, the brewery's new managing director, was given £50,000 in shares. (William's elder brother George ran the Younger brewery in Alloa.) McEwan had married four years earlier (the year before he was elected a Liberal MP for the Edinburgh Central constituency) and his share of the brewery business was inherited on his death in 1913 by his stepdaughter Margaret. As the widowed Hon. Mrs Ronald Greville she was to become a notable society hostess at Polesden Lacey, the Surrey villa her stepfather gave to her in 1907.

William Younger retired in 1924, though his son, William McEwan Younger (always known as Bill) did not join the new company's board until 1935. McEwan's was the smaller partner at first, with Younger's shareholders owning two-thirds of the equity of the £4 million new company. However, in 1942 Bill McEwan Younger inherited all the shares owned by his great-uncle's stepdaughter on Margaret Greville's death, becoming the biggest shareholder in Scottish Brewers. The Fountain brewery at Fountainbridge was considerably re-equipped, and gradually the McEwan's Cavalier trademark, first seen in the late 1930s, began to dominate over the Father William figure. The Abbey brewery was shut and converted into offices in 1955.

More significantly, the same year Scottish Brewers acquired the Red Tower Lager Brewery (later named the Royal brewery) in Manchester, moving production there of its new MY lager. Bill McEwan Younger did not really believe lager would ever sell well in Britain, but companies such as Hope & Anchor of Sheffield, which brewed Carling Black Label under licence, seemed to be having some success with the drink, and one Edinburgh brewer, John Jeffrey & Co., had been brewing lager since 1902.

It was Jeffrey's experience in lager brewing that bought it to the attention of the Canadian brewing entrepreneur E. P. Taylor, owner of the Carling Black Label brand. In late 1959 he took over Jeffrey's through his company Canadian Breweries, with the help of 40 per cent of Jeffrey's stock bought from Bernard Dixon, the former managing director of Flower's of Luton and Stratford on Avon. Capacity at the Heriot brewery was only 1,000 barrels a week, but on his visit Taylor could see there was space for expansion When Northern Breweries, an amalgamation of Hammonds United of Bradford and Hope & Anchor, finally took its first breath under Taylor's midwifeship in March 1960, Jeffrey's was transferred to it.

Jeffrey's original Heriot brewery had been on the south side of the Grassmarket, and it had at least four owners in the early nineteenth century before John Jeffrey acquired it in 1837. In 1880 a new brew-house was built at Roseburn, to the west of the city proper. In 1902 the brewery's head partner, David Jeffrey, persuaded the German brewer who had helped Tennent's in Glasgow brew lager successfully, Jacob Klinger, to come and do the same at the Roseburn site, which had taken on the name of the Heriot brewery. Jeffrey's was soon exporting lager around the world.

The newly launched Northern Breweries quickly acquired other Scottish brewers, including William Murray of Duddingston in May 1960. Jeffrey's was merged with John Aitchison & Co. of the Canongate Brewery in Holyrood Road, Edinburgh, which had fallen with its seventy-four pubs to Hammonds United in 1959. Northern, which became United Brewers late in 1960, organised its Scottish holdings into United Caledonian Breweries Ltd in 1963 with production eventually concentrated at the Heriot brewery.

J. & R. Tennent of Glasgow, the biggest brewer in the west of Scotland, had been acquired by what was now Charrington United in 1963; three years later, it was merged with the rest of the group's Scottish holdings to make Tennent Caledonian Breweries Ltd. Under the Tennent Caledonian flag the Heriot brewery ran for more than twenty-five years, surviving the merger of Charrington United with

Bass in 1969 to make Britain's biggest brewer. However, in 1993 it was announced that the Heriot brewery would be closing.

Just after the First World War, in 1919, the Sunderland brewery Vaux had acquired Lorimer & Clark of the Caledonian brewery, Slateford Road, Edinburgh, to give it a brewer of Scotch Ale to supply to the north-east of England, where the style of ale was very popular. The company had been started in 1869 by George Lorimer junior, son of a prosperous builder, and his partner Robert Clark, head brewer at Melvin's Boroughloch brewery. After the First World War, when he was seventy-three, Lorimer sold the company to Vaux for just under £34,000. Vaux continued brewing at the Caledonian brewery even when, in 1959, it swooped on two more Edinburgh brewers: Steel, Coulson of the Croft-an-Righ brewery and Thomas Usher of the Park brewery.

Steel, Coulson, which used a fleur-de-lys as its trademark, had its roots in Glasgow, where James Steel had bought the Greenhead brewery in 1853. In 1858 he acquired from J. & W. Burnet the Craigend brewery in North Back Canongate, to brew the increasingly popular pale ales. In 1865 George E. Coulson of Edinburgh was taken into partnership. The Craigend site was now too cramped, and in 1874 Steel, Coulson moved to a brewery in Comely Gardens, Abbeyhill, alongside Holyrood Palace. The premises had been erected in 1866 by the City of Edinburgh Brewery Company, which had gone into voluntary liquidation after eight years. The Croft-an-Righ brewery shut the year after Vaux acquired it.

Thomas Usher & Son Ltd began when Andrew Usher, who ran a whisky wholesaling operation in Edinburgh, set up his two eldest sons, James and Thomas, in business at the Cowgate brewery in Campbell's Close. In 1860 they moved to the Park brewery in St Leonard's Street. By the time Vaux took the Park brewery over, it had 170 tied houses. Vaux continued to brew at the Usher's premises. However, in 1980 it was sold to Allied Breweries, which closed the brewery the next year.

As Scottish brewers began disappearing into the jaws of English combines, some decided it was better to be eaten up by their local big brewer. T. & J. Bernard Ltd of the Edinburgh Brewery in Slateford Road agreed to merge with the Younger's–McEwan's set-up in April 1960. The original Edinburgh brewery, founded by Daniel Bernard, had been one of the many concerns in North Back Canongate. Thomas Bernard had run it until his death in 1874, when it came into the hands of his eldest son Daniel, then only nineteen, and Daniel's brother John Mackay Bernard, two years younger. Eventually, in 1887, the pressures of a cramped city-centre site forced the brothers to have plans drawn up for a new Edinburgh brewery to the west, off the Slateford Road. The brewery opened in 1889. However, within a short while the pair had fallen out, and by early 1890 John was running the new brewery in partnership with a Mr Pringle, while Daniel was brewing under his own name in North Back Canongate.

Ironically, the expanding activities of the North British Railway Company, which forced Drybrough's to move to Craigmillar, pushed Daniel out of North Back Canongate too. Undoubtedly to the fury of John Bernard, Daniel's own new site, which was going up by December 1893, was just a short distance from the new Edinburgh brewery, this time in Gorgie Road. Relations between the two remained broken right up to Daniel's death in 1902.

Bernard's was joined in Scottish Brewers in 1960 by J. & J. Morison Ltd of the Commercial Brewery, 160 Canongate, which had been founded in 1868. A few months later, in March 1961, Robert Younger of the St Ann's brewery, maker of bottled 'heavy oat creme stout', was taken over too – but by now Scottish Brewers itself was no more. It had been approached by Tennent's of Glasgow, but turned the Glaswegians down in favour of an offer from the North-West of England's biggest brewer, Newcastle Breweries. At the beginning of May 1960 the two firms came together to make a £50 million, 1,700-pub concern called, rather unimaginatively, Scottish & Newcastle Breweries. This was more than a regional firm: it was a UK national brewer, one of the then 'big seven', albeit the smallest by tied estate, with fewer than half the number of pubs of the next smallest, Whitbread.

Over the next six years Edinburgh's three remaining independent brewers were to fall to English predators. The first to go was the smallest, George Mackay & Co. of the St Leonard's brewery in St Leonard's Street. Mackay's had been founded in 1867 and later turned into a limited company. In 1954 it acquired Gordon & Blair, a firm with a history that went back to 1822, when John Blair established the Craigwell brewery in North Back Canongate. This proved somewhat of a poisoned chalice: Mackay's attempted to offset its new subsidiary's losses against tax, became embroiled in a legal argument with the Inland Revnue and finally lost its case in 1962. Very shortly afterwards Mackay's was acquired by the distiller Seager Evans, which sold it on to the English brewer Watney Mann in 1963, when brewing in St Leonard's Street ended.

Three years later Watney's bought Drybrough & Co. Ltd. The company claimed roots in the first half of the eighteenth century: Andrew Drybrough, brewer and 'baxter' (baker), was operating in Edinburgh 'before 1750'. James Drybrough was brewing in Tolbooth Wynd, off Canongate, before moving to North Back Canongate in 1782. Drybrough's had been the first Edinburgh brewer to move out of the city centre to Craigmillar, and by the time of the Watney's takeover in 1965, when it ran 125 pubs and two off-licences, it was the last one in the district still brewing.

Watney's started with big ambitions in Scotland. But by 1987, when it was part of the Grand Metropolitan empire, it had decided to compete no more with the Big Two of Scottish brewing, Tennent Caledonian and S&N. Drybrough's was sold to the Alloa Brewing Co., the Scottish subsidiary of Allied Domecq (formerly Allied Brewers) and the Craigmillar brewery closed.

Edinburgh's last independent brewer was Archibald Campbell, Hope & King Ltd of the Argyle brewery in Chambers Street. Campbell's brewery claimed a foundation date of 1710, though 1740 seems to be the most reliable guess for when the business started. It had a high enough reputation to be awarded a Royal Warrant to supply the households of four monarchs: Victoria, Edward VII, George V and

George VI. It exported Campbell's strong Scotch Ale in bulk to Belgium for bottling from 1890, and the beer is still being brewed under the Campbell's name by Interbrew in Belgium today. The company was registered in 1896 to bring together the Argyle brewery and Hope & King, wine and spirit merchants in Glasgow. Its independence, and that of its seventy-three tied houses, was lost in 1967, when Whitbread, the only big English brewer without a real presence in Scotland, swooped down on Chambers Street. In 1969, however, Whitbread sold the former Campbell's pubs to Drybrough's and Vaux, and in 1971 the Argyle brewery was closed.

In 1980 the Vaux group, in the start of a retreat from Scotland, sold the former Usher's Park brewery and its pubs to the Alloa arm of Allied Breweries, which closed the Park brewery the following year. In 1985 Vaux decided to shut the former Lorimer & Clark's Caledonian brewery as well, although it was still brewing some 80,000 barrels a year, more than most of the surviving small brewers in England.

However, the managing director at the Caledonian, Dan Kane, an active member of the Campaign for Real Ale, and its head brewer, Russell Sharp, felt there was enough demand for traditional beer for the brewery to be worth saving. They persuaded Vaux to sell it to the management team, and in 1987 it reopened as the Caledonian Brewery Company Ltd. It now produces more than 90,000 barrels a year, some under the names of vanished Edinburgh brewers.

Scottish & Newcastle, meanwhile, had built a new brewery at Fountainbridge with an initial capacity of nearly three million barrels a year. In May 1986 it closed the Holyrood brewery, concentrating all production in Edinburgh at the New Fountain brewery. The aromas of brewing would no longer disturb royalty when it stayed at Holyrood Palace: Queen Elizabeth II, it is said, called it 'the Edinburgh smell', and wondered after the brewery closed where it had gone.

S&N was the second smallest of the UK's Big Six brewers, with by far the smallest tied pub estate (only 1,500 houses) and 10 per cent of all Britain's beer sales in 1985 (most of that through the free trade). Its management, fearing that it was vulnerable to a takeover, decided the company needed to look more dynamic. Twice, in 1968 and 1974, S&N had tried to merge with Courage, the smallest of the Big Six with 9 per cent of the beer market, and on each occasion talks had failed: once over who would be chairman and the second time because Courage executives did not want to relocate to Edinburgh. In 1972 Courage had been bought by the tobacco giant Imperial, which in turn was acquired in 1986 by Hanson Trust. Its largely southern-based trade made a good fit with S&N, which immediately asked Hanson if it would like to sell Courage. But the risk of the Edinburgh brewer's bid being referred to the Monopolies and Mergers Commission persuaded Hanson to go for a rival offer of £1.5 billion from an overseas brewer, Elders, which owned Fosters, one of Australia's brewing giants.

Thwarted, S&N looked for a medium-sized English brewer to acquire. After trying unsuccessfully to buy the Blackburn brewer Matthew Brown, it acquired the 450-pub Home Brewery in Nottingham, which agreed to be taken over in September 1986 for £120 million. The next year S&N had another go at Matthew Brown, succeeding this time with an offer worth £190 million. This lifted S&N's tied house estate to 2,300 pubs and brought under its control Theakston's brewery in North Yorkshire, brewer of a highly regarded and popular cask bitter.

The logic that led S&N to seek a merger with Courage also occurred to Courage's new owners, and in 1988 Elders IXL made a £1.6 billion bid for the Scottish group. The Monopolies and Mergers Commission stepped in, and after four months ruled against the bid, on the grounds that a Courage–S&N merger would mean just two groups (the other being Bass) controlling more than 40 per cent of the UK's beer market. Elders eventually sold its stake in S&N at a loss of £90 million.

Ironically, the Monopolies and Mergers Commission ruling came out on the same day, 21 March 1989, that it published its report into the whole UK brewing industry – the report that eventually led to the 'Beer Orders' which effectively forced the biggest brewers to divest themselves of their tied estates. The first big result was a double shuffle in 1991 which saw Courage and its Australian owners acquire all of the Watney group's breweries from Grand Metropolitan, while most of the two sets of pubs went into a separate company, Inntrepreneur. Then, in May 1995, Elders pulled out of the UK, selling Courage to S&N for £425 million.

Scottish & Newcastle had grown in thirty-five years from two regional groups huddling together to the biggest brewer in the UK. However, this was no longer enough: there were overseas giants, such as Interbrew of Belgium, who had ambitions to expand in Britain, and S&N knew it could not stay as, effectively, a regional European brewer, any more than Scottish Brewers and Newcastle Breweries could have survived as regional British concerns: it had to grow too large to be swallowed. In 2000 it bought the French brewer Kronenbourg from the food group Danone for an eventual payment of £3.2 billion. Edinburgh may have had only two breweries left, but it was now home to the second biggest brewing concern in Europe.

A SHORT AND ENTIRELY WRONG HISTORY OF BEER

Beer is a popular subject, and the literature abounds in unsupported statements, misleading or inaccurate quotations and inaccurate references.

D. Gay Wilson, 1975

There are many incorrect or deeply dubious stories which still pop up too regularly in writings on beer. Here, in bold, is a short history of ale and beer in which almost everything is wrong, though each 'fact' has appeared in print somewhere:

Myth 1: 'The oldest known written document on Earth is a Sumerian clay tablet inscribed with cuneiform and accurately dated to around 6000BC, which describes the brewing of beer for sacrifice to the god Ninkasi.'

Nearly everything is completely inaccurate in this statement, which can be found in several sources: cuneiform writing was not invented until around 3300BC; the 'Hymn to Ninkasi' referred to was written down around 1800BC and is not the oldest known written document;

it describes beer brewing, not the brewing of beer for sacrifice; and Ninkasi was a goddess, not a god. She was, at least, a Sumerian deity.

It is true, though, that the earliest known examples of writing, found on clay tablets from the Sumerian city of Uruk, and dating to about 3300BC, do mention beer: they are clerks' notes recording the transfer of commodities such as beer, grain and livestock.

Myth 2: 'The word "beer" comes from the Sumerian/Hamitic languages.'

No. 'Beer' (or *bier*), which became *pivo* in Slavonic languages, entered West Germanic languages probably through the Latin *bibere*, to drink, which comes from an Indo-European root, *pi-. (The asterisk indicates in philology that this is a presumed form of an unrecorded ancestor-word). An attempt has been made to take the old Celtic for ale, *courmi*, back to the Sumerian *kurun* or *kurum*, the name of a type of beer. It is, however, much more likely to be linked to the Latin *cremor*, meaning thick broth, and an old Slavonic word, *krma*, meaning nourishment or food. There may also be a misunderstanding of the word for a third type of Sumerian beer, *kashbir*, meaning 'sweet beer', from *kash*, 'beer', and *bir* 'to sniff'. Sumerian and Hamitic, in any case, are entirely different language families.

Myth 3: '*Kash*, an ancient Egyptian [some accounts do say Sumerian] word for beer, is the root of the modern English word 'cash', because *Kash* was used as currency to pay slaves and priests.'

It isn't. As any etymological dictionary will confirm, 'cash' originally meant 'money-box' in English, with the secondary sense 'money' becoming dominant by the eighteenth century. It was derived from Italian *cassa* and, ultimately, the Latin word *capsa*, meaning 'box'. Beer had nothing to do with it. The Sumerians did have a word *kash*, meaning 'beer', but the Egyptian word for beer is usually given by Egyptologists as *henket* – properly *hnkt*, as we do not know what vowels the Egyptians would have used.

Myth 4: 'Jewish exiles in captivity in Babylon (in 597BC) drank hopped ale as a defence against leprosy.'

They did not. The original Hebrew description (from the fourth century AD) of the herb used in the anti-leprosy drink was 'cuscuta of the hizmé shrub', that is, a Middle Eastern climbing plant of the dodder family. By the eleventh century, rabbinical commentary on the Talmud was talking about hops, probably because these were more familiar to European Jews than cuscuta. In any case, what was drunk to guard against leprosy was *shekar* flavoured with cuscuta, *shekar* being a Hebrew word which meant any strong drink, not beer specifically (although in Akkadian, a related Semitic language spoken by the conquerors of Sumer, the word *sikar* translated Sumerian *kash*, beer). *Shekar* became, via the Bible and its Greek and Latin translations, and then French, the source of the English word cider.

Myth 5: 'Ale was introduced to Britain by the Romans.'

Not at all. Brewing was taking place in these islands millennia before Rome was founded. Commentators from the Mediterranean world always wrote with some surprise of northern and western tribes' use of grain to make intoxicating liquor.

Myth 6: 'Julius Caesar wrote about the Britons drinking a "high and mighty liquor . . . made of barley and water".'

This passage is supposed to occur in Caesar's *De bello gallico*, book 1, chapter 5. It doesn't.

Myth 7: 'Pliny, in his *Natural History*, says the Germans preserved ale with hops.'

No, he didn't. Pliny mentions *lupus salictarum*, by which we presume he meant hops, only as a 'delicacy' for eating, not as a flavouring for ale.

Myth 8: 'Diocletian's price edict of AD301 mentions British beer.'

It doesn't. Of the three types of beer listed in the edict, none is given a specific place of origin.

Myth 9: 'In the fourth century the Emperor Julian is said to have sampled British ale while on a journey to Paris and disliked it to the extent that he wrote a poem in which he compared its smell to that of a goat.'

Not exactly. Julian, or Julianus, was put in charge of Gaul and Britain by his cousin the Emperor Constantius II in 355, aged twenty-three. He spent at least six years in the west, before becoming emperor himself in 361. Very likely Julian drank Celtic beer at some time while he was head of the army in Gaul, and pushing back Germanic invaders: there is no need for it to have been British beer, however, as the Gauls themselves were brewers. A poem in Greek about Celtic beer, full of puns and jokes, has been attributed, without convincing proof, to Julian. Translated by D. L. Page, it goes as follows:

> *Who are you, and whence, Dionysos? For by the*
> *   true Bacchus,*
> *I do not recognise you: I know only the son of*
> *   Zeus.*
> *He smells of nectar, you smell of the goat. Truly*
> *   the Celts must have made you from grain only*
> *   for lack of grapes.*
> *Therefore we should call you Demetrios, not*
> *   Dionysos.*
> *rather born of grain [than of fire], and Bromos,*
> *   not Bromios.*

Demetrios means 'son of Demeter', the goddess of corn, raw material for beer, while the name of the wine god, Dionysos, was thought to mean 'son of Zeus'. The joke at the end of the last line is that *Bromios*, meaning 'roarer', was an epithet of Dionysos, while *Bromos* means 'oats', which the writer of the poem obviously felt was the name more suitable for a beer god. There is also a pun in the last line, which, depending on how you pronounce one word, means 'born of grain', as a beer god would be, or 'born of fire', as Dionysos was supposed to have been.

Myth 10: 'Braggot takes its name from Brage (or Bragi), the Norse god of poetry.'

Wrong. Braggot or bragget, a drink made from honey and ale, comes from the early Welsh *bragaut* (*bragawd* in modern Welsh), which goes back to a supposed Old Celtic root *bracata, linked to Celtic words for malt and a type of grain.

Myth 11: 'Brasenose College, Oxford, gets its name from being built on the site of King Alfred's *brasinium*, or brewhouse.'

No way. The college's name comes from a bronze knocker on the main gate of the original Brasenose Hall during the Middle Ages. Brasenose College, founded in 1509, had a brewery of its own, like other colleges (until 1889, when it was demolished). But King Alfred's *brasinium*, wherever that was, had nothing to do with it.

Myth 12: 'The first reference to hops in England is a document from AD622 by the Abbot of Corvey.'

Two problems here – 622 is a typographical error for 822, and Corvey is on the banks of the Weser in Westphalia, Germany, and not in England.

Myth 13: 'References are made to humlonaria, or hop gardens, given to the Abbey of St Denis [in Paris] by King Pepin in 768.'

Error. The deed in question names lands in the forest of Iveline in France, near Paris, that the king was granting to the abbey, which among 'diversa loca' included one called *Humlonariae*. This is a place-name, and does not mean 'hop gardens', though it does suggest somewhere noted for wild hops.

Myth 14: 'A plan exists of the abbey of St Gall in Switzerland dating from the ninth century which shows three brewhouses, brewing beer for, respectively, distinguished guests, monks and pilgrims.'

Alas, no. Around the beginning of the ninth century, Hitro, the Bishop of Basle and, from 803, Abbot of Reichenau on Lake Constance, sent to his 'dearest son' Gorbert, the Abbot of St Gall, a plan of the 'ideal' monastery. This plan, on a sheet of parchment 44 inches long, still survives. All the support services were mapped out around the abbey church, from herb garden to stables, including a guesthouse with its own kitchen, brewery and bakehouse; the monks' kitchen with bakery and brewhouse attached; and an almonry with the almonry kitchen and brewery alongside. There is no evidence, however, that Gorbert built this 'ideal' monastery at St Gall: as laid out on the map, it would not have fitted on his site.

Myth 15: 'The English King Edgar [reigned 959–75], acting on the advice of St Dunstan, Archbishop of Canterbury [from 959], suppressed many alehouses and allowed only one per village or small town.'

Almost certainly untrue. The original authority for this claim appears to be a book by the eighteenth-century antiquarian Joseph Strutt called *Horda: A Complete View of the Manners, Customs &c of the Inhabitants of England*, published in 1774. No contemporary Old English document seems to survive to verify this alleged law. Nor does it make sense in terms of social conditions and practices in Edgar's time. Ale selling was not a regular profession in pre-Norman England, particularly in villages, but a part-time service carried on by different individuals on different occasions. Thus no one place would be 'the village alehouse'.

Myth 16: 'The Domesday Book recorded in the eleventh century that St Paul's Cathedral brewed 67,814 gallons of ale from 175 quarters each of wheat and barley and 708 quarters of oats.'

No, it didn't. The great 1086 Domesday Book says virtually nothing about London, and nothing at all about St Paul's and brewing. The original reference comes from a book called the *Domesday of St Paul's of the Year MCCXXII* (that is, 1222), written by William Hale Hale (*sic*), Archdeacon of St Paul's in the nineteenth century. The figures in Hale's book were from a document dated 1286.

Myth 17: 'The expression "to take someone down a peg" comes from the peg tankards used for communal drinking in medieval alehouses.'

Very unlikely. The story first seems to surface in Elizabethan writings that claimed King Edgar (king of England from 959 to 975) brought in a regulation insisting every drinking vessel should have pins or pegs inserted in it at regular intervals down the inside. The reason for the pegs, it was claimed, was that in communal drinking they showed how much each drinker was swallowing at a time. King Edgar's law supposedly ordered that no drinker should go past a fresh peg during his turn with the ale pot. However, no contemporary Old English source is known for this 'law'.

Two-quart peg tankards with eight pegs inside, each peg marking half a pint, and with designs on the outside supposedly dating to the tenth or eleventh century, 'have been reported but not authenticated', according to Frederick Hackwood's *Inns, Ales and Drinking Customs of Old England*, published in 1909.

However, it is difficult to see how we get from drinking to pegs to 'taking someone down a peg'. The meaning of the phrase is 'to humble, to snub' (Chambers' *Twentieth Century Dictionary*). Hackwood suggests to 'take a man down a peg' meant to cut off his turn at the bowl, 'for some offence against tavern etiquette, maybe'. But how was the *man* going down a peg?

A more likely explanation of 'taking someone down a peg' has been suggested involving naval flags of rank, which were supposedly fixed to the ship's mast by pegs. 'To take someone down a peg' would mean to diminish their status by flying their flag lower. Even more likely, surely, is an explanation involving games which are scored on boards with pegs, such as cribbage. This is where 'to peg out', an originally nineteenth-century phrase meaning to die, comes from, since pegging out is what you do at the end of a cribbage game.

Myth 18: 'The first tax on beer was the "Saladin tithe" of 1188.'

Up to a point. The 'Saladin tithe', levied by Henry II to finance the Third Crusade, was paid by anyone in England who did not 'take the cross', at a rate of one-tenth of the valuation of their revenues and moveables. It was thus a general tax, not one specifically on ale or brewing. The 'fines' imposed by local courts on brewers during the Middle Ages were a de facto form of tax, but the first specific tax on ale and beer was not imposed until the English Civil War in the seventeenth century.

Myth 19: 'The medieval ale-conner or ale-taster would test an alewife's latest brew by pouring some of the ale on a wooden bench and then sitting in it in his leather breeches. After half an hour he would attempt to rise, and if his breeches had stuck to the bench the ale had too much sugar in it, and was thus impure.' (Or, depending on which version you read, 'if his breeches stuck to the bench, the ale was of good strength and had passed the test.')

This is a widely repeated story, the main outlines being given in Hackwood's *Inns, Ales and Drinking Customs*. It also occurs, in slightly different form, in German, Alsatian, Flemish and Czech tradition. However, in Britain, at least, there is no known contemporary evidence at all for ale-conners testing beer in this peculiar way, and the oaths that medieval ale-conners were required to swear spoke only of their having to be prepared to taste ale when it went on sale, not sit in it.

Another version of the tale brings the test two or three centuries closer to the present. It says, correctly, that after the first tax on beer was introduced in Britain in 1643, there were two different rates, depending on the strength of the brew, and the 'gauger' (excise man) had only his palate to tell him what was strong beer and what was weak. This was supplemented 'at one time', the story claims, by an 'official test' which involved the gauger sitting in his leather breeches in a pool of beer for thirty minutes. If he stuck, the beer was 'strong' and paid the higher duty rate, if not it was 'small' and liable for the lower rate. Again, I know of no contemporary evidence to support this claim.

The ceremony of testing the beer is supposed to take place every ten years at the Tiger pub on Tower Hill, London, when the Lord Mayor, his Sheriffs and the aldermen allegedly watch a member of the 'Society of Ale Conners' test the beer's strength by sitting in a pool of beer poured onto a stool. This is completely untrue – they don't, and never did. In 1949 the Tiger was the scene of a revival of the custom of hoisting an 'ale garland' of holly and laurel outside City of London pubs, which was attended by the Lord Mayor, the two City ale-conners, and the Master, Wardens and Liverymen of the Brewers' Company. The ale was tasted by the ale-conners, but not sat in, and there is no evidence that the Lord Mayor and the ale-conners came back to the Tiger in subsequent decades, or ever intended to.

Myth 20: 'Chaucer wrote about an ale-conner.'

A mock-Chaucerian work written anonymously in 1594, called the 'Cobler of Canterburie' contained the lines: 'A nose he had that gan show / What liquor he loved I trow; / For he had before long seven yeare / Been of the town the Ale-conner.' At least one later writer, presumably confused by the reference to Canterbury in the title, has attributed the quotation to Geoffrey Chaucer, author of the *Canterbury Tales*, who died 200 years earlier, in 1400.

Myth 21: 'English ale before the introduction of hops was generally sweet.'

No, it wasn't. The same yeast that is used to make ale and beer, *Saccharomyces cerevisiae*, is used to make wine and cider, and it is perfectly capable of fermenting those two drinks out to complete dryness. There is no reason why medieval and pre-medieval ale could not have been fermented out to dryness as well. In addition, astringent phenols and other flavours produced by wild yeasts such as *Brettanomyces*, and sourness as some of the alcohol was turned into vinegar by invading micro-organisms, would have countered any sweetness that did remain in the ale after its initial fermentation. One Anglo-Saxon source talks of *hluttor eala wel gesweted*, well-sweetened clear ale, implying that clear, mature ale (which was old enough for wild yeast and lactobacteria to have attacked it and soured it) was tart or sour enough that it had to have sweetness added to it.

Myth 22: 'Plants whose names end in the word "wort" were used in the Middle Ages as an ingredient in ale.'

No, they weren't. This is a confusion of two different, though etymologically linked words: 'wort' meaning vegetable or herb, equivalent to both the Old Saxon *wurt* and the Old High German *wurz* (modern German *Wurzel*), 'root' or 'plant'; and 'wort', an infusion of grain for the making of beer, equivalent to the Middle High German *würze*, seasoning or spice. The 'wort' ending of plants such as mugwort thus means 'plant', and is unconnected with brewing (the 'mug' bit of mugwort, incidentally, means 'midge', small gnat-like insect, and is unconnected with 'mug', drinking vessel). At least one plant with a name ending in 'wort', ragwort, is extremely poisonous to horses and cattle, causing irreversible cirrhosis of the liver.

Myth 23: 'Gruit, the mixture of herbs used to flavour beer before hops, included sweet gale or bog myrtle and marsh or wild rosemary.'

It seems unnecessary for any gruit recipe to include both bog myrtle and wild rosemary. These are similar-looking plants with similar flavours growing in similar places. Bog myrtle, *Myrica gale*, *Porst* in German, *pors* in Scandinavian languages, was one of the most favoured pre-hop flavourings in both Britain and continental Europe. Wild rosemary, *Ledum palustre*, which is very uncommon in Britain, can have serious toxic effects, and was by no means as favoured. Its second-class status is indicated by two of its names in German, *Schweineporst*, 'pigs' gale', and *falscher Porst*, 'false gale'. (In Norwegian it was called *Finnmark pors*, gale from Finnmark county, which also appears to be derogatory). Although medieval German inventories show that wild rosemary was stocked alongside bog myrtle, it was probably regarded by most medieval brewers as a poor substitute for real *Porst*, to be used only when bog myrtle was not available.

Myth 24: 'The Abbess Hildegarde of Bingen wrote about the addition of hops to beer in 1079.'

Entirely the wrong year. The Abbess was not yet alive in 1079: she was born in 1098 and died in 1179. She did, however, mention hops in her book *Physica sacra*, written about 1150 or 1160.

Myth 25: 'Hops were used for flavouring ale in pre-Norman England, and Himbleton in Worcestershire means "hop town".'

Very dubious. The archaeological evidence that hops grew wild in England before the fifteenth century is pretty good: pollen remains dating back to the Neolithic and before from what were probably wild hops have been found at Thatcham in Berkshire and Urswick in Cumbria. The authorities are split, however: Mabey's *Flora Britannica* says the hop is 'almost certainly a native', while the botanist Roger Phillips believes the hops found growing today in hedges around England are there 'probably because it has often escaped from cultivation', rather than as wild survivors.

Old English had the word *hymele*, which was derived from the same root as the word used for hop in medieval Latin, *humulus* (and the modern Flemish dialect word *hommel*). However, *hymele* 'may refer to the hop plant or to some similar [climbing] plant', the *Oxford Dictionary of Place Names* says. A tenth- or eleventh-century Anglo-Saxon vocabulary glosses the Latin *uoluula*, that is, convolvulus, bindweed, as *hymele*, and the word *hymele* was also used for bryony, another climbing plant with hop-like lobed leaves.

Even hemlock seems to mean '*hymele*-like', perhaps because both it and bryony are extremely poisonous. The best we can say of Himbleton, therefore, is that it means 'tun (or homestead) where *hymele* grows'.

Even if hops did grow here before the Normans came, there is no record of hops, cultivated or otherwise, used for brewing in Britain before the fifteenth century. There was an ancient form of rent called 'hopgavel' or 'hoppegavel' in pre-Conquest Kent, which, it has been suggested, indicated that hops were cultivated for brewing in the county before 1066. But *hoppe* in Middle English could also mean the seedpod of the flax plant, and *hoppegavel* is defined in one Middle English dictionary as a rent paid in flax pods.

There is the curious case of the Graveney Boat, which was abandoned at Graveney in Kent about AD950 and discovered by archaeologists in the early 1970s. Investigations showed clearly that it had been either loaded or unloaded with hops just before it was abandoned: there were remains of hop flowers and hop nuts in the boat and on the brushwood platform that lay beside the boat.

However, in the absence of any evidence on what those hops were used for, the Graveney boat must remain an anomaly. The sometimes violent reaction of fifteenth- and sixteenth-century English ale brewers and drinkers against the use of hops by beer brewers from the Low Countries shows that if hops had once been put into ale for flavouring in these islands, their use had been forgotten. Yet if hops had ever been used by British brewers before 1400, the advantages they gave to the product, particularly in extending the life of the drink, would surely have meant hops would have been already widespread here long before Dutch and Flemish beer brewers began to arrive.

Finally, if the Old English had a word for hop, *hymele*, it would be odd for medieval English to have to adopt the Middle Dutch word *hoppe* for the name of the plant. It seems much more likely this was a new plant to the English, which needed a new name.

Myth 26: 'The planting of hops was forbidden by Henry VI / the use of hops was forbidden by Henry VIII / in 1520 the brewers of Coventry were ordered not to use hops.'

No; no; and no. Henry VIII never banned hops: his army survived on hopped beer, and the royal household bought both unhopped ale and hopped beer, brewed by separate ale and beer brewers. While the royal ale brewers were ordered not to use hops, which were meant for use only in the royal beer, the plant itself was never banned. Similarly, the Mayor and Aldermen of Coventry were forbidding the use of hops in 'all' (*ale*), not beer. These, and similar regulations found elsewhere in England in the last half of the fifteenth century and the first half of the sixteenth, were an attempt to maintain a difference between beer and ale, and protect the ale brewers' market, rather than a bid to ban hops entirely.

Thomas Fuller, the seventeenth-century English writer, recorded in his book *History of the Worthies of Britain* that the opponents of hops liked to 'plead the petition presented in Parliament in the reign of King Henry the Sixth against the wicked weed called hops'. No such petition is known, but, apparently on the basis of Fuller's comment, writers such as the nineteenth-century temperance campaigner Dr Richard Valpy French have declared that 'in Henry VI's reign . . . the planting of hops was prohibited'. It wasn't, and it never has been.

Myth 27: 'Edward VI passed special legislation in 1552 to permit the use of hops again by British [*sic*] brewers.'

See above. As hops were never banned, there was no need to pass a law to allow them to be used. Edward VI's Privy Council in 1549 paid the expenses involved in bringing over hop setters, apparently from Flanders, to work in England, which would hardly be happening if hops were illegal.

Myth 28: 'The arrival of hops meant the Tudors were able to brew stronger beer than earlier brewers could manage.'

Wrong. This 'fact' is 180 degrees in the wrong direction: hops, because they have a preserving effect, meant brewers could make weaker beers that would still last longer than strong unhopped ales.

Myth 29: 'Bottled beer was invented by Alexander Newell [*sic*], Dean of St Paul's, who was out fishing on the Thames one day during the reign of Queen Mary when he received a warning that his enemy Bishop Bonner was out to arrest him. Newell fled England, leaving behind on the river bank the bottle filled with beer that he had taken along to refresh himself with. Years later, when it was safe for him to return to England, Newell went back to the river bank, and found the bottle he had left behind, which was still drinkable, the cork coming out with a loud bang.'

This mangled version of the tale of 'Newell', properly Nowell, and bottled beer merges two separate episodes in the dean's life. It is apparently based on a misreading by the nineteenth-century journalist John Bickerdyke of the relevant passage in Thomas Fuller's *History of the Worthies of Britain*, published in 1662: a similar misquotation occurs in Alfred Barnard's *Noted Breweries of Great Britain*, vol. II, which was published in 1889.

Fuller interjects the tale of the left-behind bottle in the middle of the description of Nowell fleeing from Bonner's wrath, which is presumably why Barnard and Bickerdyke conflated the two stories into one. But Fuller specifically states that it was *days* later, not *years* later, that Nowell found the bottle of ale he had left in the grass. Even so, secondary fermentation had built up considerable pressure inside the bottle.

The *Dictionary of National Biography* claims, on no given evidence, that the bottle incident happened by the River Ash at Much Hadham in Hertfordshire, where Nowell was rector from 1562 (eight years after he had been forced to flee abroad).

Myth 30: 'The "X" used on beer casks comes from the monks marking barrels with a cross to show they were sound / had been blessed;' 'the X comes from the excise man marking barrels to show they had to pay ten shillings in duty.'

The idea that the X is a monk's debased cross is repeated by most writers on beer: but why the monks should use an X instead of a proper † is never explained. Nor does it seem likely that the holy symbol of Christianity would be used on intoxicating liquor. It is true that excise regulations (after 1782, at least) distinguished between 'strong or X beer' and 'T or table beer', with casks of table beer having to be marked with a T. But the tax on strong beer only rose to 10s a barrel from 1802, and X as a symbol for strong beer was in use long before that. It is much more likely that X and XX are short for *birra simplex* and *birra duplex*, Latin for 'single beer' and 'double beer', the common names for weak beer and strong beer.

Myth 31: 'The "stale" beer they drank in the eighteenth century was so called because it picked up a lactic sourness during long months of storage in wooden tuns.'

No. Stale beer, etymologically, is simply beer that has stood for some time, giving it time to clear: the word 'stale' is from the same roots as 'stall' and 'still'. To brewers and drinkers, therefore, 'stale beer' was 'aged, clear beer'; the term did not describe taste per se. The sense of 'stale' solely as 'lost its freshness', 'gone sour' is comparatively recent.

Myth 32: 'Porter was invented by Ralph Harwood, a brewer in Shoreditch, London, in 1722 to match the taste of a popular drink called three-threads which involved landlords mixing beer from three different casks. This way they could draw the drink from one cask, not three.'

This long-running myth first appeared in 1802, eighty years after the events it allegedly described, and has been repeated ever since. There was a drink called three-threads, but there is no contemporary evidence to show that it came from three casks, that porter was a replacement for it, or that Ralph Harwood, who was indeed a brewer in Shoreditch, invented it. In any case there is contemporary evidence to show porter was certainly being drunk before 1722.

Myth 33: 'Three-threads was also known as entire butt, because the ends, or butts, of the kegs faced the drinker, and they began calling the drink "a draw of entire butt".'

This is a confusion between the common American English meaning of butt and the word as used by eighteenth-century English brewers, to denote a cask holding 108 gallons, equivalent to two hogsheads or three barrels. Strong beer was matured in butts, and known as 'butt beer'; beer made from all three mashes of the grain was known as 'entire'; strong beer made from all three mashes of the grain was known as 'entire butt'.

Myth 34: 'Porter got its name because of its popularity with market porters' [in some versions, specifically 'porters in London's Covent Garden market', or even 'the porters at London's Victoria Station'].

Not at all. A porter in eighteenth-century London need not have been – indeed, generally wasn't – a market porter. Porters were found all over the city: porterage involved fetching and carrying bales of goods for all sorts of tradesmen from woolmen to wine merchants, and lifting and moving heavy casks, sacks and packs in and out of cellars and yards and about the streets, as well as unloading ships on the Thames. Railway porters appeared 120 years after porter the drink.

Myth 35: 'Porter got its name because the brewers' deliverymen, or porters, used to arrive at the door of the alehouse, inn or tavern and shout, "Porter!", to say they had arrived.'

Wrong again. Porters, of whom there were thousands in London, would presumably shout 'Porter!' whatever they were delivering to your door, whether it was a bale of cloth or a side of beef. Why would this cry stick as a name to beer alone? Contemporary commentators all said that porter was so named because it was popular with the common people of London, many of whom worked as porters. No more complicated explanation is necessary.

Myth 36: 'George Hodgson invented India Pale Ale at his brewery in Bow, East London, deliberately using a high hopping rate so that it would survive the long sea journey.'

No. Although Hodgson's brewery in Bow became famous for the pale ales it supplied to India, there is no evidence at all that it was supplying anything other than a standard strong October-brewed keeping ale as would have been first made for the home market. There is certainly no evidence Hodgson deliberately invented a new type of beer for the Indian market; he seems just to have been lucky that this particular type of beer matured so well on the journey out to the East.

Myth 37: 'India Pale Ale was the name originally given to a fine pale ale made for export to troops in India, usually in bottle.'

No again. Troops were a minority of the European population in India: fewer than two out of five Europeans were 'military servants' as opposed to the 'civil servants' of the old East India Company, and other traders and settlers. The customers for the strong pale ales being exported to India from Britain from the 1790s, therefore, were mostly civilian rather than military. British troops in any case mostly drank porter, even in India: in the 1850s Whitbread was exporting tens of thousands of barrels of porter to the subcontinent. Beer was normally exported in barrels, and bottled in India.

Myth 38: 'The Scottish use of names such as 60/- (sixty shillings), 70/-, 80/- and so on for different strengths of beer derives from the amount of duty per barrel.'

A misconception. The 'shilling' names for Scottish beers come from the wholesale price per (36 gallon) barrel, not the tax paid. As a naming system it goes back at least to Regency times: in 1819, for example, Robert Stein's brewery in the Canongate, Edinburgh, held in its cellars stocks of £5 and £6 ale, and five grades of porter from

115/- through 80/- to 30/-. In the 1890s Maclay's brewery in Alloa was producing beers ranging from 24/- table beer through 41/- mild ale to 54/- pale India ale, 60/- export ale and 70/- sweet ale (a strong mild). All were named for their price per barrel.

Myth 39: 'Mild is so called because it has a lower hop rate than bitter.'

No. Mild today does, generally, have fewer hops used in the brewing than bitter, but originally the mildness of mild ale was unrelated to hop content: mild beer was simply unaged or young beer, and its taste was mild because it had not acquired the sharp, acid flavours of 'stale', or matured beer. The original opposition was thus mild versus stale, not mild versus bitter: mild as a name for a type of beer goes back many years before brewers began to sell a beer called bitter.

A WORD IN YOUR BEER

the etymology of brewing

The Anglo-Saxon (or, more properly, Old English) word for fermented malt liquor was *alu* (in Anglian) or *ealu* (in West Saxon), *aloth* in the genitive case. It became 'ale' in modern English, and it appears to come down from a Germanic root *aluth. (The asterisk indicates that this is a presumed form of an unrecorded ancestor-word.)

Words for beer derived from the same root as ale are found across northern and eastern Europe, in Finnish (*olut*), Lithuanian (*alùs*), Latvian (*alus*), Estonian (*olu*), Old Slavonic (*olu* again), modern Slovene (*ôl*), Serbo-Croat (*olovina*), Old Norwegian and modern Swedish (*öl*) and modern Danish and Norwegian (*øl*).

It also turns up away in the Caucasus, in the Iranic language Ossetian, as *aeluton*, and in Georgian (apart from Finnish and Estonian the only non-Indo-European example) as *ludi* or, in a couple of mountain dialects, *aludi*. Although the Caucasus is close to where beer brewing began, there is no evidence the word 'ale' began here and spread to Europe: it was most likely the other way round. Georgian linguists believe their language took the word from the Ossetians, who are descended from the formerly nomadic Indo-European Alans. The Alans ranged as far west as France in the fifth century AD, alongside other invaders of the Roman world such as the Germanic-speaking

Vandals and Goths, and they probably picked up the 'ale' word from one of these peoples and brought it back to the Caucasus.

Despite being so common in northern European languages, 'ale' is a mysterious word, which has given etymologists some trouble. The ultimate Indo-European root, if there is one, may link it with other words meaning 'bitter-tasting', such as alum (sulphate of aluminium), the astringent salt used in leather-making. The idea that ale was 'the bitter drink' is given support by an Irish poem from some time before the twelfth century, part of which translates as: 'The Saxon ale of bitterness / Is drunk with pleasure about Inber in Rig.' Perhaps ale was called 'the bitter drink' by northern Europeans in contrast to their other favourite intoxicant, mead, which is etymologically 'the sweet drink' or 'the honey drink'. Certainly bitter herbs were popular as a flavouring for ale: they included bog bean or marsh trefoil, and bog myrtle or sweet gale.

Another theory, put forward by a leading American Indo-European expert, Professor Calvert Watkins of Harvard University, is that the Germanic root *aluth is related to the Greek *aluein* or *alussein*, 'to be distraught', with cognates having to do with sorcery, and also 'hallucinate'. The semantic link, obviously, is that after a few jars too many of *aluth* the bewitched drinker would stagger about in a distraught state and begin to have visions.

If the word 'ale' goes back as far as the Neolithic, and if the suggestion by some archaeologists that Neolithic ale was flavoured with the poisonous plant henbane is correct, the possible etymological link between ale and 'hallucinate' becomes stronger: henbane ale will certainly bring the drinker feelings of terror, delirium and visual distortion.

None of the explanations for the origin of the word 'ale' is convincing, however, and there is not the obvious connection to the mechanics of brewing that the roots of other beery words show. The oldest known Indo-European word for beer, the Hittite *siessar*, found some 3,500 years ago, literally means 'straining', from the verbal noun of *siya-* 'to strain, sieve', a reference to making bread-beer by straining soaked bread through sieves. Many other brewing words have the sense of 'boiling' behind them. 'Brew', for example, goes back to an Indo-European root word *bhru-, connected with heating and bubbling. This root gave the ancient Thracian language in the eastern Balkans the word *broûtos*, meaning beer, and English the modern word 'broth'. 'Fermentation' comes via the Latin for yeast from a connected Indo-European root, *bher-, to bubble, to boil. *Curmi*, the old Celtic word for ale (and the root, via Latin *cervisia*, of *cerveza*, the Spanish for beer), seems to be linked with the Latin word *cremo*, to burn or boil. 'Yeast' has the same Indo-European root as Sanskrit *yásati*, to seethe or boil, and Welsh *ias*, 'seething'. *Kvass*, the Russian rye beer, looks to have a connection with Sanskrit *kvathati*, meaning 'he boils'. The connection between beer and boiling is a double one: water has to be boiled up to mash the grain, and also fermenting wort will bubble like a boiling liquid.

'Ale' looks to be an old word, at any rate: certainly another etymologist, Professor Alan Ross, found the many Slavic, Baltic and Germanic variants of the word 'ale' were 'inter-related', rather than any one showing an obvious derivation from another. Perhaps – but this is only a guess – the Slavs, Balts and Germans all took the word from another, long-vanished non-Indo-European language that once existed in northern Europe, whose speakers were already brewing something they called ale when the mead-drinking Indo-European ancestors of Slavic, Baltic and Germanic speakers moved into the ale-makers' territory from the east.

The ancestor language of modern German and Dutch also once had a word from the 'ale' family. But this was replaced around the sixth or seventh centuries AD by *bior* (modern German and Dutch *bier*, English 'beer'). Most etymologists say *bior* comes from the monastic Latin word *biber*, meaning drink: monasteries were, of course, great centres of brewing. However, the picture is made more confusing because in Old English there was a word, *beór*, which seems to have been used for cider or fermented fruit rather than ale, and the same is true of the equivalent word in Old Norse, *bjorr*: it is possible, therefore, that, like the Old English and the Norse, the tribes of Germany and the Low Countries were already using a word very similar to *bior* for another alcoholic drink, fermented fruit, before they transferred it to the drink made from malted grain.

In any case, if the theory that 'beer' comes from monastic Latin is true, why did the monks use *biber*, 'drink', rather than the regular Latin word for ale, *cervisia*? One possibility is that the use of *biber* for ale may be down to the many Irish scholars and clerics, such as St Columbanus, St Gall and St Kilian, who travelled to Germanic-speaking Europe during the sixth and seventh centuries to spread the Gospel. In Irish, the first language of these travelling saints, *lionn*, which like *biber* originally meant 'drink', had replaced *cuirm* as the word for ale. Perhaps when Irish monks spoke in Latin about *lionn*, meaning ale, they translated the word literally from Irish into Latin as *biber*, 'drink', rather than *cervisia*, 'ale'.

From the Irish monks the use of the word *biber* for ale could then have spread to others in the many monasteries where Irish influence was strong (important centres of Irish Christian authority included Cologne, Mainz, Strasbourg, Salzburg and Vienna, while St Kilian and his companions brought Christianity to Franconia and Thuringia, and St Gall gave his name to an important medieval monastery in modern Switzerland). From there the use of *biber* for beer could have spread to the early Germanic population generally. If they were already using a similar-sounding word for a type of alcoholic drink, it is easy to see how they would pick it up.

The word spread from German not only to French (*bière*) and Italian (*birra*), but also to the Slavonic languages, where it became *pivo*; Turkish, where the word is *bir*; and as far away as Chinese (where the word for beer is pronounced *pijiu*) and Japanese, where it became *biiru*.

If speakers of the ancestor languages of German and Dutch were originally using *bior* to mean another type of alcoholic drink from ale, German philologists do not appear to have found any evidence of it. But there is little doubt that in pre-Norman England, to the speakers of Old English, *beór* definitely meant something other than ale. There are many sources that make it clear the Anglo-Saxons regarded *beór* and *ealu* as very separate drinks (for example, one of the 'Homilies of Aelfric', written around the end of the tenth century, says of John the Baptist that he 'ne dranc nathor ne win, ne beór, ne ealu': that is, he drank 'neither wine, nor *beór* nor ale'), and *beór* was particularly potent; pregnant women were specifically warned in one Old English leechdom or medical tract that they must not *beór drince* at all, nor drink anything else to excess.

The most likely meaning for *beór*, which would fit in with its evident strength, is cider, fermented apple juice, which can hit an ABV of 18 per cent or more. The etymologist Christine Fell puts forward a very good argument for *beór* in Old English (and its equivalent in Old Norse, *bjorr*) being a strongly alcoholic, sweet, honey-and-fruit drink consumed from tiny cups only an inch or so high: such cups have been found in pagan Anglo-Saxon graves from the sixth and seventh centuries AD. Compound words containing *beór* included *beór-byden* or beer barrel, *beórsele* or beer hall, *beórtún* or beer enclosure, *beór-setl* or beer bench and *beórscealc* or beer server.

Some time around the Norman Conquest *beór* fell out of the English language (it is not found in Chaucer, who died in 1400), being replaced by *sither* or *cidre*, the modern word 'cider'. This comes from the Old French word *sidre*, which goes back via medieval Latin and ecclesiastical Greek to the Hebrew word *shekar*, found in the Bible to describe any strong intoxicating liquor. Confusingly, in Normandy, which, of course, takes its name from the Old Norse speakers who settled there, *bère* is the usual dialect word for cider. At the end of the fourteenth century, *beor*'s relative, *bere*, arrived in English to describe the new hopped grain drink from the continent. After a trial with the spelling 'beere' in the sixteenth century, by the start of the seventeenth century the word had settled down to the modern 'beer'.

HOW BEER IS BREWED

The brewer's mission is to take his raw material, grain (normally barley, sometimes wheat, very occasionally oats or rye), and convert the starch in the grain into sugar. Then he turns the sugar into alcohol, with the help of yeast. This makes his job more difficult, and more technically challenging, than the task of the wine-maker, who has only to crush the grapes to let the yeast on the grape skins attack the sugars in the grape juice.

The job of turning grain starches into sugars is known as malting. The grain is soaked, which tricks it into starting to sprout. As it sprouts, enzymes in each barleycorn or wheat seed turn the starch inside the grain into sugar that the grain will use as fuel to power its growth. The maltster's art lies in halting that growth with heat, at just the point where the enzyme activity is at its height but not too much starch has been used up by the growing grain. How hot the maltster makes the grain, and how long he roasts it, will have a major effect on the flavour and colour of the final beer.

The semi-sprouted, dried grain, now known as malt, is roughly ground by the brewer and mixed with hot water to form a porridge. This process, known as mashing, starts up the enzymes in the grain again, and more starch is converted into sugar. The malt sugar dissolves in the hot water, and this hot, sweet liquid, known as wort, is then drained off.

Modern brewers will then boil the wort with hops, to add a bitter flavour and a preservative effect to the final beer; in the millennia before hops, brewers might add other herbal flavourings. Then comes the final stage: introducing yeast to the wort. The yeast, a single-cell organism, feeds by turning the sugar into alcohol and carbon dioxide.

Once the yeast has finished its job, and converted all the sugar it can (normally after six or seven days), the liquid, which is by now beer, can be racked into casks. It is then stored for a while – the time varies, depending on what type of beer it is – before being drunk.

BEER WORDS:

from abroad cooper to zythophilia

abroad cooper Brewery representative who checked the condition of the beer when it was in publican's cellars.

ABV Alcohol by volume: the percentage of alcohol in a volume of liquid, the standard modern UK measure of beer strength.

ale In references from Saxon times to the end of the seventeenth century, this means a fermented malt liquor made without hops, in strict contrast with beer, which, when the word reached the British Isles in the 1400s, meant a fermented malt liquor flavoured with hops. By the early eighteenth century, ale and beer had become synonyms, both meaning a hopped fermented malt drink.

ale-draper An ale-house keeper.

attenuation As beer ferments, and sugar is converted into alcohol, the specific gravity of the liquid lowers, a process known as attenuation. Beers where most of the sugar is converted are known as highly attenuated; sweet beers where more of the sugars have survived have low attenuation.

back The traditional term for a vessel in a brewery: the hop back, for example, is where the hops settle out as the wort is run out of the copper.

barrel A specific size of cask, 36 gallons for the British beer barrel, 32 gallons (30 gallons before 1532) for the ale barrel.

beer In references from the fifteenth century onwards, a fermented malt liquor flavoured with hops. However, beer writers and beer historians follow the convention of archaeologists and historians generally in talking about 'Sumerian beer', 'Egyptian beer', 'Celtic beer' when strictly they mean 'Sumerian ale' and so on, such drinks being unhopped.

beerhouse Brought into being by the Beerhouse Act of 1830, an establishment licensed to sell beer only, not wine and spirits. Now extinct.

bitter The name first given by the nineteenth-century drinking public to pale ale on draught.

bottom-fermenting yeast More accurately, bottom-settling yeast: generally associated with the cool-fermenting yeasts used to make lager beer, although some warm-fermenting ale yeasts can be bottom-settling types.

brewhouse The part of a brewery where the mash tun and copper are housed.

brewer's pounds The number of pounds of sugar that would need to be dissolved in water to get to a particular specific gravity.

brewery tap A brewery's nearest tied retail outlet.

bulk barrel After Gladstone's Licensing Act of 1880, beer output, nationally or per brewery, could be measured in 'bulk barrels', that is, real actual barrelage produced, or 'standard barrels', that is, total output expressed as a single beer of 1057 original gravity, lowered a few years after 1880 to 1055 OG. The original gravity of the 'standard barrel' was the base point for calculating how much duty was payable on beer of different gravities, and the government liked to measure output in 'standard barrels' because it showed how the tax yield was varying from year to year.

Burton ale A darkish, slightly sweet draught beer made originally in Burton upon Trent.

bushel A measure of grain; originally a container that would hold exactly 8 gallons of water, then the amount of grain that would fit into such a container, generally taken to be around 42 pounds of malt. (The grain, when measured, would be levelled off with a piece of wood known as a 'strike', hence the pub name Bushel and

Strike.) If you hid your light under your bushel, of course, it could not be seen.

butt A cask with a capacity of 120 gallons, about the biggest that could be easily handled by one (strong) man, often used in the eighteenth century for maturing beer. The butts of maturing beer would frequently be stored in cellars, which could be dangerous: in 1758 it was recorded that the abroad cooper employed by Huck's brewery in London had died after going down into a cellar in Pall Mall filled with 40 butts of unstopped beer. Contemporary reports blamed the 'steam' off the beer, but the cooper, and the sedan chair man who went down after him, were undoubtedly suffocated by the carbon dioxide being given off by the beer as it underwent secondary fermentation in the butts.

cask Any wooden draught beer container of any size, from pin to tun.

condition The amount of carbonation in a beer.

cooper Maker of casks and other brewery vessels out of wood (although a man who specialised in vessels other than casks was known as a back maker).

copper The vessel in which the wort was boiled with hops, traditionally made of copper, an excellent conductor of heat.

currency In this book all currency references before 1971 have been left in pounds, shillings and (old) pence, shortened generally to £, s (for solidus, a Roman coin) and d (for denarius, another Roman coin). Thus five pounds two shillings and six (old) pence is given as £5 2s 6d. There were 12 pence to the shilling, and 20 shillings to the pound.

double beer Beer made from wort that has been poured back through the mash to increase its strength by extracting more sugar from the malt.

dray Properly, a four-wheeled vehicle, as opposed to a cart, which had only two wheels. Later applied indiscriminately to any vehicle, horse-drawn or mechanically powered, used to deliver beer.

entire A beer made with all the wort collected from a set of mashings on one batch of grain.

enzymes Biochemicals found in both malt and yeast which convert one substance, such as starch, into another, such as sugar. They were originally identified in yeast, and enzyme literally means 'in yeast' in Greek.

fermentation The process during which yeast converts sugar into alcohol, changing sweet wort into ale or beer.

fermenting vessel Where fermentation takes place.

final gravity The specific gravity of a beer when it has finished fermenting at the brewery. A precise relationship exists between original gravity, final gravity and the amount of alcohol in a beer.

fining Adding a substance, often isinglass, in order to clear ale or beer.

firkin A 9 gallon cask.

free house Licensed establishment not tied to one brewer and thus able to sell beers from any brewery.

grist Ground malt, ready for mashing.

gruit Herb mixture used by continental brewers for flavouring ale before hops came in.

guinea A sum of money equivalent to £1 1s (*see* currency).

gyle *(noun)* Originally, freshly fermenting wort; later, a specific brewing batch (as in 'gyle number 42').

gyle *(verb)* To add freshly fermenting wort to a batch of finished beer to raise its condition, otherwise known (from the German) as krausening.

hair A horse-hair sieve.

hogshead A cask of 54 gallons capacity, or 1½ barrels.

India Pale Ale Name given in Britain (but not India) to the strong pale ale originally shipped to the East for expatriate Europeans, which matured fast thanks to its double trip through warm equatorial waters on the way round Africa. IPA became particularly associated with the big Burton upon Trent brewers.

inn Strictly, licensed premises offering lodging, always with a full (as opposed to beer only) licence.

isinglass The swim bladder of fish, especially the sturgeon, dried and sold to the brewer. He then mixed it with stale beer to turn it into a jelly that would clarify or 'fine' beer when added to a cask, by taking suspended solids with it to the bottom.

Jacob's ladder The bucketed conveyor belt which carried grain from the grist mill to the mash tun.

kilderkin Cask of 18 gallons capacity.

lager Beer brewed under cool conditions, using a so-called 'bottom-fermenting' yeast and stored for some time to mature; named after the German word *lager*, store-room.

lead The medieval term for the brewery vessel, generally not made of lead, in which the water was boiled prior to mashing.

liquor The brewer's name for water.

long pull Serving up more beer than was asked for, to attract more custom. The 'long pull' was made illegal in 1915.

malt Grain which has been allowed to start to germinate, to encourage the production of sugars from the starches in each barleycorn or wheat seed, and then dried to stop germination before all the sugar is used up by the growing plant.

maltings The building where malt is made: generally long and thin, with a kiln at one end to dry the malt.

maltmaker A worker in a maltings.

maltster The entrepreneur who ran a maltings.

mash Mixed grist and liquor.

mash fork The wooden implement used to stir the mash in the mash tun.

mashing Mixing the grist with hot liquor to extract the fermentable sugars.

mash tun The vessel where mashing takes place. The earliest mash tuns were simple tubs, and a wicker basket (known as a strun or huckmuck) was pushed into the middle of the mash, so that the sweet wort flowed into the basket to be ladled out into the fermenting vessel. Later mash tuns had taps, protected by twigs or straw from blocking up, through which the wort would run off, and still later versions had a perforated false floor through which the wort ran to a tap.

mild   Sweetish, often dark beer, generally lightly hopped because it was meant to be served and drunk soon after being brewed.

OG   *See* original gravity.

original gravity   The specific gravity of wort before fermentation, known as OG. The specific gravity of water is taken to be 1000, and the original gravity of wort, which shows how much fermentable material is dissolved in it, is given in points above 1000, such as 1036, 1047 or 1080. The OG figure gives a guide to the likely alcohol level of the finished beer, with an OG of 1047 meaning a likely final ABV of around 4.7 per cent, depending on how well attenuated the beer is.

own brew   A less ambiguous term than 'home brew' for describing inns, pubs and beerhouses that brewed their own beer of sale on the premises.

peck   A quarter of a bushel, equivalent to around 10½ pounds of malt. One peck of malt would make, very roughly, about 4½ gallons of beer, or 36 pints.

pin   A cask of 4½ gallons capacity.

pitching   Adding yeast to the wort in the fermenting vessel.

ponto   Round fermenting vessel designed to thrown off excess yeast into a trough, a more primitive version of the union system.

porter   Originally a strong, dark brown, bitter beer popular with London's very many street and river porters in the eighteenth century. In its final incarnation, a weak but still dark beer. (Porter was always called a 'beer' and never an 'ale'.)

present gravity   The specific gravity of a beer in cask or bottle at the point it was measured some time after racking or bottling, which, after secondary fermentation in the cask or bottle had produced more alcohol and thus lowered the specific gravity, will be less than the 'final gravity' at the point the beer left the fermentation vessel.

pub   Short for public house; generally a reference to premises with a full on-licence to sell beer and spirits, but not offering accommodation (unlike an inn).

quarter   A volume measure of malt equal to 8 bushels. The exact weight of a quarter of malt would vary depending on how dense the malt was, and on the size of the grains, but it is generally taken as three hundredweight, or 336 pounds. The capacity of breweries was measured in the number of quarters of malt they could mash at any one time, a quarter of malt producing, very roughly, four barrels of beer at the 'standard' OG of 1055.

racking Running the fermented beer off its lees into casks for delivery.

round A fermentation vessel.

secondary fermentation The fermentation that takes place in the cask after the beer has been racked.

small beer Weak beer made from the last mash.

sparging Spraying hot water over the mash tun at the end of mashing to maximize extraction of sugars.

specific gravity A measure of the density of a liquid, compared to pure water. With beer, specific gravity falls as fermentation progresses, sugar is used up and alcohol (which is less dense than water) is produced.

square A square fermentation vessel, double-chambered so that excess yeast flows up from the bottom part into the top, separating it from the beer.

stout Originally a slang expression for any strong beer, later specifically a strong version of porter.

tavern A licensed establishment that also provides food, but not accommodation.

tied house A licensed establishment restricted, through ownership, or loans to the owner, to supplying beers from one brewer only.

top-fermenting yeast More accurately, top-settling yeast, since it rises to the top of the fermenting vessel when it has used up all the sugar in the wort. Most, but not all, ale yeasts are of the top-settling type.

tun A brewery vessel; a cask of 240 gallons. (The contents of a tun weigh approximately a ton: the two words come from the same root.)

union system Fermentation method particularly associated with Burton upon Trent, in which the beer is separated from the excess yeast by flowing up a pipe, and automatically returned to the fermenting vessel via a trough.

working vessels Fermenting vessels.

wort Unfermented beer; the sugary liquid collected from the mash tun.

yeast The single-celled organism that the French scientist Pasteur finally identified in the nineteenth century as responsible for turning sugar into alcohol. Yeast comes in millions of types, of which only 250 will produce fermentation, and only twenty-four are regarded as 'good'. Brewers, wine-makers and cider-makers mostly use the yeast *Saccharomyces cerevisia* (meaning 'beer sugar fungus' in Latin), which itself comes in many different strains.

zythophilia The love of beer, from the Greek *zythos*, a word for a type of ale.

BIBLIOGRAPHY

As well as the sources listed below, use has also been made of documents at record offices in Hackney, Hertford and Bedford; printed copies of Tudor and Stuart government records kept at the British Library; and archived editions of the *Luton News* and *Brewers' Journal*.

General sources

Arnold, John P., *Origin and History of Beer and Brewing*, Chicago, 1911

Barber, Norman, *A Century of British Brewers*, New Ash Green, Brewery History Society, 1990

Barr, Andrew, *Drink: An Informal Social History*, London, Transworld, 1995

Bickerdyke, John (pseudonym of Charles Henry Cook), *The Curiosities of Ale and Beer*, London, Swan Sonnenschein, 1889

Brewery History Society, *Brewery History* magazine, 1974–2002

Campbell, Andrew, *The Book of Beer*, London, Dennis Dobson, 1956

Clark, Peter, *The English Alehouse: A Social History 1200–1830*, London, 1983

Corran, H. S., *A History of Brewing*, Newton Abbot, David & Charles, 1975

Faulkner, Nicholas O., *Allied Breweries A Long Life. A Directory of Ancestor Breweries*, Allied Lyons, 1988

French, Richard Valpey, *Nineteen Centuries of Drink in England: A History*, London, 1884

Hornsey, Ian S., *Brewing*, Cambridge, RSC Paperbacks, 1999

King, Frank A., *Beer Has a History*, London, Hutchinson, 1947

La Pensée, Clive, *The Craft of House Brewing*, Beverley, Montag Publications, 1996

La Pensée, Clive, *The Historical Companion to House Brewing*, Beverley, Montag Publications, 1990

Marchant, W. T., *In Praise of Ale*, London, Redway, 1888

Monckton, H. A., *A History of English Ale and Beer*, London, Bodley Head, 1966

Monckton, H. A., *A History of the English Public House*, London, Bodley Head, 1969

Monckton, H. A., *Whitbread's Breweries*, London, Whitbread & Co., 1984

Nordland, Odd, *Brewing and Beer Traditions in Norway*, Oslo, 1969

Patton, Jeffrey, *Additives, Adulterants and Contaminants in Beer*, Barnstaple, Patton Publications, 1989

Richmond, L. and Turton, A., eds, *The Brewing Industry*, Manchester, 1990

Strong, S., *Romance of Brewing*, London, 1951

Wilson, C. Anne, *Food and Drink in Britain*, London, 1973

Chapter 1 In the beginning: how the search for a pint brought us civilization (maybe)

Barker, G., *Prehistoric Farming in Europe*, 1985

Braidwood, Robert J. et al., *Symposium: Did man once live by beer alone?*, 1953

Buhner, Stephen Harrod, *Sacred and Herbal Healing Beers*, Colorado, Brewers Publications, 1998

Cunliffe, Barry, *The Extraordinary Voyage of Pytheas the Greek*, London, Allen Lane/Penguin Press, 2001

Dineley, Merryn and Dineley, Graham 'Neolithic ale', ch. 13 in

Andrew S. Fairbairn, ed., *Plants in Neolithic Britain and Beyond*, Oxford, Oxbow Books, 2001

Forbes, R. J., *Food and Drink*, Oxford, 1956

Forbes, R. J., *Studies in Ancient Technology*, vol. 3, 1955

Fowler, Peter, *The Farming of Prehistoric Britain*, Cambridge, Cambridge University Press, 1983

George, Andrew, *The Epic of Gilgamesh*, London, Allen Lane/Penguin Press, 1999

Goodman, J., Lovejoy, P. and Sherratt, A. eds, *Consuming Habits: Drugs in History and Anthropology*, London, Routledge, 1995

Hartman, Louis F. and Oppenheim, A. L., *On Beer and Brewing Techniques in Ancient Mesopotamia According to the XXIIIrd Tablet of the Series HAR.r a= hubullu*

Katz, Solomon H. and Maytag, Fritz, *Brewing an Ancient Beer*, 1991

Katz, Solomon H. and Voigt, Mary M., *Beer and Bread: The Early Uses of Cereals in the Human Diet*, 1986

Renfrew, Jane M, ed., *New Light on Early Farming: Recent Developments in Palaeoethnobotany*, 1991

Ritchie, Anna, ed., *Neolithic Orkney in its European context*, ch. 16 'The Neolithic Fair', Sandwick, Skiall House, 2000

Sherratt, Andrew, *Alcohol and its Alternatives: Symbol and Substance in Pre-Industrial Cultures*, 1995

Sherratt, Andrew, *Cups that Cheered*, 1987

Smith, Bruce D., *The Emergence of Agriculture*, New York, Scientific American Library; Oxford, 1995

Chapter 2 Celt and Roman: how the legions learned to love British beer

Almqvist, Bo, *The Viking Ale and the Rhine Gold*, 1965

Birley, Anthony, *Garrison Life at Vindolanda*, Stroud, Tempus, 2002

Black, Maggie et al., *A Taste of History: 10,000 Years of Food in Britain*, London, British Museum Press, 1993

Bowman, A. K. and Thomas, J. D., *Vindolanda: The Latin Writing-Tablets*, Britannia Monograph Series No. 4, London, 1984

Bowman, A. K. and Thomas, J. D., *The Vindolanda Writing Tablets (Tabulae Vindolandenses II)*, London, British Museum, 1994

Caesar, Julius, *De Bello Gallico*

Findberg, H. P. R., ed., *The Agrarian History of England and Wales*, vol. 1, Cambridge, 1988

Hofsten, Nils von, *Pors och andra humleersättningar och ölkryddor i äldre tider* (Bog Myrtle and Other Substitutes for Hops in Former Times), Uppsala, University of Uppsala, 1960

Ireland, S., *Roman Britain: A Sourcebook*, London, Routledge, 1996

Logan, James, *The Scottish Gael*, Edinburgh, 1831

Niblett, Rosalind, *Roman Hertfordshire*, Wimborne, Dovecote Press, 1995

O Curry, Eugene, *On The Manners and Customs of the Ancient Irish*, Dublin, 1873

Orosius, Paulus, *Historiarum adversum paganos*, ed. C. Zangemeister, 1889

Pennant, Thomas, *A Tour in Scotland and Voyage to the Hebrides*, London, B. White, 1774–6

Pliny, *Naturalis Historia*, The Loeb Classical Library, Cambridge, Mass., Harvard University Press, 1983

Reynolds, P. J. and Langley, J. K., *Romano-British Corn-Drying Ovens, An Experiment*, 1980

Ross, Alan S. C., *Etymology: with Especial Reference to English*, London, André Deutsch, 1958

Ross Anne, *Everyday Life of the Pagan Celts*, London, Batsford, 1970

Strabo, *Geography*, book 4, trans. Horace Leonard Jones, 1927

Tacitus, 'Germania', in *Tacitus on Britain and Germany*, trans. H. Mattingly, 1967

⋄ BIBLIOGRAPHY ⋄

Chapter 3 A thousand years of ale: from the Saxons to Dick Whittington

Ball, Mia, *The Worshipful Company of Brewers*, London, 1977

Barron, Caroline and Saul, Nigel, eds, *England and the Low Countries in the Late Middle Ages*, Stroud, 1995

Bennett, Judith M., *Ale, Beer and Brewsters in England*, Oxford, Oxford University Press, 1996

Bond, James and John Rhodes, *The Oxfordshire Brewer*, Witney, Oxfordshire Museum Services, 1985

Fell, Christine, *Old English Beor*, Leeds Studies in English, new series, vol. 7, 76–95 , 1974

Firth, J., *Reminiscences of an Orkney Parish*, Stromness, Rendall, 1922

Greenaway, G., ed., *Life of Thomas à Becket*, London, Folio Society, 1961

Hagen, Anne, *A Handbook of Anglo-Saxon Food and Drink: Processing and Consumption*, Pinner, Anglo-Saxon Books, 1992

Hagen, Anne, *A Second Handbook of Anglo-Saxon Food and Drink: Production and Distribution*, Hockwold-cum-Wilton, Anglo-Saxon Books, 1995

Hale, William, *The Domesday of St Paul's in the Year MCCXXII*, London, Camden Society, 1858

Hildegard of Bingen, Abbess, *Physica Sacra*

Laughton, Jane, *The Alewives of Later Medieval Chester*, New York, 1995

Postles, David, 'Brewing and the Peasant Economy: Some Manors in Later Medieval Devon', *Rural History*, vol. 3 (1992), pp. 133–44

Salzman, Louis Francis, *English Industries of the Middle Ages*, London, 1964; first publ. 1923

Swanson, George, *Tastes in London's History*, London, 1953

Unger, Richard W., *Technical Change in the Brewing Industry in Germany, the Low Countries and England in the Late Middle Ages*

Wilson, D. Gay, 'Plant Remains from the Graveney Boat and the Early History of Humulus Lupulus L. in Western Europe', *New Phytologist*, vol. 75 (1975), pp. 627–48

Woolgar, C. M., *The Great Household in Medieval England*, New Haven: Yale University Press, 1999

Chapter 4 The early years of beer: how hops became hip

Aerts, Erik, Louis M. Cullen and Richard G. Wilson, eds, *Production, Marketing and Consumption of Alcoholic Beverages since the Late Middle Ages*, Leuven, 1990

Barker, Theo, *Shepherd Neame, A Story That's Been Brewing for 300 Years*, Cambridge, Granta Editions, 1998

Barth, Heinrich Johannes, Christiane Klinke and Claus Schmidt, *The Hop Atlas*, Nuremberg, Joh. Barth & Sohn, 1994

Boorde, Andrew, *A Compendyous Regyment: or Dyetary of Helth*, 1542

Brears, Peter, *All the King's Cooks: The Tudor Kitchens of King Henry VIII at Hampton Court Palace*, London, Souvenir Press, 1999

Eley, Philip, *Portsmouth Breweries 1492–1847*, Portsmouth, Portsmouth City Council, 1988

Filmer, Richard, *Hops and Hop Picking*, Princes Risborough, Shire Publications, 1982

Harrison, William, *The Description of England* (1587), Washington and New York, Folger Shakespeare Library and Dover Publications Inc., 1994

Hopkinson, Jean, ed., *A Pocketful of Hops: Hop Growing in the Bromyard Area*, Bromyard & District Local History Society, 1988

Houtte, J. A. van, *An Economic History of the Low Countries 800–1800*, London, Weidenfeld & Nicolson, 1977

Laurence, John (Revd), *A New System of Agriculture*, London, 1726

Lawrence, Margaret, *The Encircling Hop*, Sittingbourne, SAWD Publications, 1990

Markham, Gervase, *The English Housewife*, Kingston, Queen's University Press,

Mercer, G. E., *The Cole Papers: The Coles of Heatham House, Twickenham and the Brewery*, Twickenham, Borough of Twickenham Local History Society, 1985

Osborne, Keith, *Bygone Breweries of Kent*, , Rochester Press, 1982

Plot, Robert, *A Natural History of Staffordshire*, Oxford, 1686

Reddington, William, *A Practical Treatise on Brewing*, London: Richardson & Urquhart, 1776

Roberts, S. K., 'Alehouses, Brewing and Govenment under the Early Stuarts', *Southern History*, vol. 2 (1980), pp. 45–71

Scot, Reginald (Reynold), *A Perfitte Platforme for a Hoppe Garden, and necessarie instructions for the making and mayntenaunce thereof etc*, London, C. Denham, 1574

Trubridge, P. C., *English Ale Glasses 1685–1830*

Tryon, Thomas, *A New Art of Brewing Beer, Ale, and Other Sorts of Liquors*, London, 1690

Watkins, George, *The Compleat English Brewer: or The Whole Art and Mystery of Brewing Explained*, London, 1747

Y-worth, W., *Cerevisiarii Comes, or the New and True Art of Brewing*, London, 1692

Chapter 5 Black is beautiful: the eighteenth century

Anon., *A Vade Mecum for Malt-Worms/A Guide for Malt-Worms*, London, c.1718–20

Anon., *Trumans the Brewers 1666–1966*, London, Truman Hanbury & Buxton, 1966

Bailey, Nathan, *Dictionarium Domesticum*, London, 1736

Baron, Stanley W., *Brewed in America: A History of Beer and Ale in the United States*, Boston, 1962

Brown, Mike and Brian Willmott, *Brewed in Northants*, New Ash Green, Brewery History Society, 1998

Bryant, G. E. and G. P. Baker, eds, *A Quaker Journal being the diary and reminiscences of William Lucas of Hitchin*, London, Hutchinson & Co., 1934

Child, Samuel, *Everyman His Own Brewer: A Practical Treatise*

Explaining the Art and Mystery of Brewing Porter, Ale, Twopenny and Table Beer, London, 1790 (6th edn 1798)

Combrune, Michael, *An Essay on Brewing, with a View of Establishing the Principles of the Art*, London, 1758

Combrune, Michael, *The Theory and Practice of Brewing*, London, 1762

Cornell, Martyn, 'A Figge for Spain: A History of Brewing in North Hertfordshire', unpublished manuscript, 2001

de Saussure, César, *A Foreign View of England in the Reigns of George I and II*, trans. Madame van Muyden, London, 1902

Earle, Peter, *A City Full of People: Men and Women of London 1650–1750*, London, Methuen, 1994

Ellis, William, *The London and Country Brewer*, London, 1734

Emden, Paul H., *Quakers in Commerce*, London, Sampson Low Marston & Co., 1939

Janes, Hurford, *The Red Barrel: A History of Watney Mann*, London, John Murray, 1963

Jennings, Paul, *The Public House in Bradford, 1770–1970*, Keele, Keele University Press, 1995

Lloyd, Humphrey, *The Quaker Lloyds in the Industrial Revolution*, London, Hutchinson, 1975

McDonagh, O., *Origins of Porter*,

Mathias, Peter, *The Brewing Industry in England 1799–1830*, Cambridge, 1959

Richardson, J., *Philosophical Principles of the Science of Brewing*, York, 1784

Ritchie, Berry, *An Uncommon Brewer: The story of Whitbread 1742–1992*, London, James & James, 1992

Sambrook, Pamela, *Country House Brewing in England 1500–1900*, London, Hambledon Press, 1996

Slater, J. Norman, *A Brewer's Tale: Greenall Whitley, Warrington*, Greenall Whitley, 1980

Stern, Walter M., *The Porters of London*, London, Longmans, 1960

Thorold, Peter, *The London Rich*, New York, St Martin's Press, 1999

Watkins, George, *The Complete Brewer . . . by a Brewer of Extensive Practice*, Dublin, 1766

Chapters 6 and 7 Pale and interesting: the nineteenth century, part one; Make mine mild: the nineteenth century, part two

Amsinck, George Stewart, *Practical Brewings: A Series of 50 Brewings in Extension*, London, 1868

Anon., 'A Day at a London Brewery', *Penny Magazine*, vol 10, 21 March 1841

Anon., 'Hodgson's India Pale Ale', *Notes and Queries* 7th series, vol. 6 (1888), pp. 329, 417

Anon., *The Hook Norton Brewery Co.*, Hook Norton, Hook Norton Brewery, 1997

Avis, Anthony, *Timothy Bentley, Master Brewer of Yorkshire*, Huddersfield, Kirklees Cultural Services, 1998

Barge, John, *A Gazetteer of Liverpool Brewers*, Manchester, Neil Richardson, 1987

Barnard, Alfred, *Noted Breweries of Great Britain and Ireland*, vols 1–4, London, Sir Joseph Causton & Sons, 1889–90

Bennison, Brian, *Brewers and Bottlers of Newcastle upon Tyne from 1850*, Newcastle, Newcastle City Libraries & Arts, 1995

Buckland, Khadija, *A Brewer of Pedigree: A History of Marston Thompson & Evershed*, MWF Hurdle, 1999

Bushnan, John Stevenson, *Burton and its Bitter Beer*, 1853

Cornell, Martyn, 'Nevermore Make Quarrels: A History of Brewing in South Hertfordshire', unpublished manuscript, 2001

Davis, Fred, *The Anglo: The History of the Anglo-Bavarian Brewery*, Shepton Mallet, J. H. Haskins, 1994

Davison, Andrew P., *Justly Celebrated Ales: A Directory of Norfolk Brewers*, New Ash Green, Brewery History Society, 1991

Dennison, S. R. and O. MacDonagh, *Guinness 1886–1939*, Cork, 1998

Eley, Philip, *Portsmouth Breweries since 1847*, Portsmouth, Portsmouth City Council, 1994

Flood, R. J., *Cambridge Breweries*, Cambridge, Cambridge Society for Industrial Archaeology/Camra, 1987

Glover, Brian, *Prince of Ales. the History of Brewing in Wales*, Stroud, Alan Sutton, 1993

Gordon, W. J., *The Horse-World of London*, London, Religious Tract Society, 1893

Gourvish, T. R. and R. G. Wilson, *The British Brewing Industry 1830–1980*, Cambridge, Cambridge University Press, 1994

Harrison, Brian, *Drink and the Victorians*, London, Faber, 1971

Jacobson, Michael, *200 Years of Beer The Story of Boddington's Strangeways Brewery*, Manchester, Boddington's Brewery, 1978

Janes, Hurford, *Albion Brewery 1808–1958: The Story of Mann, Crossman & Paulin Ltd*, London, Harley Publishing Co., 1958

Jones, Michael, *Time, Gentlemen, Please! Early Brewery Posters in the Public Record office*, London, PRO Publications, 1997

Lackey, Clifford, *Quality Pays: The Story of Joshua Tetley & Son*, Ascot, Springwood Books, 1985

Langley, Andrew, *London Pride: 150 Years of Fuller Smith & Turner*, London, Fuller Smith & Turner, 1995

Lewis, R. A., ed., *Pale Ale and Bitter Beer*, Staffordshire County Council Education Department, 1977

Lynch, P. and Vaizey, J., *Guinness's Brewery in the Irish Economy (1759–1876)*, Cambridge, 1960

Molyneux, W., *Burton on Trent: Its History, its Waters and its Breweries*, London, 1869

Morewood, Samuel, *A Philosophical and Statistical History of the Inventions and Customs of Ancient and Modern Nations in the Manufacture and Use of Inebriating Liquors*, Dublin, 1838

Moynihan, Peter and Goodley, Ken, *Westerham Ales: A Brief History of the Black Eagle Brewery, Westerham*, New Ash Green, The Brewery History Society, 1991

O Drisceoil, Diarmuid and O Drisceoil, Donal, *The Murphy's Story*, Cork, Murphy Brewery Ireland Ltd, 1997

Osborn, Helen, *Britain's Oldest Brewery: Young's of Wandsworth*, London, Young & Co., 1999

Owen, Colin C., *Burton upon Trent: The Development of Industry*, Chichester, Philliomore & Co., 1978

Owen, Colin C., *The Greatest Brewery in the World: A History of Bass, Ratcliff & Gretton*, Chesterfield, Derbyshire Record Society, 1992

Parry, David Lloyd, *South Yorkshire Stingo*, New Ash Green, Brewery History Society, 1997

Pearson, Lynn, *British Breweries: An Architectural History*, London, Hambledon Press, 1999

Pearson, Lynn, *The History of Robinson's Brewery*, Altrincham, Moris Nicholson Cartwright, 1997

Peaty, Ian P., *Essex Brewers*, New Ash Green, Brewery History Society, 1992

Protz, Roger, *Classic Stout and Porter*, London, Prion, 1997

Pudney, John, *A Draught of Contentment: The Story of the Courage Group*, London, New English Library, 1971

Seton Karr, W. S. and Sandeman, Hugh, *Selections from Calcutta Gazettes 1784–1823*, Calcutta, 1864–69

Sheppard, Francis, *Brakspear's Brewery, Henley on Thames*, Henley on Thames, W. H. Brakspear & Sons, 1979

Tizard, W. L., *The Theory and Practice of Brewing*, London, 1846

Tuck, John, *The Private Brewer's Guide to the Art of Brewing Ale and Porter*, London, W. Simpkin & R. Marshall, 1822

Various, *Burton Pale Ales*: papers presented at a seminar held on 14 July 1990 at the White Horse, Parson's Green, London, The White Horse, Parson's Green, 1994

Wild, Antony, *The East India Company: Trade and Conquest from 1600*, London, HarperCollins, 1999

Wilson, George B., *Alcohol and the Nation*, London, Nicholson & Watson, 1940

Wilson, R. G., *Greene King: A Business and Family History*, London, Bodley Head/Jonathan Cape, 1983

Yule, Sir Henry and Burnell, A. C., *Hobson Jobson: a glossary of collo-quial Anglo-Indian words and phrases and of kindred terms, etymological, historical, geographical and discursive*, London, John Murray, 1886

Ziegler, Philip, *The Sixth Great Power: Barings 1762–1929*, London, Collins, 1988

Chapters 8 and 9 Gone for a Burton: the twentieth century, part one; The counter-revolution: the twentieth century, part two

Allen, Brigid, *Morrells of Oxford*, Oxford, Oxfordshire Books, 1994

Anon., *The Brewer's Art*, London, Whitbread & Co. Ltd, 1948

Arthur, Max, *When This Bloody War Is Over*, London, Piatkus, 2001

Baillie, Frank, *The Beer Drinker's Companion*, London, David & Charles, 1974

Boston, Richard, *Beer and Skittles*, London, Collins, 1976

Bristow, Philip, *The Mansfield Brew*, Ringwood, Navigator Publishing, 1976

Bruce, George, *Kimberley Ale: Hardys & Hansons 1832–1982*, London, Henry Melland, 1982

Bull, George and Vice, Anthony, *Bid for Power*, London, Elek Books, 1961

Competition Commission, *A Report on the Acquisition by Interbrew SA of the Brewing Interests of Bass plc*, London, Stationery Office, 2001

Cornell, Martyn, *The Business Guide to Cask Ale*, London, Martin Information, 2001

Elkins, Ted, *So They Brewed Their Own Beer*, Northern Clubs Federation Brewery, 1970

Glover, Brian, *Brewing for Victory: Brewers, beer and Pubs in the Second World War*, Cambridge, Lutterworth Press, 1995

Glover, Brian, *Loyalty Pays: A History of the United Clubs Brewery*, Stroud, Alan Sutton, 1995

Glover, Brian, *New Beer Guide: A Guide to Britain's Small Brewery Revolution*, Newton Abbot, David & Charles, 1988

Gorham, Maurice, *Back to the Local*, London, Percival Marshall, 1949

Gourvish, Terry, *Norfolk Beers from English Barley: A History of Steward & Patteson*, Norwich, Centre for East Anglian Studies, 1987

Hawkins, K. H. and Pass, C. L., *The Brewing Industry*, London, Heinemann, 1979

Hickey, T. J., ed., *All About Beer*, London, The Statist, 1952

Hughes, Rene, *The Old Star: A Tale of Old Stourbridge*, Ilfracombe, Arthur H. Stockwell, 1974

Izzard, George, *One for the Road: The Autobiography of a London Village Publican*, London, Max Parrish, 1959

Mackey, Ian, *Twenty Five Years of New British Breweries*, Aylesbury, Ian Mackey, 1998

McGill, Angus, ed., *Pub*, London, Longmans Green & Co., 1969

Nevile, Sir Sydney, *Seventy Rolling Years*, London, Faber, 1958

Office of Fair Trading, *The Supply of Beer: A Report on the Review of the Beer Orders by the Former Director General of Fair Trading, Mr John Bridgeman*, London, Stationery Office, 2000

Phillips, Glen C., *On-Tap: The Odyssey of Beer and Brewing in Victorian London*, *Middlesex* (Ontario), Cheshire Cat Press, 2000

Protz, Roger and Millns, Tony, eds, *Called to the Bar: An Account of the First 21 years of the Campaign for Real Ale*, St Albans, Campaign for Real Ale, 1992

Rohmer, Richard, *EP Taylor*, Toronto, McClelland & Stewart, 1978

Seldon, Arthur, *The State is Rolling Back*, London, Institute of Economic Affairs, 1994

Various, *Beer in Britain*, London, Times Publishing Co., 1960

Williams, Gwylmor Prys and Brake, George Thompson, *Drink in Great Britain 1900–1979*, London, Edsall, 1980

Wilson, R. G. and Gourvish, T. R., *The Dynamics of the International Brewing Industry since 1800*, London, Routledge, 1998

Chapter 10   The local brew

Cornell, Martyn, *J. W Green: The Brewmaster*

Donnachie, Ian, *A History of the Brewing Industry in Scotland*, Edinburgh, John Donald, 1979

Keir, David, *The Younger Centuries*, Edinburgh, William Younger & Co., 1951

Luckett, Fred, Flint, Ken and Lee, Peter, *A History of Brewing in Warwickshire*, Warwickshire Campaign for Real Ale, 1983

Ritchie, Berry, *Good Company: The Story of Scottish & Newcastle*, London, James & James, 1999

Roberts, W. H., *The Scottish Ale Brewer*, Edinburgh, Oliver & Boyd, 1837

Scottish Brewing Archive Journal, Scottish Brewing Archive

Scottish Brewing Archive Newsletter, Scottish Brewing Archive

INDEX

Page numbers in italics refer to illustrations. Breweries are located in London unless otherwise stated.